SBOOK 4:
A SOUTHAMPTON SOLENT
UNIVERSITY GRAPHIC DESIGN
RESEARCH PROJECT

Interviews with Magazine Designers

CONT

PREFACE
4 Nick Long
INTRODUCTION
6 Steve Lannin
INTERVIEWS
10 Masoud Golsorkhi
18 Tony Chambers
26 Matt Willey
36 Yorgo Tloupas
46 Gail Anderson
50 Peter Stitson
58 Carlos Mustienes
64 Andy Diprose
70 Peter Kellett
76 Hans Dieter Reichert
84 Alex Isley
90 Eva Camilla Brandt
94 Angharad Lewis
100 Amelia Gregory
106 Jop Van Bennekom
118 Danny Miller
122 Thomas Persson
130 Dennis Ortiz-Lopez
134 Stuart Holmes
INDEX A
138
INDEX B
140
INDEX C
142
1,2,3 (SBOOKS)
144
06 FINAL YEAR STUDENTS
146
ACKNOWLEDGMENTS
148

PRE

The word magazine comes from the Arabic for storehouse, and it would be hard to find a better single descriptor for its purpose. The editor will decide what is stored between its covers, but it's the art director that organises the individual elements into a cohesive whole. The success of these dual functions will largely determine if a magazine finds (and keeps) an audience. Inherent in this process is an understanding of the cultural and sub-cultural contexts in which the publication exists. This can be an ever-changing feast, as the modern magazine is a perfect exemplar of niche marketing. If there is a gap in the souk for a new title, it will be found and filled. If there isn't, one will be squeezed in there regardless. New magazines are created out of the ashes of last year's model, and the Futurist's state of constant revolution is alive and well in this part of the publishing industry. The positives of this situation are that those who have predicted the end of print, are left with precious little evidence when faced with the explosion of magazines since the invention of the Internet. Each new title creates a potential platform to launch a new graphic language and find a new way of communicating with an audience. It is no coincidence that the reputations of many of the world's foremost visual communicators have been built in such environments. The magazine is fundamentally a luxury item, using a linear structure to draw us into its congress. Page by page, it re-informs our interests, and our prejudices. It allows us to review the world in edited form, not as it is, but as we would wish it to be. It can put us in a place where; we all have a spare couple of hours to prepare the evening meal; it's easy to get planning consent to live in a glass box; makeup is always applied via an airbrush; and where all cars are made in Modena. As such, this domain need not conform to any existing design protocol. In fact, its ability to promote risk taking, aids in the formation of a parallel world that can separate us from the mundane, and surround us with the extra ordinary. And that brings us neatly back to those visual mechanics that are charged with creating this alternative nirvana, the art directors and magazine designers. They operate from the secular world of planning meetings, grid structures, type specifications and of course, tight deadlines: An unlikely alliance for the creation of radical graphic design. Yet these interviewees discuss their work on some of the most innovative and influential titles in the market place. They have helped turn this industry on its head, whilst pushing the boundaries of graphic communication, through their responses to both popular and visual culture. And we in turn are grateful that these designers have taken the time to explain how and why these changes have occurred. *NICK LONG*

NTR-

"Once is usually enough. Either once only, or every day." Beyond this introduction two strands are woven into the interviews that follow. Have I simply ignored or excluded other threads that occur through the chapters? Quite possibly, there are certainly themes that I have dismissed, but as I tell my students – leave the sink in the kitchen – and extract the essence. 'Art' is one motif returned to on several occasions, in a variety of forms, the other is 'Magazines as a social force', which, although the convivial nature of the form is seemingly obvious, has emerged in virtually every chapter without a direct question prompting this line of enquiry. As I'm about to discuss, these two elements intersect and, in many ways, help define what a magazine is and what it can be. During his interview, Tony Chambers, Wallpaper's Art Director, is asked if magazine design is an element in the history of art. His answer proposes that art is about self-expression whereas design is a means of responding to a visual problem. Similarly Masoud Golsorki, from Tank, eliminates anyone from the category of artist who is not 'solely engaged' in art production, then blots his copy book by inferring that Warhol is a fine example. He furthers this argument by opining that art cannot have 'a commercial or practical use' – otherwise, he surmises, 'it becomes design.' So, if I open a bottle of Sol on a Henry Moore sculpture, does it become a design product? Perhaps the opposite is true – when design transcends pure functionality, when it can be interpreted or possesses multiple-layers, it becomes art. This may imply that art has better a purchase on the aesthetic hierarchy than design, but I would counter that when a design object can exist on two qualitative scales, art & function – it is distinguished as the greater, rather than the lesser creative format. Andy Warhol, the late jobbing illustrator & fine artist [whose own 'Interview' magazine is still published], related the dictum that heads this section, in his collected thoughts: "a to b and back again - the philosophy of Andy Warhol". Magazines, seen in this light, like so many other cultural artefacts, usually offer only a compromise – being neither the 'daily newspaper' nor the 'once' of a book. It is one of many accommodations that the magazine must frequent, and these inform the site for its social strength and its artistic weakness. Periodicals are about creating societies, art about dissecting and investigating the social – artists can't afford to tread softly around commercial interests or worry about a competitor's content, presentation etc. Magazines veer away from making fiercely original statements for fear of unpopularity. Can they be art? Yes – if there is only one issue – for a weekly, unlikely. Mainstream publications represent one of many acts of cultural masochism, in its guise as repetition. The Chambers' chapter ends with his theory about ego as a master, [misquoting a biblical phrase about not serving two of such] but magazine creatives are always serving two authorities, at the very least, appeasing their readership and their sponsors – there's also logic, a personal design sensibility,

consistent visual identity, to mention but a few. It is a hard job in what can be an oppressive climate. Yet despite my tortuous description, Chambers' office appears to be somewhere he thrives, and [like any good masochist], savours the limitations. "Typography exists within a social context", stated Melle Hammer in Triggs' The Typographic Experiment. This aspect of a magazine's responsibility, typographic or otherwise, is reflected upon in a number of ways throughout the volume: Eva Brandt discusses how social engagement & functionality are important aspects for Fri Flyt; Danny Miller relates how a Robbie William's style down-to-earthism enables an appropriate team spirit at Adrenalin; extrovert action, like parties, helped Amelia Gregory to establish her magazine, but she believes it is through respecting the submissions from her contributors that working relations will sustain;

Carlos Mustienes views the whole world as his readership, with Colors as a flag for all easy going, international communities; Angharad Lewis, on the other hand, interprets her job quite differently, declaring a wish to push and challenge Grafik's audience beyond their comfort zones; Peter Stitson reflects, nostalgically, on the drug fuelled social order of ecstasy culture, still appropriately Dazed & Confused; from the wealthy readers of Forbes, to the intimate associations he draws with his chosen profession, Alex Isley is seeking the magazine design equivalent of an ASBO, by studiously flouting the industry's 'stupid rules'; Denis Ortiz Lopez parallels computers with magazines, proclaiming their legacy as a social force to increase and promote design awareness; Hans Dieter Reichert discusses the founding of a design democracy for Baseline, offering a visual rather than a journalistic starting point to his audience, a community of written pieces around a visual theme – and in a less formal aside, notes that a friendly printer helps him get out of bed in the morning [I don't even get offered a cup of tea by mine]; the work harder ethic drives the Map, Ra, Zembla assembly line, that Matt Willey oversees [with a communal whip?] as he targets the niche and avoids the mainstream – taking an unusually open swipe at the celebrity cattle products, gossip hungry magazines that, he implies, are a contemporary disease. However, you need only watch an ancient film like Singing in the Rain to realise these rags are a virus that have been around since the dawn of the national media, and will be furiously knitting trivial, anti-social stories at its demise. Masoud Golsorki holds a similar opinion to Willey in considering the importance of the magazine to scattered, dislocated societies, gathering likeminded people into a 'family' and making deliberately focused objects for particular communities to enjoy. Thatcher coined the post-modern phrase 'there is no such thing as society' – yet in practice 'Thatcherist Enterprising' proved the reverse. It demonstrated that we were multi-societied – this is very different to multi-cultural – cultures suggesting historical and, often, religious antecedents, societies could be founded and defunct over the course of a year, a community that comes into existence

either by design or by chance. Golsorki is delighted that magazines can cater for such different groups, but like Willey, is ultimately concerned that this form of media will not survive in its printed form. Actually in the hands of Peter Kellet & co [aka Plastic Rhino] the conventional form of magazines would probably cease to exist over-night – they would remain largely paper based, according to their current rationale, but never look the same twice. At Plastic Rhino HQ the team act as a radical cooperative with mainstream accessibility to new thinking a high priority. Their approach to magazine work is refreshingly individual and a recent project, Polished T, brings conceptual art onto the newsstands and maybe into the lives of those yet to brave a gallery space. Having returned to the art motif it seems surprising, despite an obvious relationship, that Jop Van Bennekom, [designer for RE, Butt, Fantastic Man], wasn't asked if he sees his oeuvre representing a unique strand of the art model. In RE custom is subverted to the point of revolution. Is there a difference between Sam Taylor-Wood's photographic portraits of her friends and Jop's journalistic portraits? Alice Twemlow recently discussed the work of Van Bennekom in Eye, while sensitively considering his very personal approach, she later describes the content as solipsism. In my view the self-indulgence appears evident and considered. The advertising, particularly within RE, seems, as it should, an after thought, patrons pay for the result that Van Bennekom intended, with or without their support. As an artist there would be no issue about self- absorption, perhaps the 'designer' label, via expectation, can appear less a badge of honour and more a position of constraint. I propose that Van Bennekom, through his products, explores different aspects of his own personality, often structurally: – with RE – convention-less reassessment, his critical faculties in full swing; with the quarterly Butt an almost 'anal' rigidity (of form), a nod to the conservative nature of mainstream gay culture, but with an entirely original look & agenda. [If Butt is indeed Van Bennekom's breadwinner - then he may, self-amusingly, have connoted the Freudian association between shit & money – the ability to control his arse linked to the capacity to regulate cash flow]. In RE, like the most inventive creations mentioned by the multitude gathered for this great project, social and artful themes meet. His community of friends became the content, and his social agendas direct the evolution of his works – rarely in a straight or commercial line.

As I discussed earlier, the social aspect of a magazine often undermines the artistic because moneyed investors will always attempt to ensure that mass taste is appeased. Van Bennekom's view is that anything radical and unproved is less and less likely to find backing as agencies form a bloated conglomerate. My feeling [and Jop is proof] is that, like Hollywood, maverick independents will always find funds and believers, later the mainstream will follow, in some diluted fashion. "It is Darwinian evolution," conjectured Martin Daubney, editor of Loaded, to the Guardian, "Men have realised that if they adopt the ways of the gays, they get laid more often." Perhaps if more art directors adopted the ways of Van Bennekom and the other out-spoken creatives celebrated in this volume, [personally & professionally], magazine design needn't be such a dirty word. As Warhol demonstrated and Tibor Kalman wrote so beautifully: "Good Designers Make Trouble". *STEVE LANNIN*

MASOUD GOLSORKHI

You set up Tank magazine with Andreas Laeufer. Did you both have a clear understanding of what you wanted it to become? You can certainly have ambitions and a set of priorities, but in an ever changing world your responses tend also to be ever changing. We set out to produce a magazine that we liked, that we would buy, and that wasn't already on the market. So we started a magazine that was achievable and within our means. Knowing the pitfalls of working with a publisher, we chose to become independent. **Did you market research your concept?** I don't believe in market research. I think it's nonsense. Everyone should do everything they do for themselves, and let the market decide whatever it wants to decide. If something is not feasible, it will not go any further. Market research should be done by companies making toothpaste, not by people who produce culture, especially if they have any claim or ambition to be original. Picasso did not get up in the morning and say, "hmm, I wonder what kind of painting my audience is going to want", before putting brush to canvas. **How did you finance your first issue?** We had a client who wanted us to produce an advertising campaign and we convinced him he needed a magazine instead! He sponsored the first issue and we produced four thousand copies, which we sold out of the back of a car. We sold out within a couple of weeks and we had to reprint.

It was 1998 and we were selling it for eight pounds. This was an outrageously high cover price for the time, considering an average magazine cost just two pounds. That's how the whole thing supported itself. **What makes a good fashion photographer?** Fashion is about attaching meaning to feelings. Fashion photography is about communicating the intangibility of those feelings. By definition it is impossible to describe "good" in fashion photography. It has been about different subjects at different stages in its history. At one particular stage it was all about innovations in technique and in photographic language. There have been stages where for example the art director has been the most important person on a shoot, like at Nova in the 70s. Those were iconic art directors whose concepts

PICASSO DID NOT GET UP IN THE MORNING AND SAY HMM I WONDER WHAT KIND OF PAINTING MY AUDIENCE IS GOING TO WANT BEFORE PUTTING BRUSH TO CANVAS

led the photographer. Later on we had star photographers who did concepts themselves. At another time it has been about the personality of the models that has been the most dominant message in the photograph. That gave us a public appetite for looking at a collection of twenty women at any given time, and defined what was a relevant fashion shoot after that. Right now it is pretty much about clothes. So there's no single thing you look for in a fashion photographer. You look for what is relevant at that particular time and that changes all of the time. It is a moving target and any description about what is good in fashion photography at any particular time, is only valid until the sentence is finished. **You worked as a fashion photographer for Interview, Jalouse and Harpers & Queen. What did you learn in this period that helped you to set up Tank?** I learned that I wasn't cut out to be just a fashion photographer! I was too big for my boots. I can write, I've got opinions and some remnants of an intellect. I found that I just needed to express all of those things. Secondly, I learned about the magazine system and how the whole thing worked. It occurred to me that it could be made to work in a different way, and that's what we have been doing in the last eight years. Thirdly, it helped me network and we met a lot of photographers, stylists and make up artists, who in turn helped me get Tank up and running. **Tank has been large format since 2002. Previously it was a smaller format bookzine. Did this signify a change in terms of increased readership and distribution?** I really don't believe in responding to what the market is asking for. I believe in responding to what satisfies your soul at the time. Tank has had three formats actually and we initially came out in A5. It was very cheap and easy to do, and we had very limited means at the time. The height was decided by the size of a hand, and the fact that it fitted into a coat pocket. It was also done because it was unique and there was nothing of that size on the market. When we went to the distribution companies they said, "No way, you can't put a thing like that on the shelf, because it's too short and no one will be able to see it". We produced it at that size for 2 years. One morning Andreas and I were in Magma and we saw nine magazines that looked exactly like ours. We thought, there's no way we're doing it this size anymore, and we moved to a super

jumbo size, which we produced for about a year. It was hugely expensive, crazy and insane. We were losing £1.50 on every issue and the more we sold the more money we lost. With a debt of 150 thousand pounds and rising we felt it might be an idea to change the format. At the beginning we were really interested in the format of magazines, because we were innovators in that field with publications like Mined, and everybody else followed us. Subsequently our priorities changed and we started thinking more and more about the content; what defines a magazine in terms of its interior architecture and the way it's put together. We have done everything you could possibly imagine, like textured covers etc. In the end, all of those things become boring. They are like strange sexual positions, once you've done it a few times its just not interesting anymore. The question remains "how deep is your love?" **Why have**

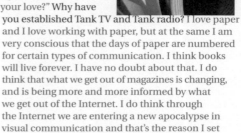

you established Tank TV and Tank radio? I love paper and I love working with paper, but at the same I am very conscious that the days of paper are numbered for certain types of communication. I think books will live forever. I have no doubt about that. I do think that what we get out of magazines is changing, and is being more and more informed by what we get out of the Internet. I do think through the Internet we are entering a new apocalypse in visual communication and that's the reason I set up Tank TV. I was on holiday in Rome and I went to have a look at a fountain. My view was interrupted by thousands of arms raised with mobile phones and digital cameras. I took a picture of all the arms obscuring this famous fountain. On the plane back I was looking hard at the image and realised this is almost where we were when the Kodak Browning camera came out in 1904 and revolutionised photography. Photography had previously been the preserve of the rich and idle. Kodak changed all that and made photography, arguably the art form of the twentieth century, universally accessible. It made the possibility of photography as Art, more relevant and more possible, not less. For me, the digital capture of images, still and moving, is a similar landmark moment. Photography can't be the same and film cannot be the same as it was. I have nothing to do with the day to day running of it but for me Tank TV is like an open window to a garden I just want to smell. It's about keeping in touch. It's a totally non-commercial proposition, but it has a huge international following. We have around a quarter of a million hits a month. **Tank Magazine was exhibited in the Museum of Modern Art's first exhibition devoted to fashion photography. How do you compare fashion photography with fine art photography?** It is a very sad state of affairs that the prefix of art anything, or anything art, has become so easy to use. I do not consider people artists unless they solely engage in the activity of producing art. By

THE REDESIGN HAS BECOME LESS FREQUENT BECAUSE IT JUST SEEMS A LITTLE BIT LIKE MASTURBATING

definition and according to people like Picasso and Warhol, a work of art must have certain qualities. First of all it can't have a commercial or practical use. When a work of art has artistic merit and is useful, it becomes design. I think a lot of the people who are going around being 'artists' are basically phonies. One of the most attractive things about fashion photography is its very commerciality. It is the interaction between art and commerce which make it so exciting- Guy Bourdin was selling shoes and Helmut Newton was selling sunglasses. I find that much more

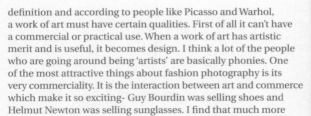

noble and exciting than if they were farting around in a gallery to an audience of 200 people. It has become a bit of a cliché that when fashion photographers make too much money they want to become artists. It's like an elephants graveyard of people who were once quite good commercial artists and who have now lost their way. I find it pathetic and irrelevant. It will be a small footnote in the history of photography and it's not going to be very meaningful. **Andreas Laeufer once stated, "We don't try to be cool, we try to be different". In today's brand orientated society do you think there is too much emphasis on being 'cool'?** You shall know a charlatan by his claim to be cool! One of the things about Andreas that attracted me was that here was an art director who didn't have his pants down to his thighs and wasn't pretending to be something he wasn't, cool was and remains irrelevant. The proposition of cool really belonged to an era where communication and mobility were very restricted. There was a sense that centres like New York, Paris and London were special. If you were living in Slough, Louisiana or Hull, you would view these centres as offering a different experience of life, and one that you were definitely excluded from. That doesn't happen in this day and age. I recently holidayed in a tiny place in the south of Spain called Rhonda. I went into an Internet café, which sold the latest copies of Tank. I met some of the people inside and they had absolutely no interest in being in London, they were just stylish, young, clever, beautiful people who were making their own lives according to their own set of criteria. They were very tuned into what was happening a thousand miles away in London, but it didn't necessarily feel like they were followers. The only usefulness for the concept of cool, is so that you can now identify the complete charlatan, and thank god there are so many of them out there. **Tank custom published, '…And?', which was heavily sponsored by Prada. How do such projects come about and what is the methodology behind such a collaboration?** They come out of a guttural need to respond to a particular situation. '…And?' came out of 2001 and the events thereof. Frankly we felt guilty working on glossy surfaces whilst all that shit was going on. I am a big fan of the Financial Times, simply because I am a committed socialist, and it's important to know how the enemy thinks! We wanted to do something that talked the language of global capitalism. Mucia was launching a New York store. I am a friend of Rem Koolhaas, the architect, who worked on that, and Prada's sponsorship facilitated that piece of work. However good or bad it was, we turned it around really quickly. Initially our plan was to get it distributed with the Financial Times, but once they saw the content they were a rather less inclined. So we just distributed it ourselves. I had a bemused retired British diplomat from Geneva who bought it thinking it was the FT because it was so pink! On page 3 it had, 'Who arte you', in big bold letters. That seemed to shake him to the core, to the point

I REALLY DO[N]
TO WHAT

ANY DESCRIPTION ABOUT WHAT IS GOOD IN FASHION PHOTOGRAPHY AT ANY PARTICULAR TIME IS ONLY VALID UNTIL THE SENTENCE IS FINISHED

T BELIEVE IN RESPONDING HE MARKET IS ASKING FOR

where he was on the phone to me from Switzerland for about 60 minutes. He wasn't offended, just baffled and angry at why he was being presented. It was really outside of his range of experience, and that's a reward in itself. **You strictly limit the amount of advertising in the magazine. On what basis do you determine which ads to include?** Initially we started by rejecting adverts we thought were ugly, because we were really making a book, not a magazine. It was a bookzine, and a book is something you're meant to keep forever. If a hideous beer ad was going to disturb the flow, then we didn't really want to include it. For a couple of grand we just didn't think it was worth it. I can't say with absolute certainty that we have never run an ad that I haven't liked, but its rare, lets put it that way. We depend on advertising money, but unlike other magazines I tend not to offer my grandmother's soul for advertising. Most magazine's economics are entirely based on advertising. We are also a commercial entity, but we allow our aesthetics sense of integrity and values to have a degree of influence over our financial decisions. **Do you think Tank's less commercialised approach, and the fact you have distanced yourselves from the mainstream, has been a key factor in the magazines success?** Absolutely yes, I'm reminded of that on a daily basis. It's a refuge and a quiet space. We really try to have a degree of integrity and an absence of the now standard bullshit, even if the

THEY HAVE GOT THEIR HEADS SO FAR UP THE CELEBRITY CULTURE'S ARSE ITS COMING OUT OF THE OTHER END

THRO
OF TH
ENTER
A

copy is talking about a new lipstick! Unlike most of our competitors we don't re-print press releases, I care about every word in the magazine and feel responsible for it, I care about lipstick. And people just love that. It's a minority interest thing, but that suits us just fine. **Unlike most magazines you refuse to use famous models or celebrities on your covers. What is the reason behind this strong rejection of celebrity culture?** It's really funny because rejecting celebrity culture has become the new big thing. One magazine recently put out a press release stating they were rejecting this idea of celebrity culture. Which was hilarious because they have got their heads so far up this celebrity culture's arsehole, it's coming out the other end! I was a huge fan of The Face in its heyday. I would go into a newsagent at the end of the month and I would see this image of a beautiful amazing girl. She had the most fantastic haircut and she was on the cover of the Face for no other reason than she was fabulous. And that made me want to buy the magazine, because I agreed that she was fabulous, although she was a single mother living in Hackney. The reason I started Tank was because by 1998 you could get a copy of the Face, a copy of Elle, a copy of Cosmo and they would all have Madonna on the cover! You can't claim to belong to a counter culture, when you are engaging in the same methods of achieving circulation as the mainstream. I don't care if Madonna is on the cover of The Face with an umbrella up her arse, she's only giving that interview because her latest song is out. I am a big fan of Madonna and I am not against celebrities, but I think if you have any claim to be an alternative voice, you must reject that PR treadmill. So from day one we banned famous models, as well as famous people from our front cover, and that has remained our principle. I am glad this view is finding popular currency, but I am also very cynical about people whose bread and butter is celebrity culture, publicly rejecting it. I think it's a fad and it will pass. With us, its here to stay, and I've got eight years of work to prove it. Of course we have worked with well known people, but the guiding principle has been that if you want to do something with Tank, you have to have something interesting to say. Tilda Swinton, worked with us recently. I just said to her, "we want to hear something about you that nobody else has heard". In the end I got her to write something, I didn't publish her picture, and I didn't print her name in large type on the cover. She's just an interesting intelligent woman and she had interesting things to say and we presented them. The idea that we would market that entire issue around the fact that she was in the magazine is just pathetic. **Has Tank been as successful internationally, as it has been in Britain?** That's the interesting by–product of market segmentation and the global village. I find the people who like Tank, tend to be roughly the same percentage of the population wherever you are in the world. There aren't that many of them in any single country, but add all the countries together and you have a viable magazine. Tank is an acquired taste, but it is globally spread and that's the beauty of it. I've been all over the world and the magazine has incredible coverage in places that you just wouldn't believe. We sell more copies of Tank in India, than British Vogue. That's a market of 1.2 billion people. The same goes for China, Argentina and Brazil. We are constantly being asked to license Tank in different markets. In Japan, foreign magazines can cost £30 a copy. So kids were buying one copy of Tank, digitally photographing every page and posting it on the web for everyone to share. Japanese publishers were getting in touch because they wanted to see how they could cash in on that phenomenon. So it's a globally spread proposition, that's not very commercial, but with horizontal coverage rather than the vertical.

And I am very interested in that as a philosophical proposition, because as the saying goes, "you can choose your friends, but you can't choose your family". An extension of that might be that you can't choose who you live next door to, but you can find like minded people all over the world. You may be the only gay in the village, but there are enough gays to go around for you to have a worldwide family. **With highly styled photography and slick graphic design, would you not agree that Tank is itself fast becoming a fashion brand.** I don't have a lot of time to discuss the whole concept of branding, because I genuinely think it's all just so much bollocks. If the people who wear too much aftershave and too much hair gel, manage to convince some dumb car company that all they need is a good marketing strategy to revive their fortunes, then that business is already dead in the water. I think 99% of people in industry think that its just bullshit. I don't really believe in the ideals of marketeers. They are just describing something that has been in common usage for a long time. Its a way of explaining an existing thing in a different way. The way you describe something doesn't change the thing itself, even though semiology tells you it does. The medium and the message are two different propositions, they exist in two different universes. So views of whether Tank is cool or not cool, or whether it's a fashion brand or not a fashion brand, is like cycling down the street; people can throw darts at you, or people can throw bouquets of flowers at you. It doesn't change who you are, I am very cynical and cautious of accepting compliments, or listening to insults, in equal measure. If Tank is a brand then I sure as hell hope it isn't a fashion brand. **How would you review the structure and look of the magazine?** Tank comes out of a strict modernist

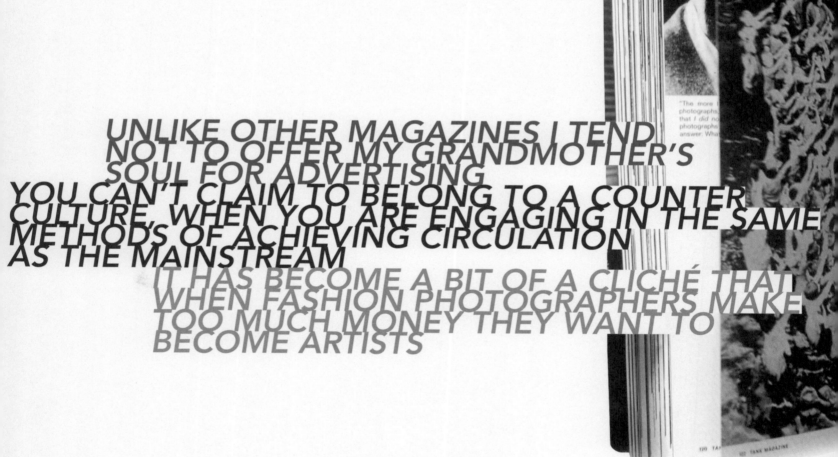

UNLIKE OTHER MAGAZINES I TEND
NOT TO OFFER MY GRANDMOTHER'S
SOUL FOR ADVERTISING

YOU CAN'T CLAIM TO BELONG TO A COUNTER
CULTURE, WHEN YOU ARE ENGAGING IN THE SAME
METHODS OF ACHIEVING CIRCULATION
AS THE MAINSTREAM

IT HAS BECOME A BIT OF A CLICHÉ THAT
WHEN FASHION PHOTOGRAPHERS MAKE
TOO MUCH MONEY THEY WANT TO
BECOME ARTISTS

family of design. Andreas is a very strict German modernist, and It always leads by function, with ease of use and ease of navigation, I guess the post modern element in that mix is that we are really interested in current and future trends in fashion. So functionality is informed by fashionability, and to be honest I feel it's imperative to have fun. Otherwise we would be like a lot of design companies, very austere and pure and never getting laid- I believe the design of Tank should have Modernist ambition but also needs to get laid, seduction and fun are totally necessary. We used to almost redesign it totally every issue, around themes. But we have become bored with redesigns, and they have in turn become less frequent, because it just seems a little bit like masturbating. It was more important to put the messages out and to improve the content. However, design is still a vital ingredient and we aim to be the most exciting avant-garde publication in global magazine design. You can't claim particular longevity for that proposition, it may come and go, but it is part of the agenda here. **Why has the magazine's masthead varied its position, colour and size over the years?** When we first started, magazines all tended to look the same. The masthead was on the top left hand corner of the cover and in red. We completely changed that and as the market followed us, we have actually gone back to an earlier proposition. The current design is homage to a magazine called Picture Post, in the 1940's. In a way it defined all magazine design subsequently. In this particular reincarnation it is about issues that we have grappled with, to do with quality and democratic access. The Coverline, 'Elitism for All', is a quote by the philosopher Jean Francois Lyotard and it sums up our thinking. That on the one hand we are obviously elitist, because we believe in producing the best possible magazine, without compromising or talking down to people. But at the same time, we believe there is a good and a bad. I was never seduced by the post modern theory that says, 'there is no good or bad, just different.' That's bullshit. I believe in the idea of quality, so I am an elitist in that sense, but I am also a complete democrat in that I think excellence should be available to everyone. Picture Post is one such example, it was mass produced and massively successful, mainstream but radical. **What is your**

prediction for the future of fashion magazines? They have become more and more insular, because essentially magazines are a dying or shrinking proposition. Fashion magazines, to be more profitable have become more and more focused on pure fashion. That is really regrettable from my point of view. The great fashion magazines like Nova and Vogue, always talked about a whole person, a whole woman and not just what she was wearing. Everybody is competing for the same amount of advertising budget, and everyone is trying to appear more 'insider' than anybody else. But essentially what they are producing is one dimensional. They haven't recognised that a woman who wears Christian Louboutin shoes is also interested in why there is a war in Iraq. That's the woman I am interested in, the one that has a job and a history, she has politics and she has a soul. Pure fashion magazines that are totally about fashion and nothing else, are frauds milking a paranoid industry inhibited by people who are always afraid the right people don't love them enough. A magazine for fashion insiders is a bit like a fart in a phone box. It might be particularly pungent to those inside, but the rest of the world doesn't give a damn. *SBOOK 4*

T

O

WALL

PAPER

Can you tell us a little bit about where you studied, and how useful you found this experience? I studied at the Central School of Art and Design just before it merged with Saint Martins in the mid eighties. They were separate colleges with two very different approaches to graphic design. So it was quite a strange merger at the time. Central had a much more academic approach to graphic design. When I was a student I was relatively unaware of these things and rather naive of how the education system worked. By the time I reached my third year I could look back with a little hindsight and begin to understand where the course was coming from. Intellectual is probably too strong a word, but the tutors tried to instil a kind of intellectual approach to graphic design. Definitely a cerebral system in comparison to Saint Martins' more commercial and culturally adept approach to visual communication. I don't mean commercial in its crudest form, but they were designing record sleeves whilst we were taking classes in map making and type legibility. It was quite a cataclysmic merger as the tutors were so different. Saint Martins' tutors were more aggressive and gung ho. So it had a bit of an effect on the course, although not directly on us, as we were still part of Central. But you could see it happening beneath the surface. Saint Martins kind of swallowed Central's approach to graphic design and to an extent that was a pity. **How long did it take you to become an art director?** I was incredibly lucky. In those days the Sunday Times was based at Grays Inn Road, which was close to the Central's building at Southampton Row. They needed some help on projects at The Sunday Times Magazine and they approached Central to send over a few students for interview. I ended up undertaking a work placement there in my second year, although at the time I wasn't really that interested in magazines. I was far more interested in typography. Graphic design generally, but typography specifically. The Sunday Times magazine was of course a very

N

Yfamous title and something I had grown up with. It was a fascinating publication partly because of its history. But I couldn't really view it as a real passion of mine. So I went into it with a slightly blasé attitude and that made me slightly more relaxed in my interview, and they probably liked that. And then on graduation they offered me three months work, which again I thought would be good, but with little real ambition to either stay there, or to stay in magazines. When the three months was up, they extended it to six, and then into a year. After about a year I began to understand how interesting magazines could be from a visual communication point of view. It enabled me to use the skills I learnt at college about typography and design, and apply them to the work of some the most talented writers, editors, subeditors and photographers in the business. This new world of journalism suddenly opened up before me, and it was just such a thrill to be working alongside this kind of person. These very intelligent people were vastly experienced and well educated, and yet they were very respectful towards this very young design graduate. It opened my eyes and I realised it would be hard to go back to just doing graphic design in isolation. That year turned into ten and The Sunday Times Magazine became my real education. It was almost like another university after Central. But I realised I would have to move on after such a long a period in one job, or my experience would be just too limited. So I went to GQ. **What were the main differences between these two environments?** I had slowly worked up the ranks of the Sunday Times Magazine. Very slowly in terms of job title. But I didn't really care about that. What's important is that you grow; that you're growing intellectually, and your talent is developing. The magazine was also growing at that time and there was a lot more to do. I think the only reason I moved up the pecking order was because I stayed so long that everyone else had left! In the end I was approached by GQ, and I thought it would make an interesting change. It was also a magazine that has always had high standards of journalism, and that's critical. Although it's a men's lifestyle title, with the now pre-requisite ladish approach, the writing is still very good and that's the glue that helps hold it together. It's given it stability and longevity. I knew I could do my bit, using the knowledge and skills gained at the Times. I was playing safe to a degree because I knew it was lacking certain things I could add, and I was sure I could improve the way it looked. It's subjective, but that's the way I felt at the time. What was drastically different was the fact that it was a newsstand magazine. I had only been used to working on newspaper magazines, which don't have the same pressures to sell. The Sunday Times Magazine had other pressures, but it's still part of a bigger package and it didn't have to survive solely on its own merits. It was important that it was well produced because people will comment and criticise if it isn't. You also felt the weight of its great history on your shoulders when you put it together. But that's still critically different to designing a monthly magazine, which has to sell to survive.

That creates its own fascinating but scary problems. If a few issues don't shift and the figures take a down turn, the pressure is on. And the editor and the art director have to respond. Much of that extra pressure concentrates on the cover. It's the primary selling device. **Who makes the final decision on the cover?** The covers are created by the editor and the art director. There's some input from the publisher and the managing director, but they tend to be hands off, unless it's going seriously wrong! If it is going seriously wrong that's when the stress kicks in. You would think it would be worse on a weekly title like the Sunday Times. But if you made a mistake on that you didn't have time to worry, as you were straight on to next week's issue. It's also not on the newsstands glaring at you for a whole month! If you've designed a weak cover on a monthly and it's selling badly, it holds you and it scares you. Having spent ten years protected by this huge cruise liner full of talented people, it was a shock to be part of a small team where your input becomes critical to a magazine's survival. **And what were the main differences between Wallpaper and GQ?** It's your reader that impacts on everything you do. GQ is a much more difficult magazine to art direct. It's a magician's act in a sense. The advertisers are funding the magazine. Therefore sales have to be healthy to attract them. But it's the type of reader you have that impacts on what type of advertising you can attract. So all these things are in the mixing bowl and it becomes a real balancing act. GQ is very difficult because the kind of advertisers you want to attract are Gucci, Prada and Armani. They want readers who are quite wealthy fashion conscious males. But if you produced a package aimed at just that market you would never sell the 100 thousand plus copies needed each month. You must attract a much broader audience that isn't necessarily within your advertisers demographic. So you have to appear up market, but flirt downmarket. But only flirt! It's a juggling act and a fascinating publishing problem. It's very hard to make a beautiful looking magazine, and appeal to that many people, in that kind of a market. It's the advertisers that want the magazine to look beautiful, but to the reader of this kind of magazine, beautiful isn't that relevant. The visually educated reader will look for an elegant layout with sophisticated photography, but to keep sales up you still need tits, ass and fast cars in a men's magazine. Oh and football! Wallpaper is completely different. It is genuinely upmarket and the readers are so sophisticated it hurts. We had one of those evenings where you meet your readers. This is normally a terrifying experience. It certainly was at GQ. As a designer you hold on to an idea of what you think your readers are like. When you meet them it can be a real eye opener. You may be presenting an aspirational design language, but when you meet them you find that approach may not be needed! The Wallpaper readers were very different. They were incredibly well educated, visually literate and knew more about the magazine than we did. They could eloquently discuss stories we had covered. They knew about the latest architecture in Shanghai and the latest design in Scandinavia. They were also passionate about the magazine. We came away knowing we could push Wallpaper further and make it even more sophisticated. This also means we don't have to do any of those difficult but necessary publishing tricks, like educating our readers. We just need to challenge them. And that's an incredible luxury. I don't like to use the word easier, but it is a more straight

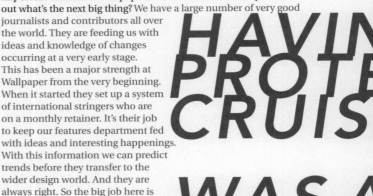

forward brief than GQ. Most magazines are much tougher. But then other pressures come with it. Our readers have real expectations of the magazine and its design. There are standards we have to reach and maintain. They push you creatively and they'll let you know in double quick time if something is below their standards in terms of design and content. **You have said the most important element of Wallpaper is to set trends. How do you find out what's the next big thing?** We have a large number of very good journalists and contributors all over the world. They are feeding us with ideas and knowledge of changes occurring at a very early stage. This has been a major strength at Wallpaper from the very beginning. When it started they set up a system of international stringers who are on a monthly retainer. It's their job to keep our features department fed with ideas and interesting happenings. With this information we can predict trends before they transfer to the wider design world. And they are always right. So the big job here is editing, as we are fed hundreds of ideas each month. It's a time consuming job to cut through to the really big stories, or to make connections between the smaller stories. **Do magazines like Wallpaper have a deeper design philosophy, which has little to do with making money?** Anyone with any moral fibre would realise that we have a certain responsibility, and without wishing to be pious about it, you can't treat that lightly. But at the end of the day the publisher expects the title to make money and not waste it. The rub occurs if you sacrifice the editorial direction just to make a bigger profit. If you pursue that thinking too far it would inevitably impact on the quality of the journalism and that would definitely backfire. Our readers are not fools and if we watered down the content to attract a broader market we would start to lose them.

SPENT TEN YEARS
CTED BY THIS HUGE
LINER FULL OF
TALENTED PEOPLE, IT
SHOCK TO BE PART OF A
TEAM WHERE YOUR
BECOMES CRITICAL TO
MAGAZINE'S SURVIVAL

Wallpaper is not an altruistic project, but we have a clearly defined readership that expects us to improve the product and keep them informed about new design cultures. We can't rest on our laurels. If we just pursued naked sales we are highly likely to end up with far less readers than when we started! You must keep building up your relationship with this kind of an audience. **Do you think this is part of your success?** I hope so. I think there have been times when we flirted with the idea of broadening the magazine's appeal, but what you gain in the short term, you lose in the long term. There was a time, a few years ago, when maybe it became a little bit predictable. Not intentionally mind you, but a pattern had formed, a way of doing things that no longer pushed boundaries. And it was noticed and changed. **Hence the need for a redesign in 2003?** Exactly. We had a rethink about how we produced our editorials and we created a more eclectic and interesting system. I think it was becoming a touch lazy. So that was the catalyst for the redesign and the change of direction. **What were the major changes?** We began by putting things into the magazine you wouldn't expect. It was a gamble. Readers and advertisers will complain if things become predictable, but if you change things too much they get mighty scared. And the unusual is always a surprise. The design predictability was useful at the start. Having a really tight consistent policy, that doesn't disorientate visually, does make people feel comfortable and gives them a strong identity to connect with. And that was Wallpaper's great strength in the beginning. It only did things in a certain way, it only covered certain subjects, and it designed those subjects using a very clear consistent visual language. However, after six or seven years people had gotten used to it and it became a bit of an albatross. But how you break tradition without scaring people away is the trick. By its nature a re-design is a revolutionary act. If it ends up looking like you've

tweaked the design rather than taken it forward, then it's not worth doing. You have to be brave. There were a few scary moments when people were genuinely worried about the changes, but we've just had our most successful year. Sales and subscriptions are really increasing and advertising has picked up. The magazine has got its second wind and it's our tenth anniversary this year. So that's an endorsement of the fact that it's here to stay. Often magazines like Wallpaper hit a moment, hit a zeitgeist, they become incredibly powerful cultural beacons, and then they burn out. They tend not to last more than five or six years, because the moment has passed. It's made its point, it's summed up a time and place, and then its boxed itself into a corner. You also get the problem of imitators who realise you've discovered a new market and will start up 'me too' titles. Just because you're the first to find a new market area doesn't mean you are going to remain the best. When starting something new, you have to be good to survive, but you mustn't get complacent. The publishing world is full of smart people who will come after you and your market share. **So are you still the best?** I think we are. Wallpaper is now an enormous brand. There have been so many that have tried to copy. But I think it's tough on them because they don't have the backing and they don't have the strength of a brand name. However, they do have the novelty of the new and that often helps them to win awards. It's new, it's exciting, and they have a six month funfair, but then many of them just die. In my experience, many of these magazines can replicate a kind of veneer of what we do at Wallpaper. But they can't replicate its inherent substance. They will look and feel wonderful. Yet they can't match our serious content and critical evaluation, and it all becomes an exercise in cosmetics. And that's why they don't last. The meat and conviction is absent, and without that, people won't come back for more. When

Wallpaper launched, it connected a type of content that had only really been approached academically. It took architecture and design, and mixed them with a little bit of glamour, lifestyle observation and sexiness. But it also had critical direction, good writing and intelligent editing. It went out of its way to find architecture and design in unusual places, it championed Swedish design in a way that hadn't been tried before. The imitators tried to use our formula without bringing anything new to the format. The same thing happened in the wake of Loaded magazine's success. Whatever you may think of the format, it did come up with a completely new way of presenting a men's fashion lifestyle magazine. It was very ironic and humorous in a marketplace dominated by Esquire and GQ, which were quite serious and maybe just a little bit dull. Loaded and Wallpaper didn't so much shake up the market, they simply went out and created a new one. Many of Loaded's competitors and imitators are still in there giving it a run for its money. Ours have sadly faded away. And that's the biggest danger for Wallpaper. There is no healthy competition. We're on our own, and it's weird. It's such an odd magazine in terms of its content and the size of the area it attempts to cover. Maybe no one else is stupid enough to attempt it! **Do you consider magazine design as an element in the history of art?** That's a tricky one. I always find those comparisons between design and art, hard. Difficult because the very nature of design is about answering problems, and magazines have to function on so many different levels. Whereas art is centred around self-expression. I have to compromise my work because of function, politics, legibility, size, you name it and there will be a reason why I might have to change it! That's bound to impact on my ability to self-express. An artist isn't subject to those restrictions and limitations. Of course all art has some restrictions. I have a feeling Pope Julius may have had something to say if he hadn't liked the depiction of God and Adam on the ceiling of the Sistine Chapel. But it ain't the same. There are so many practicalities I have to consider, and so many functions I have to satisfy, in terms of print quality and paper, distribution and advertising, that it could never be considered art. Culture, yes, but not art. It's no lesser for that. It's just different. **So how often do you feel you have to part from your design principles to create a magazine?** All the time and everyday! I don't think I have ever done anything I'm totally happy with. GQ was the trickiest. There might be some double page spreads within it I would be perfectly happy with. But within the structure of the completed magazine there's always going to be compromise. And it is right to compromise. If I was simply there to experiment with my passion for type and image, then we would lose our readership in three issues and we would all be out of a job. That would be pretty arrogant and I could never condone that. I have responsibilities to the people I work with and for. A magazine's function is to find and keep an audience. If it doesn't have one, it doesn't exist. Game over. You must walk the line between a magazine being well designed, and maintaining its readership. Many GQ readers buy a magazine to do exactly that. They buy it to read. This means they might want busy spreads containing large amounts of information. You can't say to them, "Sorry mate, I'm a bit of minimalist." **Is that the difference between GQ and Wallpaper?** There are elements of this in Wallpaper. The readers want to see some information laden pages as well. So maybe I have to compromise my artistic journey to get all that information included. They want to be visually stimulated by all these gorgeous things, but they also want to read about the twenty best hotels. Maybe I have to sacrifice a little on the award winning typographic gymnastics sometimes. But I am happier knowing we have been doing this thing properly for ten years, rather than extraordinarily for six months. **But you have still been nominated Art Director of the Year, twice.** That was with GQ and I think those things are mostly luck. It just depends who the judges are at the time. Obviously your work has to be decent, but a lot of it is down to how your magazine is being received at that moment. GQ had just got through that big change. The men's market was so fascinating at the time, with these new lads mags selling five, six, seven

OFTEN MAGAZINES LIKE WALLPAPER HIT A MOMENT, HIT A ZEITGEIST. THEY BECOME INCREDIBLY POWERFUL CULTURAL BEACONS, AND THEN THEY BURN OUT

A DESIGNER NEEDS A CERTAIN AMOUNT OF EGO TO DRIVE YOU FORWARD, BUT IF YOU LET THAT BLEED INTO YOUR WORK THEN YOU CAN NEVER SUCCESSFULLY SATISFY THE BRIEF

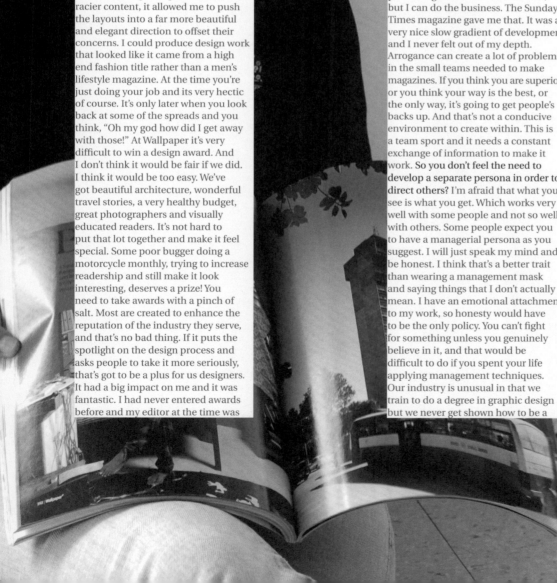

hundred thousand copies. GQ was in a very difficult position and maybe it wouldn't survive this onslaught. Somehow we had to make it sexier, whilst still looking like a Conde Nast publication. I think the judges may have been aware of the difficulty of the task! I also believe that when our advertisers began to panic over the racier content, it allowed me to push the layouts into a far more beautiful and elegant direction to offset their concerns. I could produce design work that looked like it came from a high end fashion title rather than a men's lifestyle magazine. At the time you're just doing your job and its very hectic of course. It's only later when you look back at some of the spreads and you think, "Oh my god how did I get away with those!" At Wallpaper it's very difficult to win a design award. And I don't think it would be fair if we did. I think it would be too easy. We've got beautiful architecture, wonderful travel stories, a very healthy budget, great photographers and visually educated readers. It's not hard to put that lot together and make it feel special. Some poor bugger doing a motorcycle monthly, trying to increase readership and still make it look interesting, deserves a prize! You need to take awards with a pinch of salt. Most are created to enhance the reputation of the industry they serve, and that's no bad thing. If it puts the spotlight on the design process and asks people to take it more seriously, that's got to be a plus for us designers. It had a big impact on me and it was fantastic. I had never entered awards before and my editor at the time was

very award savvy. He knew how to do it. He knew how to enter. And he knew you can use them as a selling tool, "It's official. We are the best designed magazine on the newsstand!" And people will listen. So I'm not debating their importance, they are incredibly important in the whole scheme of things. But you've got to take it with a pinch of salt as to whether you are that much better than anybody else. It's just a combination of fortune, fate and a bit of luck. **So you haven't used the awards to throw your weight around?** Who me? No never. I have total confidence in what I do, which is a useful asset in a tough industry like publishing. I know I'm not the best, but I can do the business. The Sunday Times magazine gave me that. It was a very nice slow gradient of development and I never felt out of my depth. Arrogance can create a lot of problems in the small teams needed to make magazines. If you think you are superior, or you think your way is the best, or the only way, it's going to get people's backs up. And that's not a conducive environment to create within. This is a team sport and it needs a constant exchange of information to make it work. **So you don't feel the need to develop a separate persona in order to direct others?** I'm afraid that what you see is what you get. Which works very well with some people and not so well with others. Some people expect you to have a managerial persona as you suggest. I will just speak my mind and be honest. I think that's a better trait than wearing a management mask and saying things that I don't actually mean. I have an emotional attachment to my work, so honesty would have to be the only policy. You can't fight for something unless you genuinely believe in it, and that would be difficult to do if you spent your life applying management techniques. Our industry is unusual in that we train to do a degree in graphic design but we never get shown how to be a

manager and that's where many of us end up. We don't go on to do three years of management and behavioural studies. We have to learn these skills as we go along and that's a good thing. Some companies will put you on these management courses. I tend to find them so contrived and almost deadening in their dishonesty. As long as I can lead by example, I can sleep at night. **What qualities separate a good designer from an average one?** Well let's take for granted that they have been well educated and they now have the skills to operate as a designer. Let's say they have learnt the ropes and now know the rules of typography and layout. It's also critical they have studied the history of design. You can't move forward until you've looked back. So all those things we shall say are in place. Then that leaves the ability to take a step back from your work and do it honestly. You must do what's right for the job, rather than what's right for your ego. That is the key. A designer needs a certain amount of ego to drive you forward, but if you let that bleed into your work then you can never successfully satisfy the brief. You cannot have two masters. *SBOOK 4*

What is it about magazine design that attracts designers? Can they be seen as vanity projects that can take risks and push boundaries? I don't think you can look at them as vanity projects. There are an awful lot of very egotistic and self-absorbed designers around, and some of them are very good designers. But in the end, if you're doing a good job you're responding to a brief of some sort as best as you can. In the case of a magazine especially

ZEM BLA MAP RA MAGAZINE

you're working with a group of people to make it good – other designers, editors, writers, publishers – it wouldn't work if it was too self-serving. Working as hard as you can at doing the best you can isn't anything to do with vanity. Whether they take risks or push boundaries depends entirely on the magazine and the people involved, the publisher and so on. It can happen and it's great when it does but it's becoming much harder to do I think, much rarer. There are all sorts of reasons for this but certainly part of the problem is our pervasive and crippling obsession with celebrity. It's like some sort of social disease, I hate it – and I hate the crap vacuous magazines that serve to cater for it. They're awful. There seem to be so few magazines these days with valuable and interesting content, that are well thought-out and well designed. There's a depressing lack of good writing too. It's a shame as there is so much to talk about, to discuss and argue against. Also there are too few publishers who are prepared to take the sort of risks that are necessary in order to produce something special and worthwhile. I'm not sure why I like magazines, I just do, but I'm sure they don't appeal to all designers. They can take up huge amounts of your time. They can be very stressful and they often don't pay very well. I suppose one of the reasons I like magazines is that they are often easily accessible to a large, wide-ranging audience, sometimes to an international audience. On the whole they tend to be relatively affordable and widely distributed. Potentially you can be communicating with an audience that can include very different people from very different places with different backgrounds and so on. That's exciting. The magazines that I've got involved in are about things that interest me, which is a fairly crucial point. I also just like working in print in a digital age.

Once you have got an audience to buy your product how do you keep their attention? How do magazines become collectable and build loyalty with their readers? If someone is interested in your magazine, engaged by the content, likes the way it looks and feels, then I guess you have a chance they will want to buy the next issue. I'd like to think that if a magazine had intelligent and valuable content, great writing and great design then that would be enough, and for some people maybe it would be, but that's more likely to make it collectable than make it a big seller. Some of the worst magazines, the celebrity-obsessed nonsense for example, sell very well. They wouldn't be considered, or have any interest in being, collectable. There are so many magazines out there now. There aren't any really 'big' magazines anymore, even Time magazine has seen a massive dip in sales. Vogue and Playboy don't sell like they used to 10 years ago. Magazines have to appeal to niche audiences now to have any chance.

Did you have an interest in magazine design on your degree course? No. I had a difficult time at St Martins. I did a lot of drinking and a lot of playing pool and not a lot of work. My interests had always been in painters and writers and I felt uncomfortable on the course. I hopped around from the photography course to illustration and then finally ended up in graphics but never got settled and never knew what I wanted to get out of it. Aside from fairly strong notions as to what I liked and what I didn't I had no real interest in becoming a designer, that didn't happen until much later. I was aware of magazines around that time which I thought looked good or interesting, things like Big Magazine, Raygun, Rolling Stone, ID, Eye and so on, but I didn't care who had put them together, I wasn't interested in who had art-directed them or the mechanics behind it. In fact I remember being more interested in the photographs. I used to cut out pictures from the Independent Magazine and the Guardian. The only designer who I was very aware of was Vaughan Oliver. I had come to him through the Pixies record covers and that had been because I liked the Pixies a lot, not because I was trying to discover anything about graphic design. Looking back, I can see that I had been more affected or influenced by the idea of magazines the year before

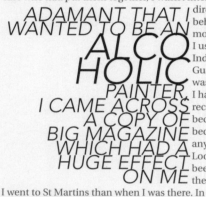

ADAMANT THAT I WANTED TO BE AN ALCOHOLIC PAINTER, I CAME ACROSS A COPY OF BIG MAGAZINE WHICH HAD A HUGE EFFECT ON ME

I went to St Martins than when I was there. In my foundation year, adamant that I wanted to be an alcoholic painter, I came across a copy of Big magazine which had a huge effect on me. I had no idea or interest in who had done it, I didn't bother to find out that Vince Frost did it until about 5 years later. I just remember thinking how wonderful it was. I had never seen anything like it. It was physically big, it had wonderful photographs including some great ones by the Douglas Brothers and Giles Revell and it was very bold and confident. It had huge letterpress titles, very masculine but beautifully and thoughtfully done somehow. It was visceral and immediate and powerful. The NYC cover Vince did for issue 7 of Big is still one of my favourite magazine covers. It's as good today as it was then. That same year my aunt bought me a subscription to Eye magazine as a present. The first issue was great in its own right, a typography special art-directed by Stephen Coates and I remember a feature on Dennis Ortiz Lopez and these great spreads for Rolling Stone magazine. It took me a very long time to work it out but I guess this was the first inkling, of sorts, that I was interested in graphic design or magazines. It was enough to nudge me towards St Martins to do a more design-based course.

In 2003 you were appointed joint Creative Director of Frost Design London. You devoted a great deal of this time to the literary magazine Zembla. Was this your first experience of magazine design? Not quite, I had just spent a year redesigning D&AD's Ampersand magazine four times. It's a quarterly members mag and we did four very different designs in their fortieth year – with a view to members' then voting for one which would then become the new design. The first one was tough, Ampersand#17, the November 2002 issue. Vince had been doing it for years, it had always been A3, all set in Franklin Gothic. We completely changed it,

Buckle Up

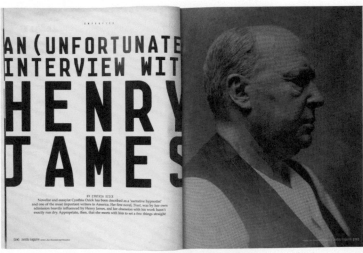

absolutely everything. It was an intimidating audience and the first thing I did with Vince. I learnt a lot doing that issue. I'm very pleased with the last one I did, Ampersand#20, the November 2003 issue, which I designed and art-directed. I think what Vince is doing with Ampersand now is great. Very interesting and very 'Vince'. Zembla was the first commercial magazine I guess. **What was your first reaction to the project?** I had seen and collected Butterfly magazine which Dan Crowe, the editor of Zembla, had done. I had liked Butterfly a lot, so I was excited by that connection when Dan came into the studio with the brief for Zembla. As I said my heroes have always included writers, it was like a dream brief.

Dan's a great bloke, a great editor and we got on very well. It makes a difference. We shared an interest in Nabokov. Butterfly had been a reference to him and Zembla is a city in his novel Pale Fire. It's difficult to impress upon people just how open the brief was. It was literally just a sheet of A4 paper with some scribbled ideas about what the magazine might be. It was an extraordinary brief. We were involved in everything from the very beginning, in every decision. There was no size, no page count, no name, no editorial structure etc, etc. That was very exciting and in some ways very daunting, a great thing to be involved with. I think magazines depend massively on the relationships between the art-director/designer and the editor. Dan gave us so much freedom to do what we wanted. I think that's probably a rare thing these days. **What spreads would you describe as your most successful?** My favourite ones are the Guillotine spread in issue#7 (p98-99), the Nietzsche spreads in issue#5 (p48-54), The Henry James spreads in issue#2 (p24-31). Zembla's aim, on the diagonal part of the Z on the cover and repeated in editor Dan Crowe's editorials, is to have 'fun with words'. **Was 'fun with words' the original concept?** Yes. It's the strapline for the magazine and the only thing that was in concrete when Dan approached us with the idea of doing a literary magazine. Having 'fun with words' both editorially and graphically. The 'fun', the humour, is an important part of Zembla, Butterfly didn't have

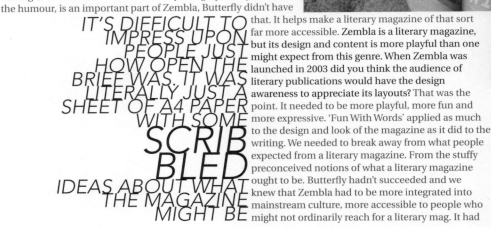

IT'S DIFFICULT TO IMPRESS UPON PEOPLE JUST HOW OPEN THE BRIEF WAS. IT WAS LITERALLY JUST A SHEET OF A4 PAPER WITH SOME SCRIB BLED IDEAS ABOUT WHAT THE MAGAZINE MIGHT BE

that. It helps make a literary magazine of that sort far more accessible. Zembla is a literary magazine, but its design and content is more playful than one might expect from this genre. **When Zembla was launched in 2003 did you think the audience of literary publications would have the design awareness to appreciate its layouts?** That was the point. It needed to be more playful, more fun and more expressive. 'Fun With Words' applied as much to the design and look of the magazine as it did to the writing. We needed to break away from what people expected from a literary magazine. From the stuffy preconceived notions of what a literary magazine ought to be. Butterfly hadn't succeeded and we knew that Zembla had to be more integrated into mainstream culture, more accessible to people who might not ordinarily reach for a literary mag. It had

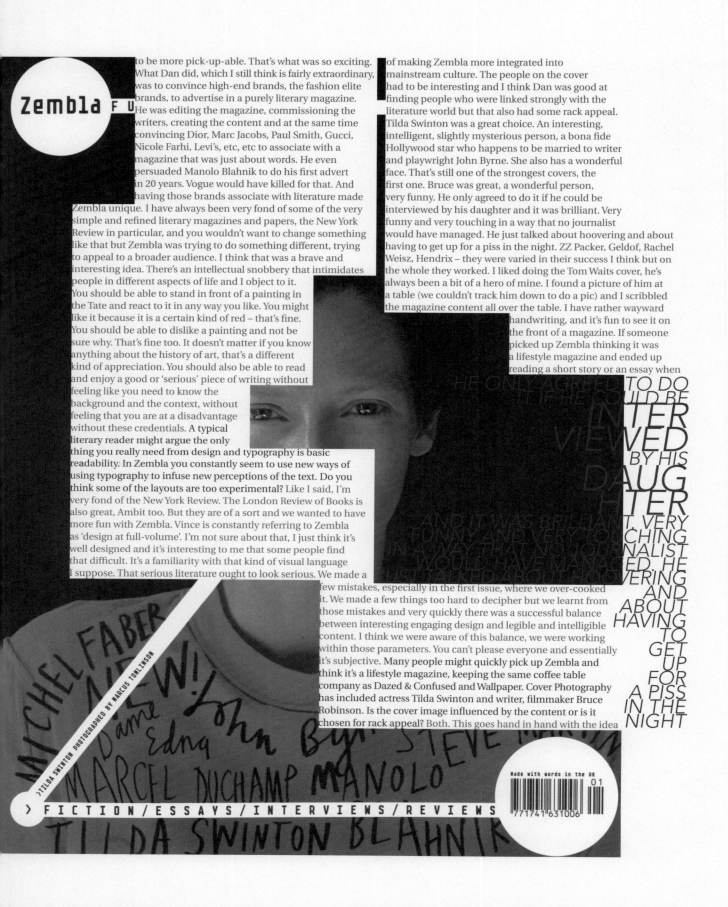

Zembla F U

to be more pick-up-able. That's what was so exciting. What Dan did, which I still think is fairly extraordinary, was to convince high-end brands, the fashion elite brands, to advertise in a purely literary magazine. He was editing the magazine, commissioning the writers, creating the content and at the same time convincing Dior, Marc Jacobs, Paul Smith, Gucci, Nicole Farhi, Levi's, etc, etc to associate with a magazine that was just about words. He even persuaded Manolo Blahnik to do his first advert in 20 years. Vogue would have killed for that. And having those brands associate with literature made Zembla unique. I have always been very fond of some of the very simple and refined literary magazines and papers, the New York Review in particular, and you wouldn't want to change something like that but Zembla was trying to do something different, trying to appeal to a broader audience. I think that was a brave and interesting idea. There's an intellectual snobbery that intimidates people in different aspects of life and I object to it. You should be able to stand in front of a painting in the Tate and react to it in any way you like. You might like it because it is a certain kind of red – that's fine. You should be able to dislike a painting and not be sure why. That's fine too. It doesn't matter if you know anything about the history of art, that's a different kind of appreciation. You should also be able to read and enjoy a good or 'serious' piece of writing without feeling like you need to know the background and the context, without feeling that you are at a disadvantage without these credentials. **A typical literary reader might argue the only thing you really need from design and typography is basic readability. In Zembla you constantly seem to use new ways of using typography to infuse new perceptions of the text. Do you think some of the layouts are too experimental?** Like I said, I'm very fond of the New York Review. The London Review of Books is also great, Ambit too. But they are of a sort and we wanted to have more fun with Zembla. Vince is constantly referring to Zembla as 'design at full-volume'. I'm not sure about that, I just think it's well designed and it's interesting to me that some people find that difficult. It's a familiarity with that kind of visual language I suppose. That serious literature ought to look serious. We made a few mistakes, especially in the first issue, where we over-cooked it. We made a few things too hard to decipher but we learnt from those mistakes and very quickly there was a successful balance between interesting engaging design and legible and intelligible content. I think we were aware of this balance, we were working within those parameters. You can't please everyone and essentially it's subjective. **Many people might quickly pick up Zembla and think it's a lifestyle magazine, keeping the same coffee table company as Dazed & Confused and Wallpaper. Cover Photography has included actress Tilda Swinton and writer, filmmaker Bruce Robinson. Is the cover image influenced by the content or is it chosen for rack appeal?** Both. This goes hand in hand with the idea

of making Zembla more integrated into mainstream culture. The people on the cover had to be interesting and I think Dan was good at finding people who were linked strongly with the literature world but that also had some rack appeal. Tilda Swinton was a great choice. An interesting, intelligent, slightly mysterious person, a bona fide Hollywood star who happens to be married to writer and playwright John Byrne. She also has a wonderful face. That's still one of the strongest covers, the first one. Bruce was great, a wonderful person, very funny. He only agreed to do it if he could be interviewed by his daughter and it was brilliant. Very funny and very touching in a way that no journalist would have managed. He just talked about hoovering and about having to get up for a piss in the night. ZZ Packer, Geldof, Rachel Weisz, Hendrix – they were varied in their success I think but on the whole they worked. I liked doing the Tom Waits cover, he's always been a bit of a hero of mine. I found a picture of him at a table (we couldn't track him down to do a pic) and I scribbled the magazine content all over the table. I have rather wayward handwriting, and it's fun to see it on the front of a magazine. If someone picked up Zembla thinking it was a lifestyle magazine and ended up reading a short story or an essay when

HE ONLY AGREED TO DO IT IF HE COULD BE INTERVIEWED BY HIS DAUGHTER AND IT WAS BRILLIANT. VERY FUNNY AND VERY TOUCHING IN A WAY THAT NO JOURNALIST WOULD HAVE MANAGED. HE JUST TALKED ABOUT HOOVERING AND ABOUT HAVING TO GET UP FOR A PISS IN THE NIGHT

MICHEL FABER
NEW!
Dame Edna John Byrne STEVE MARTIN
MARCEL DUCHAMP MANOLO
TILDA SWINTON BLAHNIK

TILDA SWINTON PHOTOGRAPHED BY MARCUS TOMLINSON

› FICTION/ESSAYS/INTERVIEWS/REVIEWS

Made with words in the UK
01
9 771741 631006

they may not have otherwise – then that's great. The big difference between Zembla and the sort of titles you mentioned is that Zembla is more intelligent. It has better writing. I enjoyed the fact that it was rubbing shoulders with much larger lifestyle titles. **Zembla was printed five times a year. What were the timescales from initial briefing to the magazine going to press?** Usually I'd get about 2 weeks to put the whole thing together. Sometimes a bit longer, sometimes less. It was always stressful. We'd try and nail the page plan as early as possible but ads would jump about, the content came in dribs and drabs. There were always problems (that seems to be an inherent characteristic of magazines) but it always got done. I remember making myself pretty ill on the Weisz issue just through sleep deprivation. I remember walking about on Tottenham Court Road and I couldn't remember how I'd got there or what I'd done for the last 2 hours. **How many designers worked on the project?** To start with it was just me and Vince. We worked inordinately hard on the first issue trying to get it right. Night and day for months. We put ourselves under a huge amount of pressure. Issue 2 was just me and Vince again and then he emigrated to Australia. I took over as creative director of the London studio and we tried to design the third issue from London and Australia. The Australia studio did the notebook section for example. Vince and I talked about spreads and ideas as much as possible, sent emails back and forth. So, depending how busy the Sydney studio was we had a few people helping out there. The London studio was small (three people) and we usually had a lot of other projects on. I enjoyed working late on my own. I found it difficult to delegate. **How closely did you work with the editorial team on Zembla, being in a different studio do they have any say over the final designs other than you being influenced by their writing?**

We worked very closely with the editorial team. We didn't have much time to put Zembla together and it benefited from us all working closely I think. The best magazines are the ones where those relationships work, where everyone is working as hard as they can to produce the best magazine they can. In terms of the design Dan was very hands-off,

MAGAZINE
DESIGN IS
HARD
I THINK
IT'S A
CR
AFT.
TOO MANY
MAGAZINES
LOOK CRAP
BECAUSE
PEOPLE
ARE LAZY
THEY DON'T
WORK HARD
ENOUGH

he allowed us an unprecedented amount of freedom to just make the spreads look as good as we possibly could. One of the vital things about how we set up Zembla is that there are no style sheets really. There's a grid which we could use if we needed to but we often ignored that too. There was nothing that made our life easy and there were no rules that got in the way of us doing what we wanted. Each spread was like starting from scratch. That was a very compelling and tough way of doing it. You had to work very hard to make each page look good. Magazine design is hard I think, it's a craft. Too many magazines look crap because people are lazy, they don't work hard enough. **Do you always read the text before you design the spread?** Yes. I think it's important on any magazine but completely essential with a literary magazine like Zembla. Zembla was unusual in that we were only given writing, lots of very good writing and we had to come up with the visual content. I don't know how you'd do that without understanding in detail what you're working with. I spent hours in coffee shops with the writing before I started on anything. **Do you receive all the editorial content before you start designing an issue or does it come in at different stages?** It comes in different stages. I always ask for as much as possible by a certain date but it never happens like that. I've never done a magazine where everything is delivered and sitting there waiting to be made into a magazine. **Is it the job of the Art Director or the Editor to build the structure of the magazine. Who decides on the placement of advertisements and main editorial features?** The structure is normally built by the editorial team but the art-director ought to be involved, ought to be able to influence it. With Zembla we had a lot of freedom to add pages to features if we thought it was necessary or remove pages, swap articles around, move an ad etc. With RA I have absolutely no control over ad placements. I'm given a page plan with ads already placed and I have to work around that. **Do you follow a similar template for each issue? How much freedom do you have from issue to issue?** There needs to be a certain amount of consistency to the structure of the magazine. People need to become familiar with the navigation of the magazine, know where things are – so yes there's a similar template for each issue. Notebook at the front, some stuff in the middle, reviews at the back – that sort of thing. **Do you think Zembla's mono-spaced, block-like display face has a similar feel to Maps angular sans serif? Is this typography an expression of your personal graphic language?** The Zembla font is called Arete Mono. I bought it before I joined Frost just because I liked it but also because it was so cheap. It was $19. I didn't have a use for it at the time I just thought it looked great. I'm glad we used it for Zembla, I think it works well – but I can't use it again, it's too tied to Zembla now. I used Hoboken on MAP. There is a similarity I guess and in both these cases I like the contrast between these big heavy fonts and the more elegant traditional bulk text font (New Caledonia in MAP and Palatino in Zembla). I'm not sure about 'personal graphic language', I'm still learning. **Whilst working at Frost you and Zoë Bather, Art Directed MAP Magazine. Are you still involved with the project now you have opened Studio8 Design?** No, I wish we were. The deal was we would design the first issue and then hand over the templates. It's a tough thing to do, to work that hard on setting it up and designing the first issue, then hand it over to someone else. Matthew Ball took it on and he's doing a great job. **How did the briefs differ from designing Map, a magazine about contemporary art to literary magazine like Zembla? How did the design reflect this?** Well the content is completely different, obviously. With Zembla we were given a load of

I BOUGHT IT BEFORE I JOINED FROST JUST BECAUSE I LIKED IT BUT ALSO BECAUSE IT WAS SO CHEAP. IT WAS $19.

words and we had to make that as interesting as possible visually. We had to invent the visual content, whether that was just doing something interesting typographically or finding a photograph or illustration etc. MAP is an art magazine, its duty is to display images, works of art, well and respectfully. The challenge is to then make good exciting layouts around that. They're almost the reverse of one another in that respect. **How long did it it take to develop the visual language of MAP? Can you talk about the co-ordinate navigation bar that was used for the page numbers? Was the concept derived from the word 'Map'?** We worked for a few months designing MAP before doing the first issue. The moving co-ordinate was one of the first ideas I had and it just seemed to work. They work like lines of longitude, plotting your position in the magazine, they follow your journey through the magazine. They also help a great deal to give the pages an identity. The visual language of cartography is wonderful and we had all that as reference material, although we were conscious that making use of it could be overdone. The strapline is 'You are here: Journeys in Contemporary Art' and the concept was very much derived from the word 'MAP'. The grid on the cover is a simple mapping-out of the area, it means the masthead can be placed in any of six possible positions. It means you have some flexibility when designing the cover, a capacity to be more sympathetic to the image.

MAP
You are here: Journeys in Contemporary Art

FRANCIS ALŸS / NATHAN COLEY / SIMON STARLING / GRAHAM FAGEN / BEAGLES AND RAMSAY / JERUSALEM / MEXICO / ARGYLL

Issue 1 / Spring 2005
£4.95

The new international art magazine from Scotland

MAP IS AN ART MAGAZINE. ITS DUTY IS TO DISPLAY IMAGES, WORKS OF ART, WELL AND RESPECTFULLY. THE CHALLENGE IS TO THEN MAKE GOOD EXCITING LAYOUTS AROUND THAT

That same square for the masthead was then taken into the magazine and used to hold the standfirsts and help announce the beginnings of features. The review section has small + marks plotting out the grid, uses Gridnik as the main font and was printed on a different stock. That helped differentiate that section. The different stock was too expensive to maintain, they dropped that after the first three issues and just printed the background colour. It still works. **How did you become the Art Director of RA Magazine? How did this project differ from Zembla and Map magazine where they were both start up jobs and you could create a completely new graphic language from the beginning?** The project came about because I had just done the posters for the Royal

Focus
São Paolo Bienal...........50

Glasgow
Torsten Lauschmann........52
Michael Fullerton.........52
Kate Davis................53

Paris
Thomas Hirschhorn.........54

Stirling
Rings of Saturn...........55

Washington DC
Dan Flavin................56

Edinburgh
Mat Collishaw.............57
Andy Warhol...............57
Ellen Gallagher...........58
Holbein to Hockney........59

Aberdeen
Urban Atlas...............59

London
Camilla Løw...............60

Academy of Arts Summer Exhibition. The publishing side of the RA saw that and liked it. I had just given up my position as creative director of Frost Design and, by coincidence, was doing a bit of work with Simon Esterson when the RA asked if I would like to pitch for the redesign of RA magazine. I was aware of the magazine from the days when Simon used to do it and was slightly apprehensive about taking something on that had already been done so well by him. But it felt like a good project to try and take on. In contrast to Zembla and MAP the RA has been around for 25 years. It's very established and it's a very different set of challenges because of that. It also has the biggest circulation of any

I GUESS I AM ART DIRECTOR AND DESIGNER, IN THE AB SENCE OF ANYONE ELSE BY THOSE TITLES (IT'S WHAT THEY CALL ME)

arts magazine in Europe. The Royal Academy of Arts itself, as an institution, can be a frustrating bureaucratic mess to deal with. Occasionally things feel like they're being designed by committee and in certain instances people are concerned only with a specific section of the magazine and will view it in complete isolation from the rest of the magazine. Thing's like that are difficult. I'm getting more used to it now. I'm working on my fifth issue at the moment, but it's very different to what I had been used to previously. I feel less like I'm part of a small team striving to make this magazine as good as it can be and more like a part of a big messy process and if I want to be heard I have to shout a lot and remonstrate. **As an Art director how involved do you get with designing spreads and kerning type? Has** this differed from the magazines you have worked on? You are both designer and Art Director of RA Magazine, do you prefer this setup? I'm a designer – I design the spreads, I kern the type, that's what I enjoy doing and that's what I've done on all the magazines I've worked on. I find it very difficult to delegate, which is a handicap, so if Art Director means coming up with ideas and then asking someone else to produce it then I am categorically not an Art Director. My role with the RA magazine is complicated and confusing. I guess I am Art Director and Designer, in the absence of anyone else by those titles, but I have far less control and less say than I enjoyed with MAP or Ampersand or Zembla. It's a different kind of beast. I have to fight very hard for what I believe in with the RA. The RA Magazine frustrates me because I know it could be better, but I'm learning and it still interests me because the challenges are so different. **Who makes the final decisions of what designs make it into RA, are there creative arguments at this stage?** There are a lot of

China

TREASURES

'China: The Three Emperors' overflows with exquisi... But beyond their beauty, these objects are laden with... On the following pages, *RA Magazine* introduces so... most ravishing riches – from enamel to jade, lacquer... asks experts to describe their deeper meanings.

arguments with the RA. Essentially the buck stops with the editorial team (this is why the Art Director title is misleading) and I think they often get it wrong. So I spend a huge amount of energy defending and explaining why I think something is right or why something is wrong. I get a lot of what I want through but it's not easy and I still think it's at a half-way house at the moment. Editorially it's strong and should compete better on the shelves of WH Smiths. They are the largest art magazine in Europe and that's because of their subscription base. It's a wonderful thing for a magazine to have, it gives them great power in regards to advertising for example but because of that there seems to be a contentedness with their situation, and maybe that's understandable, but they don't want to push the magazine forward or strive, in any serious way, to improve the magazine. It's very safe. There are elements within the RA, I think, who do have aspirations for the magazine but the way the RA is set up, as a whole, is hopeless. **You've used a red circle on the cover as a masthead and throughout on the spreads, can you tell us about this idea?** The circles on the cover can be positioned anywhere, made larger or smaller, I can add circles to hold more information, make the circles opaque, a different colour. It helps to create something which is flexible and capable of being sympathetic to the image behind. I've used the red circles throughout the magazine as page flags, to hold bullet points etc. It helps give the magazine its identity. **What magazines do you read and who are your favourite editorial designers?** I'll pick up anything that looks good. I'm interested in Newspapers and the magazines they produce. Newspapers are behaving more and more like magazines these days. The Guardian's redesign, for example, has made it far more picture-led rather than title-led. A lot of the good writing is in the newspapers now and the weekend supplements. They're so well designed and sophisticated, the photography is always extremely good and they're well edited. The Observer's Sport Monthly and Music Monthly are great. The New York Times Style magazine is great, etc, etc, etc. Favourite editorial designer? Working today? Mark Porter or Simon Esterson I guess. Not working today? Hard to look past Alexey Brodovitch. *SBOOK 4*

RA
ROYAL ACADEMY OF ARTS MAGAZINE
Nº88 / AUTUMN 2005 £4.50

TREASURES FROM THE FORBIDDEN CITY
ZAHA HADID'S FLUID FORMS
RUBENS IN THE FLESH

CHINESE WHISPERS

*YORGO TLOUPAS

**INTERSECTION

What were your initial thoughts for the design of Intersection prior to its launch? My original idea for any magazine would be to prioritise images over design. The latter has to take a step back, since it really is a technical craft rather than an art. The main goal should be to make things readable, and I hate design that comes to the forefront to end up as a decorative element. However I'm not going to deny that I have a sense of aesthetics and I want the pages to look good. For example, one of my rules when I started was to never put text on top of images. I just wanted to provide a simple and self-effacing frame for the photographs to express themselves. Issue one of Intersection had a hybrid design somewhere between a magazine and a book, with a hard cover but a magazine-like structure inside. I guess it was a homage to 1970s Nordic and Swiss design, very bold, very strict, very grid orientated with dense black columns of text, printed quite tightly to each other and near to the edge of the page. From that first issue the identity evolved into something more 'commercial', but still with this black and white, slightly retro structure. I even let colour sneak in the layouts. **What design problems did you have to solve within this very early development stage?** One of the problems lies in the temptation to follow a truly minimalist route, which in the end will only appeal to a limited group of people. It's the opposite of a commercial approach that makes the reader instantly aware of what's going on in an article. Modern magazine work uses catchy headlines and bold pull quotes to draw you in. If you look at Esquire or GQ, their layouts are incredibly complicated, reminiscent of web pages almost. They've got sub boxes, different sizes of type, and different faces for everything. This gives the impression of a wealth of information, an unlimited and vertiginous amount of things to dwell on and explore. But I'm resisting this kind of approach by keeping the design very straight forward. I am trying to find a balance between something that people would want to read instantly, and a visual language that tells the reader, he will find demanding, thoughtful and sophisticated content beyond these plain black headlines. **How important is the creative director in this process?** Well I'm very lucky because I part-own the magazine! There's no despotic or tyrannical publisher who's forcing us to decrease the leading, increase the amount of colours, add sex, or remove political content. My business partner and I make all the decisions. Some decisions might lose us money, but at least there's no one to overrule us. I've got free range to adjust things according to how I think and feel. That's a genuine luxury in this business. **But running your own magazine must be a big risk?** It's a risky hobby, albeit a very expensive one. A traditional publishing group can reduce their costs by having 10, 20, or 100 titles. They can print them on mass at the same time and in the same place. They can have grouped advertising departments. And they have a wealth of 'built up' knowledge to draw on when they want to launch a new title. Our approach is very different. Independent publishing usually means no big backers and a small team dealing with all kinds of problems. We also need to learn how to get around them on the go. I've been very lucky because Dan

MY ORIGINAL IDEA FOR ANY MAGAZINE WOULD BE TO PRIORITISE IMAGES OVER DESIGN. FOR ME DESIGN HAS TO TAKE A STEP BACK, ALMOST AS IF IT IS A CRAFT RATHER THAN AN ART

Ross, my business partner, has found solutions to many of these difficulties, including saving us a small fortune on printing and delivery. Magazine distribution systems are very corrupted and not at all geared towards small publishers. It's extremely hard to get into WH Smiths. In some instances it costs more money to get your magazine on to a newsstand than it does to produce it. So it's very difficult on that level. But it's been an amazing learning curve and it still is. **How did you set your own brief for Intersection?** The USP of the magazine resides in its theme, not its design. I didn't start Intersection to produce nice images or design nice layouts, we started it because we saw a real gap for a clever cultural approach to cars, and that became the brief. I'm not interested in engineering, horsepower or how much space there is in the boot. I'm interested in architecture, art, music, design, fashion, and how those things might link to one of our most culturally significant objects - cars. I was completely bewildered as to why there wasn't a car magazine that addressed the subject from any viewpoint other than, 'how expensive and how fast?' **How important is it for a magazine to have such a strong and unique concept?** It's crucial and that's why I'm always let down each time I flick through a style and trend magazine. I spent some time at the airport yesterday and I flicked through GQ Style and Another Man, and they just bored me to death. I hate it when GQ, for example, will try to tell you this is the woman you have to like, this is the film you have to see, these are the socks you have to buy. They pretend they know everything about everything in a very patronising way. I also call some of those magazines "tear sheet providers". Photographers work for them because they are going to get some nice pictures to cut out and put in their portfolio, but that's their only reason for existing. The same goes for Ten, Tank and that new one, Wonderland. They just seem to be created as part of a business to business model. For me content is primordial, I only get turned on by magazines that have a very strong identity. Vanity Fair is my favourite magazine because the writing is amazing. It's very well researched and very serious, but the art direction and photography is pretty hopeless. I also like specialist magazines. I'm a skateboarder, and skateboard magazines do their thing better than anyone else. There's not much to read, but at least they know what they're talking about. What we are trying to do here is to have an opinion and to back that up with our knowledge of the subject. We limit ourselves to one area that covers cars, bikes, and transport. That allows us to be truer and more respected by our readers because they know we have this passion. **You produced a limited edition 'Issue 00' of Intersection, in a luxury box set. How did this issue influence those that followed?** We started Dazed & Confused with three partners: Dan Ross, who is now the editor, Rankin, who is no longer involved, and me. So when we wanted to launch Intersection we already had a firm understanding of how to go

CAR MAGS TRY TO MAKE YOU FEEL A BOND WITH CARS; THAT'S WHY THEY HIDE ANY HUMAN PRESENCE IN THE PICTURE. THE DRIVER IS HIDDEN BEHIND A PILLAR, SO THE READER CAN IMAGINE HIMSELF AT THE WHEEL. THAT'S PRETTY DAMN SIMILAR TO A PORN MAG

about it. We also had offices, contacts and a close association with D&C that would open most doors extremely easily. But to the great dismay of Dan and to my strong regret I completely overspent the allocated photo budget on Issue 00! Since then we've learnt how to reduce these costs, and I guess that first issue was necessary to make us realise that our existence really depends on the willingness of photographers to work for very little – if any – money! Obviously that issue 00 did not carry advertising, as we wanted to use it to test grounds and see how the buying agencies would react. It was a good approach I think, but we still spent an enormous amount of our time and energy chasing these life-saving adverts. **What kind of pre-marketing did you do?**

That's a dirty word round these parts! We talked to friends and asked them if they'd ever bought a car magazine. Those that had, hid them away in their Herald Tribune like porn mags. Or they pretended they'd bought them for someone else. There was a clear hole in the market and we could see how fashion, art, design and architecture magazines were featuring cars in virtually every issue. We then used Dazed and Another to put out teaser ads, and did 2 dummies to show to the advertising and distribution world. **Do you really believe that buying your average car magazine is akin to buying a porn mag?** When people ask me what I do I always say I create magazines, and then hope they don't ask what kind! If you tell them it's about cars they think you're some kind of nerd from the back woods who just cares about massive exhaust pipes. There is a stigma attached and that's quite understandable when you meet some of people in the car industry. Of course you can accuse the fashion world of being superficial and overtly concerned with image and trends. But at least you can find the interesting and eccentric amongst their number. That's pretty difficult in the standardised, conformist world of the automobile. Traditional car mags try to make you feel a direct bond with an automobile, that's why they hide any human presence in the picture. The driver is hidden behind a pillar, so the reader can imagine himself at the wheel. That's pretty damn similar to a porn magazine. The men are cropped out so you can imagine yourself in there with that blonde with the huge breasts. It's a cruel and crude linkage, but it's there. **So who was your target audience?** Our intended audience was and still is the affluent, creative and curious urban male. But we are also unisex and we probably have more female readers than any other car magazine. Our target audience are people with creative minds. That's not necessarily creative people like designers, architects, and fashion photographers. It could be bank managers, city boys or people in less art-related jobs who still have an open-minded approach to things, and a liking for cars. **How did you create your flexible grid?** It's not that flexible! I took a few risks in that the more margin you leave around the columns, the more space you leave between them, and the more space between the lines, the easier it is to read. I wanted the text to look block-like and also to fill the page. I also wanted to keep consistency, even through the three different sections. I wanted them to feel part of the same identity and yet different. But there's room for improvement. At the moment I'm using this six column grid which can be divided into three, two, or even some half columns. I like to stick to it and never let anything escape from that grid! **Can you explain your use of typography?** When I studied we were forced to not use Macs. We cut and pasted the letterforms, which I used to find rather strange because in 1993 computers were around, but my school (ESAG in Paris) had these principles which I now completely understand. When Macintosh made layout and design more accessible, the range of possibilities became endless and everyone went wild. Magazines would have ten different typefaces, use shadows, overlay text, play with non-readability. For one David Carson, who succeeded in Ray Gun, you had thousands who failed and destroyed years of typographic tradition with an overdose of filters and layers. My goal was to only ever use a maximum of four faces with just one of those for the text. And I've stuck with that from

OUR TARGET AUDIENCE ARE PEOPLE WITH CREATIVE MINDS. THAT'S NOT NECESSARILY CREATIVE PEOPLE LIKE DESIGNERS, ARCHITECTS, AND FASHION PHOTOGRAPHERS. IT COULD BE BANK MANAGERS, CITY BOYS OR PEOPLE IN LESS ART-RELATED JOBS WHO STILL HAVE AN OPEN-MINDED APPROACH TO THINGS, AND A LIKING FOR CARS

the beginning. Mind you I've swapped that text face three times. I started with Akzidenz Grotesk, then went to Rockwell until it got overused. I switched to a face I didn't like called Johanna, before going back to a slab serif called Serifa that we still use. Our headlines are done with specially designed fonts called Hellenica, Serifight, Suisse and so on (they're all modified versions of existing fonts). I wanted something that looked like it could have been designed in 1966. I don't want to use systems or possibilities that are only offered by computers. Intersection has to look like it could have been put together by hand. **What about the structure of the magazine?** In an ideal world we would have more pages and more section dividers. It's a great luxury when you can afford to have a double page spread to announce you are entering a new section. Unfortunately it's a luxury we can't afford. So our sections are indicated in the contents page and then marked by slightly different layouts within the magazine, although they probably still need greater differentiation. I wish I had longer to put it together but I usually give myself two weeks to finish it. But of course it's mostly the last week that things get done! The process of gathering all the images and articles takes a long time. And that's the bit I'm much more involved in; making sure we get the right images and selecting these from the photo shoots. Once that's done the design is quite a quick affair. Rob Milton works with me on the design process and although we always try to get pages designed as soon as we receive shots, we always end up putting everything together at the last minute. **What do you see as your major challenge when designing a new issue?** It's the rhythm of the magazine; to balance out the small rich bits, where there are four articles on a page, against the longer features. It's also about finding the right balance between images and text. I hate the latest issue (17) because everything is equal, there's no big feature to pull it all together. There's a lot of small interesting things, but they compete and that's the problem with some issues; finding the proper rhythm. **You once said that concept cars can be as demanding as Naomi Campbell. Was there a particular incident that brought you to this conclusion?** Everything in the car industry is multiplied by a factor of ten in terms of difficultly. Concept cars cost up to two million pounds, they're one-offs and they've got very tight schedules. At the moment I've been waiting to shoot an Aston Martin. It's been out since January, so its not even that new. It has been in Geneva, then it came back to London for repairs, and now it's going to New York! They can't even find us half a day for a photoshoot. And when they finally give us a slot I guarantee it will be in some godforsaken hole where you can't create interesting imagery. When you do finally catch up with some of these concept cars, they come with uncooperative minders, the wheels don't turn, the doors won't open, or the electrics don't work. I'd say that's pretty near to working with a supermodel. **Do you use photography to create a narrative within an article?** That's very hard to do sometimes, but it's a really crucial approach to our photography. There's nothing more boring than a car put in front of a plain white background. It's amazing how many angles a cinematographer can find to shoot a scene in a movie. That's where I find my source of inspiration and I always try to find photographers with the same mindset. I guess I'm also really interested in bringing a new eye to events that have been done to

WHEN YOU DO FINALLY CATCH UP WITH SOME OF THESE CONCEPT CARS, THE WHEELS DON'T TURN AND THE DOORS WON'T OPEN. I'D SAY THAT'S PRETTY NEAR TO WORKING WITH A SUPERMODEL

death. For example, we once did a photoshoot with Martin Parr, sending him to the Japanese F1 Grand Prix. Obviously he took these weird, amazing shots of people caught off guard, their vanities laid bare by his strong flash. What was quite funny was the fact that Jaguar paid for this trip, and they asked if we had more flattering pictures of their drivers, to which we replied that Martin Parr was never going make anyone look their best. They knew of his work beforehand so there was really nothing to argue about on this… **Isn't it strange art directing car shoots with fashion photographers?** However good the fashion photographer is, and they are usually very good, they still find it a daunting challenge to shoot a car. They all want to do it, because they either like cars or they think they might go on to be asked to shoot a car campaign for fifty grand. But once faced with the actual object, many struggle to find creative ways to photograph vehicles. Unless they search for ways to be inventive, they will end up with the same pictures as everyone else. We brief photographers tightly, but that's also a problem because of the freedom they are given at

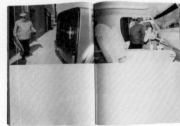

fashion magazines. They normally get asked to go to a disused flat in Hackney, take a stylist, and come back with something interesting. Whereas we tell them to go to Detroit, in some unlit car park, shoot the car from this angle and that angle. "Oh and don't forget to include this detail and that detail from the interior." Some of them just freak out and complain that, "I'm not used to being given orders". **Do you feel your work at Intersection has influenced how other car magazines look?** My partner Dan thinks this is the case, but I've never really seen it that way. Every designer knows this stuff is in the air, and I've designed things that came out at the same time as something done in exactly the same way by someone else. British car magazines generally look good. Top Gear doesn't look too modern, but it does contain good articles. Car Magazine does look quite well designed. But England is an exception and if you go anywhere else in the world, it's a catastrophe. In America, the design, writing, photography, everything, even the quality of the paper is terrible. In France I can't describe how bad it is. **Why does an independent magazine need to get involved with advertorials?** Well I would agree it's a slightly perverted way of creating content, because you don't actually tell the reader that what they're looking at is an ad. But it satisfies the clients, as they gain credibility if it looks like part of the editorial. Of course they pay us, but we would only give them this kind of 'biased' coverage if it was something we intended to cover anyway. **What was it like studying at an art school in Paris?** The school was called ESAG and I had some amazing teachers. We had to draw constantly for the first two years. Nudes, still lives, and sketches in the streets. It's a very demanding programme in terms of workload. And very different from somewhere like St Martins where you hand in your dissertation when you can! They seem very relaxed in comparison. We got fired if we didn't work hard enough. Every week I would have at least one sleepless night, and that really taught me how to work hard. I discovered how you must work non-stop until the job is done. We also learnt photography, typography, calligraphy, drawing, illustration, and design. In fact everything you might need to create a magazine. In Paris there's a small mafia of ex-students from that school who always end up working together because everyone knows they have the same work ethic. The guy who directed the Honda "cog" ad was from Esag for example. **When you art directed Crash, you took a very different design direction from the majority of French magazines of the time?** Crash was a

owner who is also a true car nut. We now think it's better to promote this connection through exhibitions and events. Car related art usually involves monumental sculptures or interactive work that's best viewed or experienced in the real, rather than on the page. **Is the cover the most important**

kind of a multi cultural fashion, art and design magazine. They had only completed one issue when I joined, and it looked terrible. They hadn't a clue. They were really clever people but they had no idea about design. In the France of the late nineties there were no well designed magazines. They all looked Apple Mac generated with fonts and effects everywhere. So I moved in completely the opposite direction. My Crash magazines looked like they came out of a 1972 Graphis annual. I'm completely influenced by that period. As a craft I don't think the minimalist design work of that time has been bettered. Even the ads were superior. Marketing has taken over modern magazine work to the detriment of design. In those days there was a rigorous approach to the design process formulated by some of the very best Swiss designers at the summit of their powers. People like Josef Muller Brockman. His influence was everywhere. Helvetica was in wide usage and I think it's still one the best typeface in the world. You can do anything with those classic sans serif fonts. At Crash I was effectively working for nothing and that gave me a lot of freedom. We debated the look of the magazine, but in the end I took a hard line Swiss approach. And of course people thought it difficult to read because there was little change in type size and very few elements to break the long patches of text. Some people got a bit put off, but most really liked its alternative approach. I worked there for two years and it opened a lot of doors. There was nothing else like it. Crash was really my portfolio coming out every month and it allowed me to get good clients, who asked me for a similar approach – but who paid me for it. **One of your initial ideas for a magazine was to bring car culture and contemporary art together. Do you feel you've achieved this at Intersection?** It depends on the issue. We always have contemporary art in there somewhere and we are planning a special art issue. In fact I had a meeting earlier today with a major art collector and gallery

THE PROBLEM IS MAINLY THE COVER; TO GET THE COVER TO ENCOMPASS EVERYTHING THAT IS IN THE MAGAZINE. BE CAUSE THERE IS SO MUCH AND IT IS SO HARD TO SUM IT UP IN ONE IMAGE. OUR COVERS ARE ALL LET DOWNS FROM WHAT THEY COULD HAVE BEEN

mechanism for selling an issue? The problem is to make the cover encompass everything that's in the magazine. There's so much in there that it's hard to sum it all up in one image. We put a lot of effort into Intersection's covers, but in a way many fail to convey the extent of content. **Why did you feel the need for a redesign after issue 13?** At the moment my redesigns occur whenever I get a new computer! I'm currently using this ancient Mac and it can't be upgraded to OS 10. I have a vintage attitude, of which I'm far too proud. When I get my new laptop and In-design there will be a complete rethink. Although I've said I wanted the magazine to avoid looking like it's been influenced by a computer or a program, it's going to be much easier to do some of the things I've always wanted to do. **Why have you teamed up with Surface magazine to launch a US edition of Intersection?** Everyone's been telling us that's the next logical step. You have to reach the states, as it's such a big market. They don't have any cool car magazines and yet everyone owns a car. Dan looked into it and Surface came out as a good partner because they already have an audience not too dissimilar to ours. They also have offices in New York and San Francisco and most importantly they have advertisers who might want to appear in Intersection. We are still in discussions about contracts, but its proven useful so far and they've got solutions to some of our problems. But we are not in the states that often and so it's likely to be hard to keep track of what's going on. I haven't been to New York in six months, although Dan is there every month. Luckily our content is international and that means we don't have to make major changes between English and American editions. In an average issue we would shoot in 20 different countries. We do try to make our content a little more USA friendly by having less English landscapes and licence plates. And of course we Americanize our English. **Who are your favourite art directors?** Nova was amazing when Harry Peccinotti was the art director. It was very risk taking for its day. I remember seeing this double page spread of breasts, lots of different types of breasts. It was an article about feminine identity. It just showed diversity. Provocative for the era, but not in anyway vulgar. Quite the opposite of the way modern magazines treat the female form. Because of my personal obsession with logos, I tend to hold identity designers in higher esteem than magazine designers. People like Paul Rand or Chermayeff & Geismar are amazing. There's much more to designing a great logo than to designing a magazine. A good logo must reach an enormous audience and yet contain the essence of a company in a single image. I think the

SLA CIT

WHAT IF RETIREE FULL-TIME RV'ERS WERE TO SPEND THEIR WINTERS ON A REAL-LIFE MAD MAX MOVIE SET? IN THE SELF-GOVERNED PIECE OF DESERT KNOWN AS SLAB CITY, CALIFORNIA, THEY DO. AND THOSE FREE-SPIRITED SENIORS LOVE EVERY SECOND OF IT.

Habitat logo by GTF is one of best I've seen in the last decade. It's one single line in one colour, it's thin, it's elegant, and it can be used in many ways. It's mind blowing and I absolutely love it. For magazines, Henry Wolf's work at Esquire in the 60s is also worth a look, as for contemporary influences then Jop Van Bennekom is probably a genius. There's no excesses in his design work for Fantastic Man, Re- and Butt magazines. His layouts are so strict, so Nordic, but really intelligent and logical at the same time, making the structure and sense of the issue apparent immediately. I also liked The Face before it closed. It was poppy and entertaining in a way we've never managed to be. It was like eating candy. Really well designed and truly of the moment. Better than Dazed and Confused or Sleaze Nation at that time. Interestingly enough, Vanity Fair has got terrible design but I still think it's the best magazine around, and the only one I buy every month. **What are your short term goals for Intersection?** The biggest satisfaction from making a magazine is meeting the people who read it and know about it. And so our goal is always to preach to the unconverted. We are very happy when some garage owner in Alabama loves the magazine or when some internet billionaire in South Africa loves the magazine. Of course we are even more flattered when Karl Lagerfeld says he adores it. **Do you have a favourite car?** To be perfectly honest I'm obsessed with my bicycle at the moment. When I do drive it's more about the freedom than the vehicle. It's the lack of limits and the ability to change your decisions at midday or midnight. Paris or Rome. But I would take an Aston Martin if given the choice! **So do you believe that cars define our character?** It's really like dressing up isn't it? I once had a black cab for the weekend and it was just complete freedom, you're completely invisible. No one looks at you because you are part of the landscape, until you put that amber light on. And then everyone starts raising their hands. I took my girlfriend out to diner in it and I had to speak to her through the glass partition. It's like choosing to wear a special outfit; people are going to react. A car is a second shell worn above your clothes. I guess if I had to choose something to represent my character it would probably be a worn out old Alfa Romeo GT Junior. Yesterday I was driving a rather quick Maserati in the Italian Hills, but today I'm very happy to be back here on my skateboard. *SBOOK 4*

THE BIGGEST SATISFACTION FROM MAKING A MAGAZINE IS MEETING THE PEOPLE WHO READ IT AND KNOW ABOUT IT AND SO OUR GOAL IS ALWAYS TO PREACH TO THE UNCONVERTED. WE ARE VERY HAPPY WHEN SOME GARAGE OWNER IN ALABAMA LOVES THE MAGAZINE OR WHEN SOME INTERNET BILLIONAIRE IN SOUTH AFRICA LOVES THE MAGAZINE

PHOTOGRAPHY **KATIE CALLAN**
TEXT **SÉBASTIEN CARAYOL**

What did you study at the School of Visual Arts? I graduated with a BFA in graphic design in 1984. At SVA, I was exposed to the best and some of the most well-known designers in the industry, including Paula Scher, Louise Fili and Carin Goldberg. Their work influenced my type choices and the way I looked at graphic design in general. My classmates were pretty incredible and have gone on to hold important jobs at record companies, publishing houses and magazines. Ironically, I work for one of my classmates now; Drew Hodges, the owner of SpotCo. You worked for Vintage Books and at the Boston Globe Sunday Magazine. How did these compare to your role at Rolling Stone? Rolling Stone was in the public eye, so everything we did, both good and bad, was up for scrutiny. While I enjoyed and learned a lot from my year at Vintage, I feel like I really began to come into my own as a young designer under Lynn Staley at the Boston Globe Sunday Magazine. I learned so much from her and built up some confidence and real passion for the work. By the time I got to Rolling Stone, I'd effectively learned how to juggle several projects at once, though I had to learn to slow down and focus on details like letterspacing and perfect mechanicals. At Rolling Stone, Fred pushed us to experiment with words and let them play off the images we worked with. I learned that a great type treatment could do the work of giving the reader real information about a story. It was more than a decorative device. It could tell a story. How did you become part of the design team at Rolling Stone? My editor at the Globe, Ande Zellman, worked with Fred in Texas at a Sunday magazine there. She talked about him all the time and said that we were similar in temperament and style. I subscribed to Texas Monthly while he was working there and then to Regardies when he moved to DC. When he moved to NYC to do Rolling Stone, I wrote him a letter and asked if he'd look at my Globe work. I wasn't sure if I was looking to move home or just to get some feedback; I think it was more the latter since I was still pretty happy in New England. Anyway, he flew me down after work since he actually had a position, and after I left the interview, I told myself that I'd definitely work for him, given the opportunity. I liked him from the minute he came out to get me in the lobby. He had this huge mane of hair, an even bigger smile and a very dry wit. He ended up hiring someone with more experience, but then called me a few months later when he was settled in and could make a less seasoned hire. What did your role as Art Director involve? I started out as an associate art director, became the senior associate and then deputy and finally, senior art director. I was there for over 14 years and knew I'd stay as long as Fred was there. We worked together on lots of stories, and almost always on the cover, which I always looked forward to since we got to hang out and chat a little. Some designers worked very independently, some enjoyed collaborating, people had very different styles and Fred skillfully accommodated all. I was the one who managed deadlines and people's schedules so the work was distributed fairly. And I made about a million illustration assignments. How do you think you changed the design of Rolling Stone? I hope that I helped to make the design smarter and more fun, but who knows? Dennis Ortiz-Lopez was brought back to Rolling Stone for a second stint whilst you were Art Director. Was there a need for the magazine to recapture its typographic identity and what was he like to work with? Dennis was crazy, crazy, crazy–but in a good and very endearing way. He was game for anything and liked to try out new techniques. Dennis would stay up all night to get a job done; would forget to eat and take little naps on a mat in his living room. But he knew the type vocabulary we were working with really well and had tremendous respect for it. He helped us to revive some of the classic fonts that were sitting in the typositor room getting dusty and was an important part of at least half of the time I was at the magazine. Once we were up and running on the computer in the mid-nineties, our needs and the technology shifted. We were able to create things like connected drop shadows on our own and relied on Dennis less. Even he had to relearn the way he worked

and while it was sort of bittersweet, it was the reality of the new world we were entering. **How important is typographic design in a magazine like Rolling Stone where readers may not be visually literate?** While we were doing it, we believed that it was the most important thing ever. I mean, we never talked down to the reader through our design. We made an assumption that the reader had a sophisticated eye and could understand our feats of type magic as well as the classical stuff. We never dumbed it down. Ultimately, who knows if the reader really can see the difference between the good and the commonplace? I guess I believe that they get it, even if they're not really sure what the "it" is. I think they can't always pinpoint the type as being key, but it's there. It's more subtle or even unconscious, sometimes. **Were your timeframes constrained by the fact you were working with high profile music stars?** The timeframe was the same no matter who was on the cover. We produced each issue in about a week and a half, though at times special stories or sections got worked on a week or so ahead. Most of the time, though, we were flying by the seat of our collective pants. **What sort of grid did you use and how flexible was it when dealing with type heavy articles?** The grid was a basic three and four column setup, with an oxford rule around the page. That never changed over the years I was there, and probably exists in just about the same format now. We broke the grid on our opening spreads, but always followed it on the turnpages. **Was there ever any input from the interviewees?** There was seldom input from the subjects of the stories and if there was, it was more about the photography than the design. While the stars never had official approval, occasionally they got to see the art as a courtesy. **In a recent AIGA career guide, you have talked about the need to develop a 'visual voice' to keep the reader turning the pages. How do you think this works?** I think that good design can draw you into a magazine. Look at Martha Stewart Kids. It has this incredible voice that oozes sophistication and style, but it's also playful. It keeps me looking at it and even reading it and I don't have kids! I'm completely seduced by its look. **What was the process of evaluation and criticism before it was decided a spread was ready for print?** Fred gave the design his thumbs up and then the managing and assigning editors gave their approval. Often, the owner and executive editor, Jann Wenner, weighed in, too. There was enormous trust during many of the years I was there, so the work wasn't dissected or done by committee. For most of my tenure, it was pretty painless. **And was the process of bringing the magazine together equally trouble free?** It began with story idea meetings, then meetings to figure out what would fit in an issue. We negotiated space and dummied the magazine and refined that over the following days as the edit and design process began. We turned our designs in by the end of the first week or the beginning of the closing week, and wrapped things up by that Thursday or Friday. Then the whole process began again! **Did the magazine ever need to change its design philosophy due to changes in public taste or in response to the launch of other music magazines?** While we were aware of other music magazines, like Vibe and Spin, they weren't much of a concern. Over time, though, the philosophy of how to attract and maintain a readership evolved, as MTV and then the internet took hold. Information was doled out in soundbites for people who could not or would not commit to long, ponderous pieces. You had to hit them with more entry points into the page so they'd have reason to stay with you. It was frustrating, but at the same time, fascinating. **How much of a 'Rock 'n' Roll lifestyle' was attached to working at Rolling Stone?** I'm about the last person you should ask about the rock and roll lifestyle. I was a hard worker and rarely a party person. I was way too shy and self-conscious to hang out. Some of the younger editorial assistants lived it up a bit, but I know as I got older there, it became more and more difficult to remain interested in some of the subject matter. I mean, I came of age as a designer during the Tom Cruise and Madonna years, but knew it was drawing to a close for me when the Britney Spears years rolled around. **So are there no intriguing memories from your time at** the magazine? Some memorable moments include seeing John Kennedy Jr. and Jackie Onasis, meeting James Taylor, and telling Tom Cruise where the men's room was. As a department, we had a few really fun and boozy nights out that still make me smile years later. Is it easier to get on the cover of Rolling Stone now? It certainly seems like it's pretty easy to become famous for a short stint these days, thanks to reality TV. And what better way to capture someone's fifteen minutes than on the cover of Rolling Stone? Do you think Rolling Stone still has the potential to become a leader in contemporary typographic design? My sense is that the emphasis has moved away from the typography in recent years, but they get a lot more mileage out of the department pages than we were ever able to. The pieces are a lot shorter, so the reader gets more to chew on in, say, the movies section, than they used to in my day. 'In my day' ha. I sound like I'm 100 years old. Your Axl Rose spread was ornately designed with lovingly crafted type. Was all the typography hand rendered? The Axl spread was easy. I knew instantly that I wanted to play off the vines that covered his legs and figured out a trick in Illustrator that I used to wrap the type around the letters. I drew some of the flowers by hand and then used them as a pattern in Illustrator, as well as some of the flowers that came with Illustrator 6. I kept going and going and couldn't stop. In what ways did your experiences at Rolling Stone, make your move to Spot Design easier? I learned to love typography and letterforms at Rolling Stone and created spreads that existed as sort of mini posters, so the transition totally made sense. I was still working with pop culture and celebrity, still solving problems and still fighting the clock. It felt like familiar territory. You have won many awards and taken part on judging panels for the Art Directors Club and Typographic Designers Club. Do you think it is more prestigious to judge an award or to win one? Both are flattering and nice pats on the back. I've met some really nice people over the years in judging competitions, so I've grown to enjoy the process. Being cooped up with someone you barely know for a few days in some strange city can make for some fun bonds; like you fought a battle together or something. So do you think that once you have been a judge for an award it becomes that much more difficult to win that award again? I can't imagine why judging would prelude you from ever winning again. Judges' having work in competitions can be awkward, but I've never judged a show where you were allowed to vote for yourself or your co-workers. The chair of the show usually steps in and does the deed for you. I admit, though, that it's almost always awkward. Can you tell us about your work for the National Down Syndrome Society and the American Anorexia Bulimia Association? I have a nephew with Down Syndrome and became more aware of it when he was born. I wanted to get involved in an organization connected to it and knew that I could at least contribute design. I didn't know a lot about eating disorders when I started doing the American Anorexia and Bulima Association newsletter, but again, thought that I could use my abilities to do something good. My goal was to take on a pro bono project every year, but my good deed days may be behind me for now. I've been slacking off on that front, I guess, though I have been working pretty hard teaching. You have worked with Steven Heller on both 'Graphic Wit' and 'American Typeplay'. How did this collaboration develop? I met Steve years ago through his wife, Louise Fili. I mentioned to her that I'd like to help him out with a book project at some point. He actually took me up on it, and we worked together on 'Graphic Wit' and three other titles. In fact, we're working on a new type book for Thames and Hudson right now called New Vintage Type. I teach for Steve in the MFA program he co-chairs at SVA, too. He's about as smart as it gets. Is it the 'vintage' typography that attracted you to old bottle tops? The bottle caps started about seven years ago and then got really out of hand thanks to eBay. I even travelled to the South to meet collectors and was part of a bottle cap collectors club. I went to several bottle cap conventions in Pennsylvania and got to hold up the letter A in the group picture! I was totally engrossed and amassed a collection of about 2000 caps. That's NOTHING, though, compared to the diehards. I fell in love with the design and typography on the older caps and just threw myself totally into collecting. That replaced the salt and pepper shaker hoarding I'd been doing about ten years before that. My apartment is home to about 300 pairs displayed on shelves, and my house upstate has about 100 more and all of the bottle caps. I'm not collecting anything these days, though. Time to pare down in my old age. *SBOOK 4*

PET

ER

STIT

SON

DAZ

ED

AND

CON

FUSED

'Dazed & Confused', took its name from a Led Zeppelin song, and started life as a limited edition fold out poster. How many copies were made? I'm not sure of the print run, but the concept behind the poster was to keep it open with no cover, almost like a blog. It was meant to be a place where people's ideas come together. Ian Taylor, the co-founder, borrowed a Led Zep tape off Jefferson Hack at the time they were looking for a name. That song pretty much summed up the mood of their generation. I think that's how the story goes, but that was before my time at Dazed. **Was Dazed and Confused influenced by magazines like I-D, The Face, and Interview?** Almost certainly, but Dazed and Confused has always been different. Ian Rankin and Jefferson Hack, who now work mainly on Another Magazine, were the catalysts for the magazine. That's different to people like Terry Jones who created I-D. He had worked for Vogue, and Nick Logan from the Face, had previously worked for Emap; but Jefferson, Rankin and a small group of aspiring London creatives, did it all by themselves. **How did Brit Pop and Brit Art affect Dazed and Confused?** In the terms of photographers and writers, there was a real explosion of young British creative talent at the time of the launch. It was the start of ecstasy culture and all the creative disciplines seemed to cross over in the creative community. At the time there weren't many opportunities for that generation to gain exposure for their ideas, and in some ways the magazine became their voice. It was spearheaded by the likes of Damien Hirst, Alexander McQueen and bands like Blur and Radiohead. **Do you think you are creating a culture as well as a product?** It's an indifferent period for magazines, in the age of digital TV and the internet, I think the craft of making magazines is in danger of being lost. When Dazed was founded, magazines were the place to find out about new subcultures, fashion, film and art, but now the internet can supply this information. It makes us work harder and push the magazine further. **What was the brief for Dazed and Confused new look?** The re-design took a couple of months, and we had to do it whilst producing the other issues of the magazine. It was quite intense and you end up with a very busy schedule when you undertake a re-design. It involved not just the art department, but also the fashion department and the editorial department. We all decided to think about the whole structure of the magazine and the re-design came out of that. The main structural change we wanted to complete was to make the magazine larger again, as it went down in size before I started. The thinking behind that at the time was to make it a more immediate read. I personally found it was very difficult to design in that

smaller space. I think there is an optimum size for a magazine, especially when you have a lot of fashion and it's image heavy. The larger size gave us more space for the content and the magazine now flows much better. We were trying to cram in the same amount of content in the smaller size and it didn't do justice to the amazing photography and illustrations. When I design I always think about clarity for the reader and how I am going to navigate them around the information. The sections should have a clear recognition factor. You should be able to open the magazine anywhere and realise where you are. Its not just about the typefaces, its about how you write the headline, and the old headlines were unclear. We have made sure the sections art/film/music/fashion are very clearly sign posted for the reader. The front section is general news and then there is a fashion news section called Eye Spy. The earlier version of Eye Spy didn't differentiate itself enough from the rest of the magazine. We wanted to make it more of a street and youth fashion section, so the design had to echo that. Previously we had just done straight shoots and that was it. Sometimes we would format it like news pages but there wasn't really a structure. The idea when re-designing this section was to make it a magazine in a magazine or maybe more like a fanzine. We applied bordering, letting the reader know this is a separate section of the magazine. Again there is a long fashion shoot but

I THINK THE CRAFT OF MAKING MAGAZINES IS IN DANGER OF BEING LOST

you can still tell its part of the same section because we use this graphic language throughout. The redesign has given the magazine a new momentum internally and that need shouldn't be overlooked. It's critical to keep the energy up on a title like Dazed. We've got really good feedback from readers, the industry, and advertisers. Its also not just about redesign, its about a constant awareness of your photography and illustration, to keep the magazine fresh. **Did you consider changing the paper stock for this section?** I would love to do something like that, but unfortunately there are budgetary and time limitations. If I worked on a smaller niche magazine that was a quarterly I might have the flexibility to sort out these things. A big monthly needs constant attention and fast working methods. Paper changes within an issue would be a bit of a luxury. **How important is the design of the main feature?** The idea behind the main section is that the design comes out of the content. With most magazines you have a house style, you have typefaces that you use throughout

MOST MAGAZINES PRODUCE FAIRLY SUPERFICIAL ARTICLES, A PRETTY PICTURE OF AN ACTOR AND SOME TEXT

and it's the same every month. Our main feature is placed in the centre of the magazine and its design changes every month. Its directly influenced by how the article is written and what it's trying to achieve. We still keep the basic grid template for body copy but the typeface changes. I usually use a three column for the back and front sections and then a two column for the main section. For the Yeah Yeah Yeah's main section I produced something a little punky that reflects the content. Although I keep the grid for the body copy, its size might change just to keep it moving. The main features are large and vary from thirty to forty pages, depending on subject. Most magazines produce fairly superficial articles, a pretty picture of an actor and some text. We think people are getting bored with that style and editorial approach, as even the Sunday supplements do that now. It was important for us to achieve breadth and depth, to give the reader more value. When we put the Red Hot Chilli Peppers section together we still did a beautiful shoot in the Dazed and Confused fashion, but we also built in archive shots, and images of all their album covers. This contextualises the article and gives the reader a real understanding of the subject matter. We are now competing with the net. You can google Red Hot Chilli Peppers and have enough information to keep you searching for a week, but it's our job to make information more intimate and digestible to the reader. The Yeah Yeah Yeah's archive was equally immense and you can easily let it slip into information overload. Keeping that balance is one of the most difficult and enjoyable challenges in editorial design. **How did you decide on your typeface changes?** Before the re-design we used Interstate as our house typeface. I felt we needed something a bit more poppy, and characterful. I've used this face called Rub-Down that was designed by a guy called Neil Wiss. The rounded type was a slight reaction against Another Magazine and Another Man. They use quite hard, straight typefaces. Dazed has a slightly younger audience and it needs more energy, more pop. There are a lot of weights to the typeface and I like the quality of the heavy font. It's a bit 'inky' and reflects the slightly cut and paste aesthetic of Dazed and Confused. The rounded font also has good contrast with the headers. These are set in both serifs and sans serifs. **Did you consider adapting the masthead in the redesign?** Not really, I had already changed it for the 100th issue and I

Photography Magnus Unnar

was very happy with the result. I wanted clean lines and so I put Dazed on the side. In the past it was squared off, but I thought it would fit in better with the rub down face, if it was rounded. It's such a well known logo, it's hard to change it. Everyone calls the magazine Dazed, but it is actually Dazed and Confused. Ian Rankin originally wanted to call the magazine, 'Did you get the feeling you are being cheated?' But it didn't really work on the masthead! **You have said that Dazed and Confused is naturally eclectic. Where do you think it should be placed on a magazine stand?** That's a difficult question, as I don't really know who our rivals are anymore. There's ID, but they have a different energy level and approach. I wish there were more magazines like Dazed and Confused. If you had asked me six years ago, I would have said The Face and Sleaze Nation. It's very sad they no longer exist. New York has more magazines similar to ours, like Tokion, Flaunt and Nylon. London has smaller niche magazines that tend to be quarterlies or bi-annuals. There's a new one called Super, but it's really about street fashion. Even Arena, Pop, Homme Man, are heavily fashion orientated and don't come out every month. I grew up on the Face, ID and Dazed and Confused and it was a really exciting period. I guess people get the same excitement out of the quarterlies, but I'm not sure how up to date you can be if you have a gap of 3 months between issues. **How did Dazed and Confused expand from Fashion, Music, Film, Art, Literature, into international social and political themes?** Dazed is about creating culture. Most magazines are little more than expanded press releases. If someone writes a book, releases a record, or opens an exhibition, that kind of magazine repackages it and puts it out as content. We do that as well, but we also instigate special projects and themed issues. Such as a recent issue based on South Africa, where all of the contributors were South Africans. The issue was associated with Aids in Africa and helped raise awareness with a campaign endorsed by Bob Geldof and Archbishop Desmond Tutu. Basing the issue around that theme is something most magazines wouldn't touch. We produced a similar issue, with a feature called, 'Do the Red Thing'. This is a project setup by Bono, and its aim was to raise money from companies to support Aids programmes in Africa. He approached Dazed and we decided to get our contributors to supply an inspiring piece of work based on the colour red and the word red. We have an up coming issue on human rights and it will be called the freedom issue. It will cover, human rights in China, and a global arms campaign from Amnesty International. We are creating a special piece on the UN's declaration of human rights. It states that everyone has a right to a free trial. There are a number of countries who signed this document back in 1948 and who now have little interest in obeying its rules. I have commissioned six art directors and typographers to take a section of this declaration and each one will create a unique piece of typography. It should hopefully produce an exhibition as well. Tomato, Ed Fella, Alan Kitching and Trevor Jackson are amongst those working on the project. That's the amazing thing about working on Dazed, it can be used to create that kind of a culture. I have worked at Arena, and those magazines are valid, but it's not like working here. It means there are lots of meetings and you have to come up with the goods very quickly. I would never have met all these fascinating people if I had been working on a different magazine. **How much forward planning do you have to build in, to create these complex issues?** We start thinking about what is in an issue two months prior to its print date, but we actually think even further ahead. Everyone on the whole team contributes to the magazine and anyone can pitch an idea. The freedom issue was planned six months in advance, but it's pretty vague at that point. When the ideas become more concrete, we might fix shots 3 months in advance. Obviously the magazine has to be 'of the moment' and we need to be able to chop and change at the last minute. We could end up shooting something a couple of weeks before we go to press, which can be quite stressful. Inevitably the fashion section is commissioned quite far ahead, because we need to take an overview of the season and decide what we want to shoot. The news section is worked on a couple of months ahead, but will

change a month ahead. Some of the features are time sensitive and others are bubbling under for a while if they are not so time critical. The cover design reflects the main feature. If it's an actor or a musician, they will be on the cover. But also because of the fashion bias of the magazine we'll have regular fashion covers throughout the year, usually in conjunction with a fashion season. But its always a 'Dazed cover' and must have that continuity, whether it's an actor or fashion cover. Sometimes a fashion photographer will shoot a musician, to help keep the same aesthetic on the cover. For example with the Red Hot Chilli Peppers we wanted to get a certain feeling from that shoot and from the brand. We also wanted to shoot the lead singer for the cover. But it's all about choosing the right photographer for the subject matter. **Dazed and Confused has an online creative directory. Do you commission illustrators through this?** When we re–launched the website we decided to have a forum, where illustrators and photographers can up load their work and leave an email or web link. It's part of Dazed supporting new creative talent and it's completely open. We don't edit it in anyway. It's a platform for people to be part of the Dazed community. But from that, we go through an editing process in the magazine and pick out our favourites. They get put into a page in the magazine. Quite a few of them end up with commissions for the magazine. **Can you talk about T2 magazine?** Sometimes we get clients approaching us to produce custom projects. When we did T2 the client wanted something that reflected their involvement in the music industry and the T Festival. We made a music based magazine that only used illustrations. When you do a one off, it's nice to have one illustrator or photographer work on the whole project, because it adds to the overall aesthetic. This client was really open and gave us a lot of freedom. I pitched a variety of illustrators that I felt were suited to the job and they choose the one I wanted to use. It was a limited edition magazine and it came with a picture disc. This gave the overall product more value and turns it into a collectable object. It goes back to your question about using different paper stocks in Dazed. With a sponsored one off like T2, everything becomes possible because the sponsor is helping to fund the concept. *SBOOK 4*

I WOULD NEVER HAVE MET ALL THESE FASCINATING PEOPLE IF I HAD BEEN WORKING ON A DIFFERENT MAGAZINE

What makes Colors different from other magazines?
Colors is a magazine about the rest of the world, wherever
you're reading it. It tries to tell you something you did
not know, about somewhere else. For the last 68 issues,
that has been our goal. Colors has always been a nomadic
magazine. Since enfant-terrible Oliviero Toscani set it
up in 1991 it has moved around the world from New
York to Rome to Paris to Treviso. The fact that it is itinerant
has given the magazine a very global feel. The staff always
changes and is very international. Researchers and writers
came from New York, Rome, Beirut, Dublin, Tehran, Paris,
Sydney, Madrid, Manila, Cape Town and Barcelona. The
magazine has always been bilingual and has been translated
from English into Italian, Korean, Spanish, Japanese, Russian,
Greek, Croatian, Swedish, Slovenian, Serbian,
Hungarian, German, Spanish and French. Colors
is not a traditional form of journalism. It contains no
celebrities, no news, no columnists and no by-lines.
We prefer to feature fashion you won't see on the
catwalk. The celebrities are ordinary people like
Ms. Stigma Free in Botswana, an elephant carer in Sri
Lanka, an aspiring astronaut in Moscow or a garbage
sorter in China. Each monothematic edition of the
magazine explores a social issue and follows it faithfully
around the world. We treat everything with the same
naivety. So far we have made issues about Immigration,
Evolution, Race, The Street, Ecology, AIDS, Religion,
Shopping, Sports, Travel, Heaven, No Words, War,
Wealth, Cuba, Jobs, Shopping for the Body, Animals,
Weddings, Smoking, Hair, Gifts for the Family, Death,
Fat, Time, Home, Touch, Toys, Heart, Water, Night,
Venice, Status Symbols, Mother, Monoculture, Prayer,
Fashion, Trash, Refugees, Gypsies, Elderly, Public
Housing, Star City, Volunteers, Madness, Schools,
Tours, Prisons, The Road, Patagonia, Slavery,
Food, Birmingham, Violence, Slums, Photo Studio,
Telenovelas, Energy, Fans, Drugs, Borders, Lust,
Freedom of Speech, Best Wishes, AIDS/HIV and the
Amazon. They all attempt to give a
glimpse of what is currently going on in
the world. Do you believe globalization
diminishes cultural diversity? We all
know that globalisation is continuing
unhindered which is why we are still
trying to tackle global issues and local
solutions. Clearly globalization has a
far-reaching effect on cultural diversity
and it is changing the world. Part of
the work of Colors is to look at what is
happening now. The magazine is also a
way of documenting changing cultures
as well as highlighting global issues. We
probably are preaching to the converted

CARLOS MUSTIENES COLORS

most of the time but from the mail we get it is also
obvious to us that at least occasionally someone will
pick up the magazine and feel like their world has been
changed. That alone is worth all the trouble. How do
you think visual communication can influence people's
perspectives on the world? Big pictures and few words
convey information as powerfully as a page of newsprint.
The graphic pictures, clean design and clear language
led some to call it the magazine for the MTV generation.
Tibor described it as "a mix of National Geographic and
Life on acid". Luckily we have a patron that foots the

bills. Benetton sponsors us and follows us. They do not have any effect on the editorial integrity and direction of the magazine. They let us choose whatever we like as the editorial and tend to stay out of the way. We collaborate though and have researched and produced issues to supplement their institutional campaigns including Volunteers and Hunger. Our Editorial Director has always been very supportive of our choices. We try to report what is going on with first-hand interviews and photography. We also try to complement our visual editorial with the Yellow Pages, which is a listing of organisations inviting the reader to get involved and do something about the situation. As a reader you might be invited to adopt a goat for a family in Uganda, buy recycled computer screens from China, send used eyeglasses to Chad or visit the AIDS-amma shrine in India. The Yellow Pages were so popular that we were asked to make a book featuring all the ones ever published in the magazines. **Is it difficult to choose the topic behind each issue?** Art Directors come from different countries including Norway, Spain, Italy, Argentina, USA, UK, Germany, Japan and Brazil. Researchers and writers are from the Philippines, Spain, Iran, UK, Australia and the USA. Likewise for the Photo Editors, Photo Researchers and Designers. Everyone has different points of view, backgrounds and experiences. So we get lots of feedback and fervent discussions. We have an ongoing list of possible social and global themes to tackle. Normally we just sit down and pick the one we think is relevant at the time and we feel like doing. **How did you join the magazine?** I got started with Colors in Rome when I read the classifieds one day and saw an ad for an internship at Colors. I had seen the magazine and went in for an interview. Because I spoke Spanish, French, Italian and English, I was instantly hired even though I had no journalistic or editorial background. I found myself working for a communal magazine, which was extremely international and easy going. I loved the fact that my job changed every day. One day I was interviewing an expert about cricket balls, the next I was at a photo shoot in Fiumicino airport interviewing and photographing people about fashion with Toscani. The following week I would be wallowing in and sorting through the 6,000 possible photos chosen by Tibor for the upcoming Photo Essay. What started out as an internship turned into a career in editorial production dealing with concepts, budgets, photo consignments, stringers, photographers, staff placement and a vast knowledge of design, printing, writing and distribution. **How critical is teamwork in the creation of an international magazine?** Job descriptions do not apply at Colors. I am Executive Editor in charge of editorial production but I might write captions, flow text into the design grids or translate headlines. Designers might conduct interviews in their native language. Researchers might find themselves scanning and fighting with Photoshop or Illustrator. We all share the responsibility of making the final magazine. We try to spread ourselves around and avoid cornering ourselves into roles or hierarchies. Our editorial team is extremely varied. We are a very small core group that centralises the editorial production. The

magazine always keeps an international staff and that is what makes it work well. You should speak at least three languages. Not a snob thing but a facilitating thing. Oliviero Toscani is famed for his use of visually arresting photography, and this a key feature of the Colors identity. **Is there a secret behind capturing a thought provoking magazine image?** Oliviero's rule of thumb was to use photos that will not be forgotten, regardless of the quality. Tibor wanted simple text that any meathead would understand. We assume we are writing for everyday people. We always try to make a magazine for everyone. A magazine without age barriers that can be read by either a six-year-old or a sixty-year-old. We have also made a magazine that can be 'read' by people who cannot read. The images speak for themselves and nothing was gratuitous. This included nudity if it was relevant even though it got us banned a few times in Japan and Singapore. On another level you can complement these images with short, concise texts. The text is simple yet inspires you to find out more if the idea captures you. **Can you tell us about Color Films?** Colors has brought many of our themes into a series of documentaries, including Trash, Retirement Homes and Patagonia. Film is just a diversification of the printed material. The fieldwork and contacts were already done. Just like our website. We have also produced many other printed projects such as 1000 Extra/Ordinary Objects, 1000 Signs, Cacas, Hunger, Tuberculosis, the Yellow Pages book and many more. We have held several photo and object exhibitions in galleries bringing the magazine into another dimension. **How do the Colors journalists initially investigate their stories?** Colors would be nothing without our network of local correspondents and photographers worldwide. There are about 60 correspondents at the moment. They are not all journalists, but people who believe in the philosophy of the magazine. As soon as we decide on a theme we let them know and they brainstorm on how and why the issue is relevant to their country. It is up to them to find out what is really going on around the world. We cannot solely rely on in-house research by internet or telephone, we need locals finding the stories. We have developed a system of communication with our correspondents that works well, and everything is commissioned by e-mail or telephone. Sometimes Colors packs up their suitcases and goes on a big trip. We have done location issues in Baracoa, Venice, Birmingham and now the Amazon. These issues are done entirely on location and examine, explore and meet the locals and see what they are up to. We want to know what they are eating, where they work and where they go out on Friday nights. We also work very closely with Fabrica, which is the Communications Research Centre for Benetton. We have used many of their young photographers, writers and researchers to contribute on issues. Fabrica is great because it is composed of over 40 students from all around the world. Colors also provides Fabrica with lots of research, info and writing abilities for their projects. The availability

THIS SPREAD HAS NOTHING TO DO WITH DRY CLEANING, BUT THE DUMMY TEXT DID

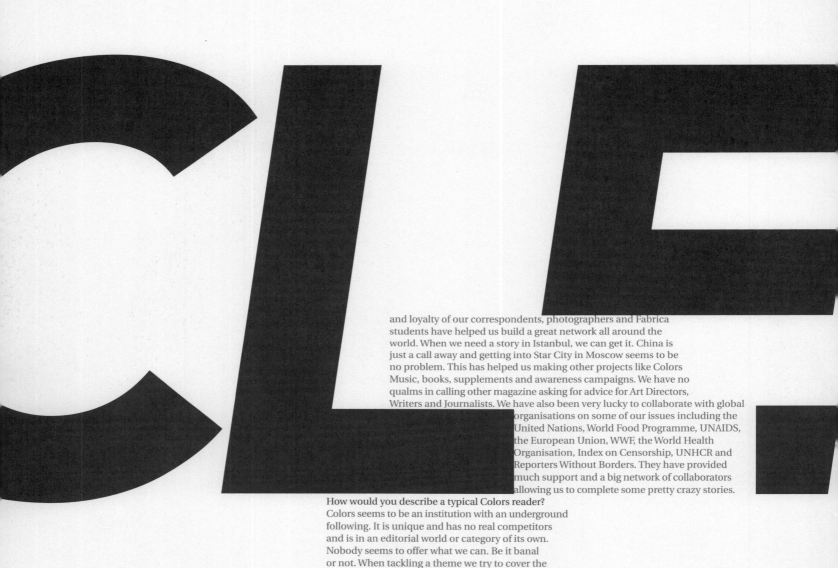

and loyalty of our correspondents, photographers and Fabrica
students have helped us build a great network all around the
world. When we need a story in Istanbul, we can get it. China is
just a call away and getting into Star City in Moscow seems to be
no problem. This has helped us making other projects like Colors
Music, books, supplements and awareness campaigns. We have no
qualms in calling other magazine asking for advice for Art Directors,
Writers and Journalists. We have also been very lucky to collaborate with global
organisations on some of our issues including the
United Nations, World Food Programme, UNAIDS,
the European Union, WWF, the World Health
Organisation, Index on Censorship, UNHCR and
Reporters Without Borders. They have provided
much support and a big network of collaborators
allowing us to complete some pretty crazy stories.

How would you describe a typical Colors reader?
Colors seems to be an institution with an underground
following. It is unique and has no real competitors
and is in an editorial world or category of its own.
Nobody seems to offer what we can. Be it banal
or not. When tackling a theme we try to cover the
world, as mundane as it may be. We try to open up
to everybody and anybody. We get lots of feedback
and letters from our readers. Many of our readers
become contributors. Many of them offer suggestions,
give us praise or send us hate mail. We obviously
cannot please everyone as many issues strike up
controversy. That is one of our goals though, to make
people discuss and talk about the issues. **Do you have
a policy on which advertisements you will include?**
The magazine is published quarterly and available
in 65 countries. We sell in newsstands, bookstores
and through subscription. Every once in a while sold-
out issues can be found on e-bay. Unfortunately the
readership is very niche and unless the world goes

crazy there will not be a boom in sales. But we have our faithful fans, subscribers and readers. Even though we do not have any policy towards advertising, it is very hard to find. Why would someone invest in the Benetton magazine? Sometimes we design ads that are placed in the magazine which are usually for NGO's and non-profits. **Has the Colors philosophy changed since the years when Tibor Kalman was Editor?** The beauty of Colors is that the philosophy of the magazine has never changed, the presentation obviously has. Toscani came up with the idea and concept. Tibor came in and played with disposition, typography, stock image and short poignant captions. Through the years it evolved into the communities issues with Adam Broomberg and Oliver Chanarin, including Prisons, Retirement Homes, Refugee camps, Asylums. These featured longer stories and a more personalised angle on the characters. These issues were also 100 percent produced by us, both text and image. Then we worked with Stefan Ruiz, who put a huge emphasis on the photography. The current Editor-in-Chief is Parisian Grégoire Basdevant who is returning to a mix of agency photo and production. We use photo researchers in New York, Milan and Paris to go around and look through agency stock. **How do you choose which art directors you will work with, or do they approach you?** The choice of Art Direction goes both ways. Sometimes we recruit people, other times people contact us. It has always been quite flexible. We have had brilliant people like Paul Ritter, Scott Stowell, Mark Porter, Thomas Hilland and Fernando Gutiérrez. It was great working with Tama Tetsuya, who spoke almost no English yet managed to communicate through his sketches, image choices and typefaces. Lots of great people have passed through the magazine bringing different insights and points of view; and fonts which then had to be adapted to the Croatian and Hungarian versions. Many of the players of Colors have moved on to get really interesting jobs. They have gone to advertising firms, newspapers, magazines, photo agencies and public relations companies. One became a Franciscan monk and another a chef and physical trainer. We are a bit of a crazy family and always keep in touch and when necessary scratch each other's backs every once in a while. **Do Colors journalists and photographers ever experience problems in collecting material?** With time and organisation we usually have no problems getting access to information and meeting the deadlines. It is positive work for both our journalists and photographers. One stringer trekked through the hills in Kenya just to get some lip plugs used as decorative body art for the Touch issue. Others have contracted malaria and been arrested for photographing illegal subjects during shoots.

What are the primary challenges facing the production team? Our biggest challenge is time and design. Since the magazine is bilingual, Art Directors have to fit in double the text and take into account that the French version is much longer than the Spanish or English. We have also recently switched from Quark Xpress into InDesign making things a bit slower. The Art Director is free to do whatever he likes. Obviously to avoid design schizophrenia we try to stay semi-consistent. Time-wise we are always late. The themes are so broad that anything goes, so the editing is difficult, in the sense that you can never say stop. As soon as we lock an issue a better picture comes around. It currently takes about three months to produce an issue between brainstorming, editorial, translation and production. We usually decide the theme, send out the brainstorming, decide on a story list, research and commission photos. Once all the photos and images are in we edit the text in around two weeks and send it to Copy Edit and proofreading. As soon as the English is final it all gets sent to the translators around the world who then translate and edit their copy in their respective countries. In the meantime we order any last minute images, do any photo corrections and final design tweaking. **Colors website enables people to access the content of the magazine. Aren't you worried this might replace the printed version?** The internet version of the magazine is very well done and works well as a teaser or another option for the paper. It will absolutely not replace the printed version. For the avid readers a screen version of anything will never replace a solid paper copy of a magazine, which you can leisurely read on the tube or on the toilet. Regardless of the price. Every time we print an issue we make donations and send copies to schools, prisons, organisations and places that do not have regular access to the internet. **What projects are the Colors team currently working on?** We are currently working on several projects. Colors 68: The Amazon is out in Summer 2006 and will focus primarily on life in the Amazonian Rainforest in Brazil. It deals with the life of the river, the people around it and what is happening with the environment. We are also preparing the Colors Notebook project. Basically we printed a blank issue of Colors and have invited people all around the world to make an issue of Colors. These notebooks will be displayed at the Pompidou Centre in Paris in October. At the same time we are completing the third volume of 1000 Extra/Ordinary Objects to be published by Taschen. *SBOOK 4*

You decided to enter magazine design straight after graduating. What made you so interested in this area, this early? When I was at college much of the work I was producing moved towards printed matter. And although I had completed multimedia projects, my real interest lay in making little limited runs of things, a bit of book binding and of course magazines. Like most design students I was a big magazine fan, and I became genuinely fascinated by the subject after Scott King visited the college to give a lecture. He was at Idea magazine at that time. It was wonderful to hear him speak with such enthusiasm about his work and to see his ability to bring intelligent concepts to this format. I remember thinking, 'I want a piece of that'. So I organised some work experience at Idea and ended up getting a job at Smash Hits straight after graduating. It was 1994 and I was a junior magazine designer. You completed your degree at Southampton Institute. What was the most important thing you learnt there, that you were able to take with you into magazine design? It was unusual in that we were the first year of the new degree course in graphic design. This meant there were no second and third year students to use as role models. This was actually really good, because there were no preconceived ideas and no notions of what the course was going to be like, or the standards that could be reached. Many of the students who were in that first year were just really good people to work alongside. I think we sort of bounced off each other and set ourselves quite high standards. We found that we could work as a group and create an interesting studio environment. That was really useful, as working in magazines is a lot like that at times. Co-operation with other people is a critical part of my job. Putting a monthly magazine together is one big collaboration, and Southampton equipped me for that. How critical was your work placement in clarifying your career choice? It was very important in helping me make that decision and also in deciding the kind of work I wanted to create in my final year. I undertook the placement between my second and third year at college and

WHEN YOU ARE A DESIGNER ON A MAGAZINE, EVERY DAY SEEMS TO TEACH YOU SOMETHING NEW. OR IT MIGHT JUST BE A DIFFERENT WAY OF APPROACHING AN OLD PROBLEM. IDEAS GENERATION IS CRITICAL AND EVERYTHING I WORK ON IS PART OF MY PROGRESSION AS A DESIGNER

ANDREW

HAVING AN IDEA AND THEN BRINGING A TALENTED GROUP OF PEOPLE TOGETHER TO CONSTRUCT IT THROUGH TO THE FINISHED PAGE, IS VERY REWARDING DIPROSE

GQ MAGAZINE

I had a great time at Idea. It was a fun, creative environment and I was suddenly just thrown in. I was really into the fashion part and it was very hands on. I just thought, 'I could get used to this. Now all I need is to get paid!' **Can you tell us a bit about the process of developing from a junior designer to an art director?** When you are a designer on a magazine, every day seems to teach you something new. Or it might just be a different way of approaching an old problem. Ideas generation is critical and everything I work on is part of my progression as a designer. Inevitably coming out of college and moving straight into a very busy magazine was a bit like being dropped in at the deep end. But it was so creative and you were only constrained by your ideas. Smash Hits was a great place for that and it was a really fun magazine. It had a college style working environment and it was full of very talented writers. Creatively it was a great springboard and I just kept working on and up. I tried to retain the fun element as part of my working process, whilst making sure I kept producing good ideas and concepts as I progressed up the design ladder. **What is your favourite part of being an art director?** It's taking an idea from conception to the printed page. I'm in a great position in that I can work on the major features within the magazine and also the funny single page grooming feature. If I have a relevant idea, I can commission a photographer or an illustrator, work with a writer or the section head, and just have that satisfaction of making the whole thing happen. Having an idea and then bringing a talented group of people together to construct it through to the finished page, is very rewarding. It's the reason I am in magazine design and the reason I wanted to become an art director. **What are the major differences between working as an art director and working as a deputy art director?** I used to be the art director for Sky magazine, but now my position at GQ is as a deputy. GQ is a much bigger magazine and it's an older established Conde Nast title. I moved up really quickly from being a junior designer, to designer, to deputy art director and then to art director. I think I was an art director at twenty six years of age. Going back to being a deputy on this kind of title has been incredibly valuable. I've soaked up so much more experience by working with these great older designers. I wouldn't have been able to do this if I had remained as a big fish in a little pond. Working with other people and moving around as a freelance magazine designer taught me so many different ways of designing, approaching design, and approaching problem solving. I've gained a great deal from stepping off my pedestal and getting back into the thick of things. Inevitably part of my job is to ensure that what the art director wants, he gets. And the other part of my job is to make sure everyone else is happy! These might appear thankless tasks, but in fact keeping the production of the magazine running smoothly, by working with a talented team, is no chore. Obviously I'm also designing pages at the same time. So I'm 50% designer and 50% working between departments. An experienced magazine designer can see the product as a whole, simply by laying out a few pages. You can't wait until it's completed to decide whether it's any good! **GQ magazine has a very complicated layout. Can you tell us a little about this?** GQ is a large title and there's a lot of work in there. The way we structure this is to break down the main sections and allocate them between staff. Pretty much all of the commissioning of photography and illustration is done from the art department, and not the picture department. Designers are responsible for the commissioning of their sections. Whether it's the front section, style section, action section, grooming section or the talk section. This really helps because they have a complete overview of their section and its construction. It would be too much work for designers to pick up single pages with GQ. I would agree that it is a complicated layout, but there are structures in place that run throughout the magazine and help hold it together. There are types of rules, copy styles, grid styles, that unify it into a coherent framework. Obviously we have to strike a balance between these things becoming a straight jacket, or for that matter, a free for all. The idea is that each section can have its own personality whilst still being seen as part of GQ magazine. That's the plan anyway. **How long do you have to design each issue?** Well it's a monthly title so that kind of determines the timescale! In theory we have four weeks, but we also have some five week issues. Sometimes we might have a four week issue with two supplements, and we have to design those as well. If we also have a sports supplement and/or a best dressed supplement to produce, that will seriously eat into the time available to design the main magazine; even with the help of freelance designers. Four weeks is not a long time to create something this big and it can make you feel like you're on a hamster wheel of design. While we're finishing one issue, we've already started on the design of the next. It's not a job for the work shy. **So what are the biggest design challenges when starting a new issue?** That would probably be time and money! We don't have the luxury you might have if you were working on an advertising job or something that is a long term project. We've got four weeks to do it and in that time the whole magazine has to be completed. There's no putting it off to next week and there are no extensions. The date it goes to the printer, is the date it goes to the printer. So even if you come up with some wonderfully crazy idea, that needs to be shot in an odd location. If you can't organise it in time, at a price you can afford, then you have to forget it. You just have to trim back your ideas to work within realistic time and money constraints. We have a page rate. Effectively it's a budget per page. We juggle page rates, but some ideas and some solutions are just too damned expensive. It's the same across most of the magazine industry, and I'm sure that we at GQ are in a very privileged position money wise. In fact I know this to be the case when compared to some of the titles I've worked at in the past. We also benefit because people want to shoot for GQ, they want to be in this magazine, and they want to work for us. So we won't be paying the rates that some titles have to pay their contributors. They think it's going to benefit their career by being in GQ and it probably does. But even with good will, we're still under money restrictions. **You have worked as a freelance designer for magazines like Arena , Elle, and FHM. Is this a difficult activity?** It's like everything, there are plusses and minuses. One benefit is that you're not sucked into office politics, and people are hopefully pleased to see you. This means you can get on with the job and you can get your head down. You might be asked to work on a new title. It's fresh, you're free, and you can book yourself a month long holiday at the end of your stint. You're your own boss, in theory. But on the flipside you haven't got the security and you haven't got your holiday time paid for you. You're also doing other peoples work, and in my opinion it's less creative,

IT'S ALL ABOUT FINDING THE TIPPING POINT. IT'S NOT THE BALANCE. IT'S ABOUT HOW FAR YOU CAN PUSH SOMETHING BEFORE IT STARTS TO BECOME SOMETHING ELSE

because you are making someone else's vision come to life. Often you will be working in a magazine that is not really your cup of tea, or one that matches your design background. You may also have very different opinions to those you are working with, but you just have to grin and bear it, and get on with the job, because you're the freelancer. You're rarely able to influence the design direction of the magazine or sometimes even the issue. Don't get me wrong, I enjoyed freelancing, but I'm happier being fulltime. You can build long term working relationships and exert greater control over what you create. Besides, it's nice to have your own desk, that way you stand some chance of keeping it tidy! **What are your views on the need for a magazine to opt for a redesign?** I think redesign is possibly the wrong word. That makes it sound like just a design led solution. Rethink would be better. You spend so much of you're time making sure the product gets out there, that you rarely have time to consider which direction you want it to move in. Too many people think a redesign should be handed over to the designers to whack in a bit more white space or change the sub heads typeface. It has got to be about more than just changing the design. It has to be a re-evaluation of that magazine's function in that marketplace. The decisions made from those discussions should be used to determine the new graphic language. It's a grown up approach. It has to start with the editor, include the section heads and then run across the whole editorial department, rather than just the design team. It's a fundamental mistake that people make. I personally think that if you've got your wits about you, and you genuinely understand your audience, then a kind of rolling redesign should be put in place. That means you are addressing problems as they occur, rather than letting them build up and then be forced into making big changes. Men's lifestyle magazines are in a tough marketplace, and we have many competitors. Major redesigns are risky adventures, they can go wrong and leave you feeling very vulnerable. Every designer sees things they want to change, month in and month out. But you can't isolate the reader. They pick up GQ magazine and to an extent they want to be surprised, but if they're regulars they also want to know what to expect. It's all about finding the tipping point. It's not the balance. It's about how far you can push something before it starts to become something else. If it does become something else, something the reader doesn't look forward to buying, you've pushed too hard! What we've been doing recently is tweaking the sections before people think they need tweaking. Too many magazines get into a situation where they feel they've gone off the boil and they're not looking so great anymore. Or worse still they've started to lose readers. Then they want to undertake a complete redesign. Whereas what we are trying to do, is while people are still saying, "Hey, GQ's front section is looking great", we'll start to rethink it. We're moving the sections on constantly to keep them fresh and appropriate to the audience. **If you could choose any magazine to redesign, what would it be?** I am not sure if I should answer that question. If things don't work out here, I may need a job there! The truth is I like far more magazines than I dislike, and I don't go out of my way to find things that need redesigning. I haven't got that much spare time on

IN ESSENCE YOU ARE SEARCHING FOR TYPEFACES THAT ARE APPROPRIATE FOR THE PERSONALITY OF THE MAGAZINE

my hands, and besides I do enough of that at work. I've always loved magazines and even if I'm not that enamoured with their design, there's always something in their content. I like Elle Decoration and I really like an American magazine called Outside. I'm into bikes so I buy American bike mags. But I could pick any magazine off the shelf and see how it could be moved on, or how it could be taken in a different direction. It's not always about good or bad. Its really about where you want to take a magazine, and a redesign is just part of that journey. If you're going to lead people, you've got to have somewhere to take them. **You have worked on some major magazines that no longer exist, like Sky. Why do you think that after being very successful it didn't survive?** Sky was a unisex style magazine. Ultimately, the market changed drastically with the advent of the lads mags, and much of magazine publishing splintered back into men's and women's titles. Sky was a down to earth version of the Face, and designed to be a little more relevant to its audience. But even the Face didn't survive these changes, which is hard to believe after effectively inventing this formula in the early eighties. Girls who were buying Sky started buying More or Just 17, and the boys went to Loaded and FHM (For Him Magazine). The market no longer really existed, and to prove a point here I am working on a men's lifestyle title! **Do you have any spreads that you look back on with particular affection?** When you're turning out a magazine every month for a dozen years it's good not to get too precious about these things. There are a lot of pages I like and a lot of pages I don't like. It's just the good creative ideas that I look back at with some fondness. Like Supergrass shot by a school photographer, animals wearing backpacks or the Incredible Hulk showing off stretch cream. Taking a difficult page, like a competition prize, and making it interesting can be satisfying. Or maybe putting together a six page feature on a high fashion brand, without making it snobby. And of course there are always memorable covers. The greatest thing about magazine work is that feeling you get at the end of the month, when you know a hundred thousand plus people are going to buy it and a lot more are going to read it. I think many creative people have a need to put their work out there and know their efforts are being seen. I still think magazines are the perfect form of mass communication. They combine portability with desirability. I get a real kick from sitting on the underground, seeing someone leaf through GQ and enjoy something I've helped construct. Mind you I don't travel by tube for that exclusive purpose. **And what about your favourite magazine designer?** I don't put people on pedestals. Let alone another magazine designer! There are a large number of individuals doing great work, from small independent publishers through to national newspapers. Of course I pick up magazines and newspapers, look at a spread or a section and wish I'd designed it. But that's just professional respect, or jealousy, depending on what kind of day I've had. You've got to keep up and raise your game incrementally. You don't want to suddenly wake up and find your design work, or that of your magazine, has got left behind. That's what keeps you invigorated. Blind terror! **Is there a secret to successfully art directing photo shoots?** Photo shoots are a tough one. They are satisfying, but you should have a crystal clear concept before you arrive. There's nothing worse than putting spreads together back at the office, and realising you didn't get the images you needed. I've seen designers turn up at photo shoots without knowing what they wanted, or how to get it. It's a skill you learn through doing. Confidence, not arrogance, is the key to handling those situations. The clearer your idea, the more confident you will be. There are a lot of people there to help you on a photo shoot: So you have to get the photographer, the stylist, the prop person, the photographers assistant, wardrobe, whoever, on side and on track. They need your direction, because only you know what you are trying to achieve on the page. You could be standing alongside one of the greatest photographers in the world, but unless you've arrived with a strong concept you can still come away from that situation very disappointed. You might have great photos, but they may not be what you require. I am not saying you can't bluff it, because you can. After all, you're the person who's probably paying for all of it! But then again you're the sucker who's got to scratch something together if you don't come back with a coherent set of images. In an ideal situation you try to work with people you trust, whilst bearing in mind that they are also creatives within their field. So although you need to explain what you want, you must leave them enough space to add their skills and ideas. **How did you choose typefaces for your magazines?** That question needs its own interview. In essence you are searching for typefaces that are appropriate for the personality of the magazine, and the context in which they will be used. GQ is a masculine stylish men's title and you need typefaces to reflect that. And then you need to consider the physical constraints. How big the typeface is going to be used, how small, how legible, etc. I've chosen faces I thought were suitable for a publication at that particular point in time. And although I consider myself a magazine person and not a typographer, I think I have enough typographic skills to set the tone and personality for a magazine. And that's a very serious business because that's what people are buying into every month. **Do you design any of the advertisements in the magazine?** No. But sometimes I wish I did when I look at some of them! Magazine designers generally have an odd relationship with ads. They pretty much pay for the magazine and yet you have to continually balance their relationship with your editorial work. Your work has to be strong enough to avoid the magazine from looking like its just made up of the advertisements. You want quality ads that can be added to your work, without detracting from it. **What is your view on current magazine design?** It's healthy and I enjoy the variety from the small independents and the mass market titles. I'm always looking out for something new and fresh to come along. To be honest I've got a bit tired of small indy fashion titles that appear to be facsimiles of the last small indy fashion title. Someone needs to go in there and take some risks. That's not to say I'm not excited every time I look at a news stand. Particularly if you can find somewhere that stocks international titles as well. Go and visit Barnes and Noble, in New York. The amount of magazines they stock is awesome. You could spend several days just working your way through the aisles. You don't need to go that far. Go to a Borders bookshop or RD Franks in London and there's some fantastic work in there. We may very well look back on this era as a bit of a golden age for magazines. But like everything else, you have to pick the wheat from the chaff. **What magazines are you reading at the moment?** Well, I'm doing up my house so I'm reading interior design magazines! Some of the type work by Tony Chambers at Wallpaper is wonderful. But I am a magazine nut and I read so many different types. I love Paris Vogue, that's amazing. US GQ is very good. I think the Sunday supplements are great, so maybe I'll move on to one of those sometime. *SBOOK 4*

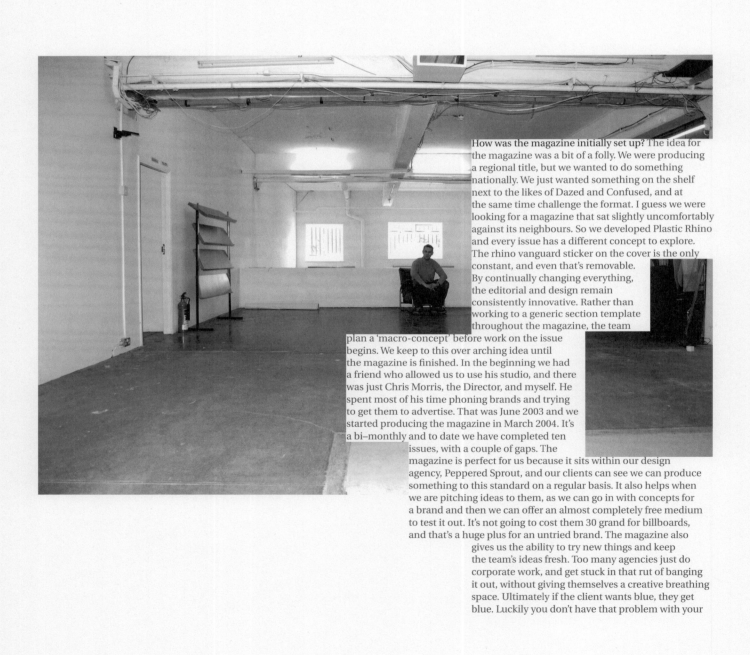

How was the magazine initially set up? The idea for the magazine was a bit of a folly. We were producing a regional title, but we wanted to do something nationally. We just wanted something on the shelf next to the likes of Dazed and Confused, and at the same time challenge the format. I guess we were looking for a magazine that sat slightly uncomfortably against its neighbours. So we developed Plastic Rhino and every issue has a different concept to explore. The rhino vanguard sticker on the cover is the only constant, and even that's removable. By continually changing everything, the editorial and design remain consistently innovative. Rather than working to a generic section template throughout the magazine, the team plan a 'macro-concept' before work on the issue begins. We keep to this over arching idea until the magazine is finished. In the beginning we had a friend who allowed us to use his studio, and there was just Chris Morris, the Director, and myself. He spent most of his time phoning brands and trying to get them to advertise. That was June 2003 and we started producing the magazine in March 2004. It's a bi–monthly and to date we have completed ten issues, with a couple of gaps. The magazine is perfect for us because it sits within our design agency, Peppered Sprout, and our clients can see we can produce something to this standard on a regular basis. It also helps when we are pitching ideas to them, as we can go in with concepts for a brand and then we can offer an almost completely free medium to test it out. It's not going to cost them 30 grand for billboards, and that's a huge plus for an untried brand. The magazine also gives us the ability to try new things and keep the team's ideas fresh. Too many agencies just do corporate work, and get stuck in that rut of banging it out, without giving themselves a creative breathing space. Ultimately if the client wants blue, they get blue. Luckily you don't have that problem with your

PLASTIC RHINO *PETER KELLET*

own magazine. You have complete design freedom and that's an increasingly rare thing in a competitive world. Now our clients can buy into ideas, rather than us just selling them. **How did you get the distribution deal with Comag?** We couldn't have got the Comag deal without having the magazine printed. There was way too much red tape. So we decided to print the magazine with the bar code and the price, as if we were going to sell it. We also produced stickers that said, "free, usual price £3.50". Then we sent a copy off to all the big distributors. Two weeks later we got a call from Comag to say they had an allocation to fill for 300 London outlets, and would we be interested. This guy was about to go on holiday and we had to get 3000 issues to him by the next day, or he wasn't going to fill his allocation. We went straight into Borders, HMV, Virgin and we have since set up an export deal with Comag. Now we print ten thousand and we distribute through 400 outlets in Central London, throughout the UK and in 15 countries. We also started a subscription deal with a magazine café. **What percentage of your sales are made through subscription?** We only have about a thousand subscribers, but that's mainly because it's readily available and we don't push subscriptions. We initially started sorting it out ourselves, but it's a big job and a logistical nightmare. **You have promoted the concept of, 'nothing being permanent' by having a removable sticker for the masthead. Can you explain how this idea was conceived?** Every magazine carries its typographic masthead loud and proud. Because our concept changes from issue to issue, we thought why not have a masthead we could move around and change too. We also didn't want a typographic masthead 'ironed' on to the front of the magazine and we loved the idea of having a removable 'vanguard', a throw away identity. Once you've bought the magazine you can peel it off the cover and the identity goes with it. The plastic rhino sticker came from a series of daft ideas. Originally we told people it was based on the theory that rhinos are close to extinction, and very soon only plastic ones will be left! Its quite funny because our distributor completed an 'image' review, so they know what titles are going to sit where and what magazines sit next to each other. There are logistics on height and width. When we printed the first issue of the magazine we stuck the rhino on the right hand side. Then we realised all the newsstands only display the first 30mm of every title on the left. All you would see of ours was a blank white strip! It certainly made it look different, but we got told off and we've put the rhino on the left ever since. Rejecting a typographic masthead meant we weren't nailing the magazine down to a particular typeface or fashion.

Spelling out plastic rhino was just too obvious and we wanted to attract the kind of people that would pick it up and say what's this thing with just a sticker on it. Our target audience came to find us, and they were the inquisitive ones. It doesn't actually say the name anywhere except down by the bar code. We liked the idea that's it's that subtle. **Where did you find the actual plastic rhino?** We picked the rhino up from a charity shop but we've lost it since. We tried to find another one and ended up contacting plastic animal manufactures everywhere. They sent us dumpy little things that looked nothing like our rhino. I don't know where it is but I hope it's happy. **How do you generate the unique concept for each issue?** Well we generate random ideas as a team. The original idea was to have a filing cabinet and you put your concept for an issue into its own file. As you gather more content it goes into that file. As it gets thicker the file moves nearer the front of the cabinet, until it finally gets made. Nothing we do is really time sensitive. We don't do features on new bands or the latest fashion trend. Although we did pass up the chance to interview the Artic Monkeys awhile back, which now looks like a bit of a mistake. **How do you manage change in the magazine?** We got to the point where we were working on a pun angle for most of the issues. A play on words, but I personally wanted to change the format and the visual presentation. I think we got to the point in the last few issues where the linear narrative reintroduces itself and you can struggle to break free. That's why we really needed to take those ideas and put them into a different format. We almost wanted to be anti-format from the start, but we got into a comfort zone and that's easy to do when things are going well. Now we change everything and there is no grid structure. It's all done in illustrator as eps's. We don't use Quark or InDesign and its not page set at all. However, there is a generic template and each designer has their own section to do what they wish. That means it comes together as a juxtaposition of styles and ideas around one concept. We are now looking at packaging and in the next issue, called Lucky Bag, we will have a series of contributions from our designers. Each of us has been given 1000 pounds to come up with something that will go into 3000 goody bags, and we will distribute them as the magazine. We have scaled down our distribution for this issue and in the future it will fluctuate depending on the budget, which will be dictated by how we develop the concept. There's a printer who can print a ten metre long constant strip. We are going to have 5 ten centimetre high, ten metre long strips and we will deliver editorial, graphic or fashion sections. Each strip becomes a different part of the magazine and clear plastic tubes will house the strips. We are looking at all sorts of ideas, different inks, edible magazines, and just challenging what a magazine can be. A different format for every issue, that's the plan. It will be more sporadic, but more interesting. The processes have to be researched and everything we do will be a challenge for the manufactures involved. When a client comes along, they can also get involved, and specify what they want from a magazine. It turns the entire client designer relationship on its head. **What do you mean by a 'linear narrative', in relation to Plastic Rhino?** Because Plastic Rhino is based on a concept that's explored and evolves as you go through the magazine, each issue naturally follows a linear narrative. We did produce one that was not strictly linear. It was called Interwinterwarmer and as it was a winter issue, we decided people needed warming up. It had a thermal colour chart with the pages in a gradient from blue to red. As you read the magazine it warmed you up a bit. The content followed the thermal colour chart and information was placed in a section that was applicable. Editorials were placed relating to their temperature. A story would be warm or cold. Our ice cream story could have gone either way, because its cold but you eat it on a hot day. Ultimately, certain stories won't sit comfortably together and if you have a spread that uses a lot of negative space, the next layout might need to be busy. And because the magazine doesn't follow a generic template we have the freedom to move anything, anywhere. The

fashion section often gets moved around more than a sheep being chased by a crazy farmer with a stick. The problem is a magazine is an inherently linear device. Its pages are numbered, and one page follows another. If we are to remove this restriction, we are going to have to apply more radical innovations to the basic format. **Why did you base issue 8 on a coast to coast train journey from Liverpool to Scarborough?** You must mean the 'Trans Pennine Express' issue! That was another linear narrative and the idea came from 'Keeping it Rhyl' in issue 2. That started from a railway station and documented the walk around that station's town. The original concept was called 'ftp' and the idea was that you can make a magazine anywhere in the world, as long as you can hook up to an ftp connection and put up the pages of the magazine. We thought we could get a series of artists to roll a dice and that would allocate them an amount of pages. They could design whatever they wanted and then upload the pages to an ftp, which would then go straight to the printer. We would never see the final publication before it goes to print and we couldn't predict the final outcome. This extraordinary piece, that no one has edited, would go straight to the newsstands without ever being seen! This idea will happen, but we worried someone might highjack it. If something went seriously wrong, we are not really in a position to get ourselves out of trouble at the moment, but we'll get there. Issue 8 is really a watered down version where we asked people to explore the surrounding area of every railway station stop between Liverpool and Scarborough. It was completely random on the day and we pulled the names out of a hat. They didn't know what they

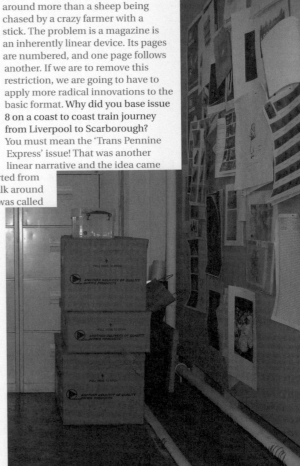

were going to do or where they were going. They were only armed with whatever they had on them. Reggie just got off at his stop only to find it was just a service station. At the end of the day everyone got back on the train, with hangovers and had different stories to tell and hopefully that reflects in the magazine. Everyone wanted to find something unique in their adventure and there was definitely a deliberateness to each story. Bumbling into any English town and discovering its secrets in x amount of hours is almost a social experiment. **Can you explain the cover images, and why you have no cover lines?** We have kept one constant, and that is we want Plastic Rhino to be sat on the shelves next to the fashion and lifestyle magazines. So we purposely put a female model on the cover. If you don't know the magazine and you scan the newsstand you could mistake it for a fashion publication. It has this strange quality to it and we have played on that for first nine issues. The models we choose aren't the best and we like the idea of the them not being airbrushed, therefore not quite right. But again its understated and I don't know how obvious it is to people. As for cover lines, we don't even like having to carry a bar code on the cover! Even the masthead peels off. It's been our ambition from day one to put a cardboard tube on the magazine rack with just our rhino sticker stuck to it. It wasn't possible to do that from issue 1. We have since realised the power of PR and we will be generating our own press for experimental issues. If there is going to be a limited print run people need to know about it. **How do you organise the workload for the magazine and your design group?** The team collectively drop tools for a solid week or the equivalent in hours. It's always produced in a really intensive flourish. Two weeks would be a luxury. The biggest job is planning the issue and keeping them different. As we have got busier as an agency, the magazine has been put on the back burner. It's a bit chicken and egg, because the more we do with the magazine, the more clients we get and it's finding that balance. A new system is needed to help find new techniques and new ways of developing costings for unusual issues. We now need to be more structured about how we deliver the magazine. Getting it to the printer usually means working up to the wire, but that's usually when the good ideas start to flow. I think that's due to the squeezing of the creative process! We always do a final edit to make sure everything is spelt roughly correctly and the grammar is kind of alright. I always tear up the first issue when I get it back from the printers. It's horrible to look through something and find mistakes. We aren't particularly fastidious, but we do care about the final outcome. But because its not done in Quark, the pages drift out slightly and there are imperfections. It goes with the nature of the magazine. A large percentage of it is produced in-house, but we also have a lot of contributors. It sounds corny but you want to support the people you like and to provide them with a network. Writers always moan it's hard to get their work into publications, but surprisingly we get more illustrators and artists contributing. Maybe they are all sitting under a tree with pen and paper ready, waiting for us to contact them! The magazine is in this transitional phase and hopefully more work will be completed internally. Maybe we need it to be more of a thumbprint of our agency and used as a mechanism to show people how we can take risks with the format, as much as with the content. **How has your relationship with the magazine's advertisers evolved?** We had big brands like Puma involved from day one. The idea has always been for us to develop the ideas and then take them to the brands. We simply don't have the usual advertising spends on single page ads, because brands want to get involved and support us in different ways. For the first issue we did leisure wear hair and we cut up Puma products and made them into hair pieces. It was easier after that, as brands understood where we were coming from. When we designed the first issue we took a series of ideas to different brands. From there we have developed relationships and

we can now rely on a number of them for support. And in turn they rely on us for ideas. We find brands are happy to be part of the magazine and help support us, as opposed to just dumping single page ads in it, like most magazines. Now that we are challenging the traditional magazine format, we are going to have to change the way brands advertise in magazines, and completely re-write the pay per page system. As we've been speaking brands, we've realised they've been pulling out of mainstream magazine advertising. They are spending their money on things like shop fits that create a sense of theatre. The way we involve brands interactively with the magazine, means we build strong personal relationships and that in turn builds loyalty. Brands generally want to back creative things and not standardise their brand. **Can you tell us about your new magazine, Polished T?** Its been a mad time really because we have literally just published issue one. The whole thing is about getting artists, graphic writers and designers, all in the same 'gallery', which is Polished T. We are bringing conceptual art to the high street and making it more accessible. The Editor Jonty O'Conner has done a great job in putting it all together. We've found a great 1940s building at the same time we launched the magazine. It's just brilliant as an open studio and gallery space. We've leased it for six months until they bulldoze it! That gives us a hundred and eighty days to programme as many things as possible into that space. We have just teamed up with an agency in London who are going to help us develop the future of the magazine, and to build online sales of prints of the artists. Issue 2 is sitting on our hard drive waiting to go to print. We really want to develop the brand Polished T as it can go to any city in the world, and lend itself to any art community. We are looking to do an issue from Jamaica next summer. It will come out bi-monthly, but we don't have to generate it from scratch every issue, like Plastic Rhino. Getting everything working together with the website is the difficult part, we'll just have to work harder! *SBOOK 4*

Why have you accumulated such a large design library at Bradbourne Publishing? When you are producing a magazine like Baseline, a design library becomes a very useful resource. Many of these books are from my own personal collection, and I have accumulated them over a number of decades. There are rare out of print books, from the 1960s and a large proportion are German and unavailable in the UK. Visual communication is directly related to the culture of a country. If you take a book like 'A Smile In The Mind', much of its humour is embedded in English culture. Many of its visual puns only really work here. Show it to a German and he does not find it funny. For instance, in England the Arabic numeral 4 can be used replace the word 'for'. That isn't going to translate into German culture. You might find another numeral in Germany that could make the same link. However, there is a deeper problem, in that Germans are generally more serious and would tend to think, "Oh, here is an attempt to manipulate our language". **How would you describe the working environment in your studio?** Maybe you should ask the people who have to work with me! It has probably changed over the years. I used to be very tough, but that is a product of the way I was taught. If I didn't get it just right the problem would go home with me, and that would happen with every job. Now it only happens with every other job! **What were the major obstacles you faced when setting up Bradbourne Publishing, 13 years ago?** Many people asked, 'Can you exist outside of London?' But we knew the 'virtual' relationship between clients and designers was on its way. You don't need a big studio anymore and you don't need to be within walking distance of your client. Some studios still insist they need to be in London, to manage their client/designer rapport. **Do you think moving out of London, to Kent, changed the identity of the company?** The identity of a design company is based on the kind of designers that work within it. Personality is a more useful word. I think 'identity' has hijacked 'personality'. In the end, design is a person to person game. You must talk with your client about the design problem and get on the same wavelength. Trust is critical in this process and that has to be built. They are entrusting you with the visual appearance of their company, and to an extent, the intellectual property that it contains. This kind of work needs to be undertaken with senior managers working at the highest levels. These are the people who are usually in a company for the long haul. If you start dealing with marketing managers, there is always the risk they are creating work that's useful to their career, rather than the companies. In a couple of years they're gone. Some marketing managers want to make their mark by changing the logo of the company and the direction of the identity. Then the whole thing gets diluted and the graphic design gets hijacked. It doesn't serve the companies needs at all. **Can you tell us about your bookwork for the '20th Century Composers' series?** '20th Century Composers', is part of a collection of books we've completed for Phaidon. The series was launched about eight years ago and we created the style for

BASELINE
HANS DIETER REICHERT

each cover using portraits of the composer. The idea is that when these portraits face you on a bookstore shelf, they will create a strong impression and a curious feeling. On the back you see the composer as a young person and that's the last image people will remember. Phaidon were one of our first major clients after we settled here in Kent. We were producing Baseline back then, but it wasn't making enough money. **How often did you publish Baseline at that time?** Only once or twice a year. We began work on the magazine on issue 17, when Mike Daines was the editor. He started the magazine way back in the Letraset days. The original idea was to produce a magazine that would keep Letraset in touch with the design community. Those magazines were A4 and two colours. It was text heavy and set on a rigid three column grid. Mike was a managing editor, and invited guest editors like Erik Spiekermann. In fact the first nine issues were all guest edited, leaving Mike with the task of getting it out. The design agency Newell and Sorrell was asked by Letraset to help out. Rodney Mylius and Dominic Lippa came on board. They had designed some major identities, the last big one being for British Airways. Letraset wanted to change the magazine and produce something outrageous, something big. After a few issues it just became a self indulgent exercise for graphic designers. For example some feature articles were set in 4pt black type on a dark blue background. It was completely unreadable. As you can imagine the contributing authors were seriously pissed off. They took a 'wallpaper' route. Much more decorative and with a, 'oh this looks fantastic, lets do another page!' approach. Five Baseline issues were created like that, and one of those was the very controversial Bodoni issue. After that one Mike Daines said he wasn't going to continue, as the design process had become so superficial. You can't just say, 'oh, this is my space now and I'll do what I like'. Needless to say they lost the job, and then we became involved. I'd worked with Mike previously, and he knew I was serious about the design process. When issue 17 came out, we placed a hand on the cover as a symbolic way of saying, stop. We then formed an editorial group consisting of Mike Daines, Alan Fletcher, Dave Ellis from Why Not, Michael Anikst who came over from Russia, Martin Ashley from the London College of Communication, Colin Brignall from Letraset, and myself. The idea being that these external consultants would provide an objective view of the magazine's core values. I think it worked quite well for a couple of years and it helped to establish the magazine's independence from Letraset. In the middle of this period Letraset informed us that they would probably be dissolving the company in a couple of years time, and the magazine would have to go! We thought, 'Oh bloody hell, just when we've got it working.' **What happened to Letraset?** You could just see them going downhill. They were the market leaders in rub down lettering in the 70s and early 80s. It was a massive company. They cut down half the trees in Norway just to make the paper for those transfer sheets. Steve Jobs came to them and said,

"I've got this idea for an Apple Computer. Are you interested?" They turned him down and of course the Macintosh effectively put them out of business. We put forward a business plan to take over the magazine rather than let it die and Letraset, after some deliberation, agreed. **Did it help, having worked on some of the previous issues?** The costs were easy enough to estimate and we knew how many copies we had to sell to break even. We also had to buy the name, the trademark, and a lot of unsold copies of every issue. In the end we had to bin them all! **Wouldn't they be valuable now?** That action probably made any remaining copies still in private hands a bit more valuable! Letraset used to heavily subsidise the magazine and the 20,000 print run per issue never sold out. They would put them in the middle of shops like the London Graphics Centre and hope for the best. They also had a very small number of monthly subscribers. Once we separated from such a big organisation things got a lot more expensive. Now we were paying the print bill, the designers and the authors. You discover pretty quickly you have to sell a certain number of units to survive. Number eighteen was the first issue under our own ownership. The next seven issues were similar cost wise, until issue twenty six, when we added the jacket. **What was the idea behind the development of the fold out jacket?** We started working with Phaidon and we looked at how they produced their jackets. They fold them inwards from both sides. This makes them quite tactile, and of course it also hides the binding or the staple. Then we began to think that this jacket could be made to fold out into a much bigger object, and size is very important in graphic design! It meant we could turn the jacket into a poster, a wall chart or almost anything. Later on we thought about how we might promote it as a completely separate thing. It meant we could ask someone like Alan Kitching, Sigi Odermatt or Helmut Schmid just to design the fold out jacket. Influential designers could produce customized designs to any size, and they would become desirable items in their own right. Then we found out from our new American distributor that shops in the states don't return unsold copies of magazines, as it is too expensive.

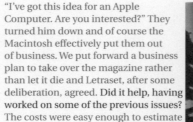

I THINK THE WORD 'MAGAZINE' COMES FROM THE ARABIC FOR 'BAZAAR', AND TO AN EXTENT, THAT IS WHAT IT SHOULD BE LIKE... **How many are distributed in the UK?** About 50% percent are sold here, some on the continent, and quite a few go to Singapore. Central Books distribute it in the UK, but they deal internationally as well. We are sent a list a few times a year and we can see who's taking them. But like most magazines we would prefer to sell direct to subscribers. When you sell to distributors or shops they take fifty percent of the money! **What was the magazine's print run when you first started art directing Baseline?** We were still with Letraset on issue 17 and they printed 20,000 copies. I doubt whether half of them were sold. You need to get the price right to successfully sell and distribute a magazine. W.H.Smith won't take a magazine if it costs over six pounds, so that counts us out of that market. We sell mostly through bookshops, where people have

a different attitude to design magazines. Where it sells and doesn't sell is really a science. We know design students buy it, but we have to make sure it's available to them. It also sells quite well through museums, but they can be quite aggressive, asking for sole distribution and sales rights. Some outlets say: 'If you supply us, then don't supply to anyone else', that sort of crap. Then odd things occur, like when the Paul Smith store in New York asked to sell Baseline. They have a broad-minded manageress who thinks about lifestyle and how you can make a clothes shop more interesting. They sold out in a week. The Paul Smith shop in London took another year before they stocked it. It is all about how different cultures view design. You can guarantee if you have an article about the Spanish design scene, then the issue will create a lot of interest in that community. Of course we try to keep a certain balance, but occasionally, as in our last issue (49), we got carried away. It ended up a little bit heavy on Swiss

A CABINET FULL OF DRAWS, AND YOU DON'T KNOW WHAT'S INSIDE UNTIL YOU OPEN THEM

design, with major features on Herbert Matter and Armin Hoffman. **Wouldn't it be easier to build a design magazine around themed issues?** You can lose the surprise factor with themed issues. I think the word 'magazine' comes from the Arabic for 'bazaar', and to an extent, that is what it should be like. A cabinet full of draws, and you don't know what's inside until you open them. **Do you ever worry there might not be enough in an issue to interest your target audience?** Finding your audience and keeping it is an art. Clearly we are not designing for the masses, but we also need to survive. We could bring a high level of academic research to the subject area and make the magazine very serious and possibly boring. I've been involved in the educational environment for over 14 years, and I could provide articles that would work well for university lecturers. Our approach is not to be elitist, but to be engaging and interesting. In the end design is not just theoretical, but also practical. **Do mistakes creep into Baseline?** I am afraid we have more spelling mistakes than we would like. I think the days of copy proofing are almost over. Obviously it shouldn't happen, but again it tends to be a cultural thing. If you have an article full of Swiss surnames it can be very difficult for an English only speaker to get these right all of the time. Making sure dates are correct is also a problem. You try to cross reference, but you can easily find three different sources with three different dates. Maintaining editorial standards is hard work and very time consuming. **How do you commission Baseline's articles?** Sometimes stories are generated by myself, and sometimes people come to us with ideas. We generally commission people to write four, or eight page articles. Four pages are about 1500 words and eight pages 2500 to 3000 words. This leaves us with enough space to explore the visual material. That is another example of where we differ from Eye. We are visually led, not word led. I believe in getting people involved in a theme by creating visual curiosity. Then they want to read more, just to find out what it's all about. The visual communication acts as an

IF A STUDENT 'NEEDS' JUST ONE GRAPHIC STYLE, THEY MUST BE A PRETTY STUPID STUDENT initiator, like a poster. It's rather different from an academic approach where the images are there only to support the text. That is why we design each story differently and why we don't have a very strict grid. We work with twelve columns throughout which gives us the possibility of 3 fours, 4 threes, 6 twos, 2 sixes and so on. It means we have a very wide palette of columns and references to explore. There are articles and artwork where you might want spreads to appear very lively by having narrower columns. Or you might have a more bookish story that needs very wide columns and will appear quieter in contrast. It just depends on the story. Of course this means a great deal more work is needed, to constantly create new ideas for layouts. It is a very different environment to somewhere like Creative Review and Grafik, where everything runs similarly from page to page. I personally don't believe in putting style over content. Style should be embedded within the story. If an article requires round corners, you can't square them off because that is your style. A visual language needs to be flexible enough to represent the 'soul' of the piece, rather than sacrificing its contents on the altar of a corporate 'look'. You can create a very strong identity for a magazine, but this can be hard on the individual elements within. Although quick recognition is useful in marketing terms, in the long term it becomes very dull. That's why there are so many re-designs in this business. **Many of Grafik's readers are students. Don't you think a magazine's design should reflect the needs of its audience?** If a student 'needs' just one graphic style, they must be a pretty stupid student. Surely at that time in their design career they want to be exposed to many different ways of solving a visual problem. I remember seeing North Design's RAC identity. It looked very 70s and the entire support material was created using Helvetica. It was very interesting. Then I found out they used Helvetica whatever the job! I cannot understand that concept. Why not use Univers? It's more humanistic, as it's slightly softer. Or what about Akzidenz, it has much more character. Helvetica is mechanical and it's useful in creating an optimised greyness on a page, if you do it properly. And that's a big 'If'. It's very mono-line, has no swelling, no quirkiness, it can look very nice and very neutral. Many texts start to come alive in Akzidenz, and begin to 'speak' their contents. **So do you change your typeface for the different items in Baseline?** We also need to remain neutral in certain parts of the magazine. For instance the editorial section has its own typeface. In an article like, 'The Book Nobody Sees', by Sue Walker, we used Gill. It's about English books and you would just rip the soul out of the piece if you set in Helvetica. The article on 'Pocket Penguins' in the same issue is set in Sabon, because Tschichold designed that face and he established a certain recognition with that series. The numbers on the first page of that article are set in Garamond. Nobody knows that. Mono-line numerals do not exist in the Sabon typeface, but Sabon was modelled on Garamond. So type knowledge and its history are quite important, because it just makes graphic design more interesting. You can't say, "I'm in a Helvetica mood for the next two years!" Of course the feel of an article is not just determined by type usage. In an item by Steven Heller called 'Dancing Type and Music Videos', again from issue 48, we printed 'black on black'. We wanted to create a dark environment because of its filmic content. We experimented with inks to see what happens when you print 70% yellow behind the black, or a 70% magenta behind the black. It was quite fascinating to discover all of these other blacks. **Do you often experiment in this way?** It's one of the reasons we work on Baseline. This current issue is quite experimental. The cover artwork started with a line thickness half of what you see now, and then we had the nightmare of getting it registered. The printer didn't really want to print it, but we persuaded him, and he came up with a solution. We ended up printing the thin black lines on top of the silver ink, rather than try to drop the lines out of the silver. It meant the black lines would be greyer because they wouldn't be sitting on white paper. It's useful to have a friendly printer who works with you to solve these kinds of problems. There's quite a personal attachment to this kind of work and that makes it worth getting up in the morning. **Are the jackets designed in house?** Sometimes we produce jackets with other people. Alan Fletcher produced a cover illustration about drawing, that included all of the letters of the alphabet and we had an article inside about his collages. Alan Kitching did a jacket for that same issue no. 29. It was originally produced by letterpress and then he signed it. Alan is a print designer, he's not a printer, actually he's a typographic artist. A lot of letterpress people think he's a printer, but he prints only to create letter images. We also commissioned a 'swiss' jacket by Sigi Odermatt for issue 35. The cover in contrast had a rather difficult to read quote from David Bailey. It said, 'We visual people read more than you literary people look'. We wanted to deconstruct the phrase with grid patterns. Odermatt's accompanying jacket was not particularly experimental, but when you use transparent paper it's always limiting because the ink doesn't dry easily. The jacket for issue 45 was just a page straight from the sketchbook of French designer, Jean Widmer. We even included the jagged torn edge of the sketchbook. He develops his logos in a methodical and hand drawn way and the jacket summed that up. You can see a little bit of his formal education in Switzerland coming through in his strong abstract graphics for the Centre Pompidou. We think it's important to showcase designers who work through the design process using an analogue approach, the pen as well as the computer. Or maybe even the mark you can make when you smudge pencil sharpener droppings! **Is the editing process difficult?** Obviously we have to check for accuracy, but each text is individual. We have to be careful of 'hype' driven subject areas, as they are likely to have little long term significance. We try to encourage a holistic approach to commissioning texts that can showcase the breadth and depth of visual communication enquiry. This does mean that someone from an academic environment will write a feature in a very different way to someone who is a practitioner. We see this as a positive rather than a negative. However, if a text becomes very repetitive, or if entire paragraphs can be summarised in a sentence, then of course we tell the writer and make adjustments. Over the years this has happened only twice. Inevitably you find people who you want to work with, and who want to work with you, and it can be a fascinating process of discovery. For instance, in issue 45 we designed a story by Dr. Caroline Archer about Anthony Froshaug's tenure at Watford College and we found a collection of his work from this time period at St Brides. **Is it the written or the visual content that determines the structure of each issue?** We design the articles independently and at the end of this stage we don't know where they will appear in the magazine. It becomes a discussion and it's really a visual, rather than a political process. We don't put articles about American designers up front in the hope that we can sell more issues in the USA! We do try to avoid putting two predominantly 'white' articles together. Helmut Schmid wrote and designed an article about his former teacher, designer and friend Armin Hoffman and straight after there was an article on Jan Tschichold! At least Hoffman's article was fairly structured and its use of colour pretty sparse. The Tschichold article was quite a classical design, so they did look different. At the moment we are planning issue number fifty. We haven't got a clue about how we are going to celebrate this milestone. **You must have some ideas?** Well we were thinking of printing every page, and every sample, in gold on gold! Just joking! **Have you thought about changing the format for the issue?** No, but now you come to mention it, we could do an issue in the golden section. The question is how do we leave an impression and make people remember it as a very special issue. After all there aren't that many design magazines that make it to fifty! **Four of you work on each issue. Do you take an article each?** We normally work with one or two designers per magazine, but it is not like, 'you do this, you do that'. If there's some work available then one person can start, and if it turns out to be a larger job than expected, then someone else comes in to support. Of course if it's an article about someone's favourite designer then they will want to take it on board. Sometimes it is just down to whether you have an interesting idea for the article. When you walked in the studio you met Paul, who designed the Wilhelm Deffke article in the last issue no. 48. His idea was to have all the captions on the bottom and the background structures related to the symbols Deffke designed. He created many of these symbols in the Germany of the 1920s and 1930s. His style was very stark and dramatic, and he redesigned the swastika for the Nazi party. This article was followed by a piece on Herbert Matter, and then an article about publications from the 1970s. One of the magazines featured was 'Oz', and the article was about sex and sedition. The design is a bit gritty and tactile. I don't think the printing industry of the 1970s was quite ready for 'Oz!' It's funny to think it appeared at the same time Weingart was re-freshing Swiss graphic design at the design school in Basel. **Have you considered a virtual version of the magazine?** The design group 8VO produced the final edition of their Octavo magazines electronically. They only ever intended to produce 8 issues. The first 7 were print based and they were tremendously influential. Very post-modern minimalist Swiss, and a real antidote to Brody's magazine work. The first issue was released in 1986 and they decided to produce their final issue on CD Rom in the early 90s. But it was too early and it paled by comparison to their print based issues. I think they were trying to say something about the crudity of screen resolution typography, by making it deliberately low resolution and using one bit colour. The question still is whether the Internet is a useful medium to visually explain graphic design and typography. It started as an experimental medium but now its commercial potential has been exploited and it's become quite boring. The messages have to be concise and come quickly to the point or most people will switch off. I was at the last AGI (Alliance Graphique Internationale) meeting last week and we were putting new UK members forward and looking at individual websites. One person's site would be straight down the line, "this is who I am and this is what I do," and another's would be playful and interactive. It was interesting to review people's reactions. Some would switch off after 30 seconds if they couldn't get to the 'meat' within the site. They weren't prepared to explore, even if the site was visually stimulating and based around their subject area. I have a feeling that graphic designers prefer to see print based work in print. I believe the web will be good for referencing, and we have an e-Lexicon that runs in parallel to Baseline. In an educational environment this sort of thing could be used to source designers, their circle of friends and their interests in one go. You can make links and create a mini library. Maybe even link with the designers direct. I think it is about creating a network. For example Rian Hughes designed a range of typefaces for comic books. His CV is amazing, with music work and teaching at different colleges. With the e-lexicon you have the possibility of linking colleges and finding out so much more. This will never have an extensive visual library for showing samples, because the copyright issues would always get in the way. That's when the magazine comes into its own. They should work in parallel. In some ways a design magazine is a luxury item and the internet is always going to be more mundane by comparison. **Baseline's personality is multi layered. Do you think the Internet is too 'flat' a medium to reflect its interests?** The Internet is really about movement and motion and when the band width is available to exploit this, it will truly come into its own. It's still very early days for this technology and its applications. The navigation systems are still very crude and unfriendly. A serious interface discussion needs to take place and visual communicators should be right in there, determining its future. Otherwise we might end up buying into 'an ease of use' system that will stifle the design process. **Is it true the Mafia controls most magazine distribution in America?** It's quite sad. We are talking big money and I am sure it's partly related to their distribution of pornography. Some magazines go to one side of the block and not to the other. Someone looks after downtown and someone else uptown. There was an independent bookshop in New York and the owner wanted us to supply him directly. It did not work out for him. The Mafia had their hands in the game. On

THE QUESTION STILL IS WHETHER THE INTERNET **IS A USEFUL MEDIUM TO** VISUALLY EXPLAIN GRAPHIC DESIGN **AND** TYPOGRAPHY

a lighter note, we are now selling into Singapore and China. Shanghai and Peking have got their own mega satellite towns with populations of 10 million plus. They're vast and they have their own graphic design communities growing at an insane pace. But the Chinese are still controlled by the State. The Rolling Stones had to skip a couple of their more provocative songs on a recent tour or they couldn't perform. It's the same with magazines. The state will censor if the contents are deemed inappropriate for the population. It's a vast market, but you can guarantee that if a magazine becomes successful there, they will copy it. It's a totally different mentality and they don't understand that things have an intellectual property. Counterfeiting is just another industry. A couple of Chinese publishers/printers approached us and said they wanted to produce a design book. They wanted to include our graphic work alongside many others. I spoke to some AGI members here in England and asked if they had received the same email. They had, and we decided not to send them our work. Well, our magazine has its international readership and followers and we obviously try to distribute in China successfully, but it will take some time. *SBOOK 4*

Your father was an architect. Did this influence your decision to become a Graphic Designer? I also wanted to be an architect, essentially because I didn't really know what a graphic designer did! I knew I wanted to have something to do with design, as I was exposed to design from such an early age. My father ran his own business, which helped, as it took the mystery out of having a business. I didn't see it as an intimidating career move. **So what did you study at University?** I went to North Carolina and their programmes are set up very differently to those in the UK. You don't really specialise in any single design discipline. You study a general programme that might include architecture, product design or even landscape design. After the first year you have to 'declare' your major. I went in thinking I wanted to be an architect, but after I was exposed to graphic design I changed my focus. I liked the way graphic designers communicate directly with people and the immediacy of the end product. If you're an architect it can take years to see your vision. You have to collaborate with a lot of people and in many cases watch your design get modified. In the end I was prepared to give up the permanence of architecture for the intimacy of graphic design. **Did you take an interest in editorial design at North Carolina?** I knew what it was, but I hadn't really made the distinction between the different disciplines in graphic design. I can't say I ever wanted to just be a magazine designer, but I thought it might be a fun and interesting thing to do. But as I have grown older I have definitely seen a split in the design world, with people that see themselves as editorial designers or conventional graphic designers. I think being an editorial designer, forces you to think quickly and not fall in love with your designs. But I also feel it limits your exposure to clients and printers. Younger designers have to be careful about entering this part of the publishing business. I have seen very talented people get trapped because they have stayed too long as an editorial designer, and it's become hard for them to get jobs in regular studios. Sometimes it's difficult to move on, as it's also a relatively sheltered existence, as long as your magazine is selling well! But if you're a good designer you can design anything. **Do you think there are fundamental design problems to solve in this form of art direction?** There are many problems to solve in editorial design and if you use your imagination you can overcome them all. But for me, if you're a designer on a magazine, the editor is the boss. If you're lucky you can work in a partnership, but in a lot of publications the editor takes the lead and your job is to help execute that vision. Inevitably your solutions are going to be limited by page size, page count and the placement of advertising. However, it's still a rewarding activity and I still really enjoy creating publications. You could argue that every design brief has constraints, but with a magazine you have to help communicate the story, address the reader appropriately, whilst making sure you convey the spirit of the magazine. Those are very specific tasks that make this a very difficult discipline. That's why there are so many terrible magazines out there. It's also why the ones that are fresh and unique break through and become influential. **How did you become art director of Spy?** They had a company make the prototype, but they were looking for an art director. Steven Dole, who was working on the prototype, asked if I was interested. The introduction was made and I met the editors. I'd been working at my previous job for two and a half years and I needed a change of scenery. I liked the idea of producing something with my name on it, and I thought a magazine would be a good thing to be put in control of the design process. **Was the prototype a useful template to create the first real issue?** The first issues were similar to the prototype. As time went by we added layering to create something more visually complex. After I finished at Spy, maybe four or five art directors worked on the magazine. And although there have been some layout changes, the overall spirit has remained remarkably consistent, and that's a testament to the editor's vision. So they were always clear on what they wanted. **How would you describe this spirit?** It was about tailoring the visual structure towards the curious and inquisitive reader. This was conveyed editorially and visually. **How much of this visual structure was created in the first few issues?** I think the graphic Language was 75% in place at this point. As the writing and story telling became more multifaceted in subsequent issues, I had to expand the structure in tone and attitude to convey this change. **Do you attempt to convey humour in the layout of a satire magazine?** I think for a humour magazine the type and imagery used was a little unconventional, but for the formal aspects of the layouts it was very straight forward. When some people are trying to design a humorous publication, website or identity, they fall into the trap of using bright colours and wacky angles. We kept the grid simple and we avoided using too many typefaces.

SPY
MAGAZINE

But the attention to typographic detail telegraphed the humour in small ways. The editor would always say, "what's funnier, a guy in a clown costume telling a joke or a guy in a good suit telling a joke?" And I think that's very true, as it's the unexpected that creates a lot of humour. So we used very traditional and classic typefaces like Garamond, Alternative Gothic, Metro, and just put a slight twist in there to accent the humour. But it was subtle and you would have to be a regular reader or another designer to receive the messages! **Did the magazine follow a similar structure every issue?** The placement of the different sections were all pretty permanent. However, the feature stories were each designed in their own way, but used the same typefaces. There are a couple of different approaches you can take when designing a magazine. Rolling Stone would do something different typographically for each story. For example if they were designing a story about the wild west they might use wood type, and if the story was delicate they may have used a thin script. I think it's more effective to convey a sense of a consistency in a publication. That's why I tried to use a limited palette of typefaces, and it's what I did with the type that reflected the story. My goal was always, "whatever page you open, you know it's spy magazine." **Why didn't you try typefaces that were new at the time?** I picked typefaces that worked well together and those

I WAS PREPARED TO GIVE UP THE **PERMANENCE OF ARCHITECTURE FOR THE INTIMACY OF GRAPHIC DESIGN**

that gave me enough flexibility to manipulate different stories. I didn't want them to have a personality of their own. It was my job to create the visual persona of the spread, not the typefaces. **How did you use the column 'The Fine Print' and can you explain the graphic shorthand you incorporated within it?** 'The Fine Print' used really small type around the outside column of the magazine. They could be anything from restaurant reviews to extracts from legal documents. And of course we got a lot of complaints about the type being too small, and as a result we had complaints about the whole magazine's type being too small. When we checked other publications our type was bigger than most, but people refused to believe it. It was a chain reaction, but 'The Fine Print' was something the editor wanted to include from the beginning. **Can you explain your theory for**

designing the perfect magazine spread? I try to integrate the headlines with the images and if possible make the 'attitude' of the story permeate the entire spread. I therefore usually avoid the rest of the article being set in straight columns. It's hard to do and requires the editor to make an early decision on the final stories. When you begin work on a magazine you quickly realise that editors will change headlines right up to the print deadline, if you let them. It's impossible to design around that, so I think many publications leave a blank spot at the top third of the page just so the editors can keep changing the headline until the last second! They did that at spy, but I tried to force them to make a decision as soon as possible. That extra time allows you to design something much more sophisticated and a little less lazy. **Did you manage to create an advantage out of working on a tight budget?** I had to be a little more resourceful, create the artwork myself and use a lot more typography. It's great to commission things if you have the money, but if you don't have it, you don't have it. Spy used a lot of typographic led spreads and many of the photographs I shot here in the studio. Sometimes I took photographs on location and used them to complete illustrations. And sometimes we could convince illustrators and photographers that the project was worth being associated with. After spy had been out for a few months it was easy to get contributors, because they wanted to be involved. The hardest time is when you are trying to use a photographer or illustrator and you have to go through their agents. They never want to lose money. If I could contact them directly they would always say, "I'm dying to do it and I really want to work with you". Then I would tell them their agent said, "No way", and they would usually get upset. An agent's job is to make as much money as possible. We still had some problems getting people on board because the money was really terrible. But if we could get them excited, they would do it. **Back in the 80s Spy's copy had to be sent out to typesetting houses. Did this complicate the design process?** These were pre–apple mac days and we had to send the copy out. We would take a manuscript and character count to figure out how much space the story would take up. Then we would specify how we wanted the type set and send it off. When we got it back we would paste it on to a board mechanically. Then you would make two or three rounds of

THE ATTENTION TO TYPOGRAPHIC DETAIL TELEGRAPHED THE HUMOUR IN SMALL WAYS. THE EDITOR WOULD ALWAYS SAY, WHAT'S FUNNIER, A GUY IN A CLOWN COSTUME TELLING A JOKE

OR A GUY IN A GOOD SUIT TELLING A JOKE?

photocopies, so the editor could proof read it and make sure it would fit. And then when the copy was finally approved you would paste it down as double page spreads and send it off to the printer. It was a different world back then. We were just about to switch over to computers at the time. It's much faster now, but it's easy to be lazy and do a sloppy job. The craft of the typographer is really a lost art. Good kerning and letter spacing are virtually a thing of the past. Designers aren't usually given the training to do it properly and it takes a lot of effort to make type look good. I think people are just starting to realise what they've lost. Because typesetting at its most basic level is now so quick it means less planning takes place and people leave everything to the last minute. That inevitably leaves the designer with less time to think and refine. **Your stay at Spy only lasted a year and a half, but your work**

remains influential. Why do you think you made such an impression? It was a good time to take risks and the magazine made a major impact in the world of publishing. It had a talented, knowing group of editors and writers. They knew they were good and they knew exactly what they wanted to achieve. Second best wasn't going to be an option. Editorially, a very special working environment was created and I think the visual structure went hand in hand with that. If Spy had been about a slightly different subject matter, maybe it wouldn't have captured the imagination of the public in quite the same way. **Who worked with you at Spy?** There was an associate art director and a production artist or two. Then we would have freelancers come in when we were closing an issue. Sometimes it was up to five people, but usually it was a core staff of three. The art department was really only the corner of an office with three drafting tables and a filing cabinet! It's amazing what you can achieve with so little. **What was your relationship like with the editor?** There were two editors of Spy, Graydon Carter and Kurt Andersen. They were the guiding spirits behind the magazine and we worked closely together while I was there. **Were the deadlines tight?** It came out ten times a year and we worked pretty much non-stop. There was a deadline where we needed to ship it to the printer, and the week before we would shift into a higher gear. But we would also be working an issue or two ahead, to make sure the stories were art-worked properly. It gave us time to think about the designs and make sure they were something special. It was always an ongoing development project. **Why did you publish it only ten times a year?** Quite a number of magazines in America only produce ten issues per year. They might have a double issue over Christmas and another double issue over the Summer period. It allows people to take some time off. The readers and the publishers. It's also a standard way of saving money. **How much does the cover art influence the circulation?** I think it does to a certain degree, but not as much as most Circulation Directors would like you to believe. Some try to turn it into a real science. They will say that you have to put numbers on a cover, or use a piece of artwork that follows a popular trend, or that a portrait must have a clear line of sight in and around the subject's eyes. But I always think the content and presentation of the previous issue determines how many people are likely to buy the next issue. The trouble is everyone knows if you put an attractive person on the cover it's not going to harm circulation numbers. And if you lack courage or vision you can fall into this trap. That's why so many magazines have beautiful people staring out at you. Of course if every magazine uses a pretty face as the cover art, then any benefit is reduced or nullified. Celebrity culture is with us, but that doesn't mean we shouldn't search for alternative ways of presenting it to an audience. We might still use a celebrity on the cover, but we would use them to illustrate something about an article inside the magazine. Unfortunately getting a well known person to pose became difficult. They began to realise we might be trying to make fun of them! **Can you give us an example of this 'alternative presentation' of a celebrity cover?** I remember we went in for a bit of Kennedy bashing at one point. We designed a cover with a bucket of water being thrown over Senator Edward Kennedy. Members of his family had been involved in all sorts of scandals over the years. When he was younger he had driven his car off a bridge, resulting in the drowning of his female passenger. It was a major scandal here in the States, and the cover gained a notoriety all of its own. We retouched his head on to a stock image of a body and then photographed a bucket of water on a black background. It was, as always, done on the cheap. It definitely caught people's attention. **Aren't you supposed to avoid black backgrounds on a cover?** They say that magazines with black covers don't sell well on the newsstand. It's another one of those stupid rules that I don't believe or follow. You very rarely see a black cover because everyone says it has be bright. A white or an off white. Complete nonsense of course. **Where does your fascination with meat come from?** Ha, I can't say. I just enjoy the taste, and I started to incorporate it into my work. I haven't really used meat in my work for a couple of years now, so I really need to work some in! I just like meat. **Spy was an independent magazine. How did this affect its working practices?** Lack of money was definitely part of the problem, and difficulties with distribution didn't help. If you're with a bigger chain you can get better distribution and good placement, because you have the clout. If not, they stick you at the back of a newsstand so no one can find you. I think our print run got up to one hundred and sixty thousand at the time I was there. In the states that is considered a tiny circulation for a general interest magazine. Most American magazines from the major publishing companies need to circulate between 750,000 to a million copies to make it worthwhile for them to publish. Anything less and they wouldn't bother, as they say they can't make any real money from smaller numbers! I have a feeling they are probably not in this business because of their deep held belief that magazines are a useful form of modern communication. **You have also Art Directed FYI for Forbes. How did this compare to working at Spy?** Forbes is a business magazine for

SPY

KENNEDY BASHING!

HAPPAQUIDDICK:
The Unsold Story

HAPPAQUIDDICK GIRLS:
SPY Goes on an Update

THE KENNEDY MEDIA CONSPIRACY

Experts Decide:
WILL TEDDY GO TO HELL?

chief executive officers and financial people. It's a biweekly and FYI was its supplement that came out with it, four times a year. The deadlines were therefore slower and we had much more money to commission photography and illustration. However, the audience was very limited with a demographic focus of mainly wealthy men. The magazine would show them how to spend their money, living the good life. It contained fun articles for executives, like how to buy a really good shotgun! The editors of Spy rather harshly described it as 'Spy for old people'. At least it took a humorous approach, as it was edited by Christopher Buckley, who wrote the book, 'Thank you for Smoking'. But there were more differences than similarities between the two magazines. That's why I enjoyed working there as it gave me an opportunity to stretch as a designer. I directed the FYI for about five years from the studio I set up straight after leaving Spy. Being a quarterly it wasn't that pressurised, although I had a full time person working as the art director, whom I supervised. **Do you still take on editorial assignments?** We will undertake redesigns and the making of prototypes, but its rarely ongoing. We might do another quarterly if it came along. A monthly is a full time occupation and it's just too

YOU VERY RARELY SEE A **BLACK** COVER BECAUSE EVERYONE SAYS IT HAS TO BE BRIGHT. A WHITE COVER OR AN OFF WHITE OF COURSE **COMPLETE NONSENSE**

much work to run through our studio. Besides, I think I've had enough late nights for one lifetime. **What do you supply in a prototype?** We give the client the format, the overall visual style, artwork, standards and rules, in short whatever they need to continue with the redesign. Firstly we will try and sort out the approach for the magazine by meeting the editor and the publisher. Then we will think about the format, try some sample stories and a few sample covers. We will show them 3 or 4 different approaches and then focus on one. Usually we act as a consultant rather that an Art Director. But we have also been hired to produce the first few issues just to get the title up and running. **Is it important to keep some of the original design features?** Sometimes they really want to start from scratch, but more often than not they want to phase in the changes over a few issues. If a magazine is doing poorly editorially, they often ask if it's possible just to tart it up a bit. This might work for an issue or two and it may allow them to get a bump in revenue from new advertisers. At the end of the day this is a short term fix and readers realise it still sucks. **Isn't that design process called, 'polishing a turd?'** I like that phrase, because they think it's cheaper to hire an art director and do a re-design, rather than fire the editor and sort out the editorial staff. It happens all the time and it never works. You can always tell when a magazine is about to go out of business because three months before they'll unveil a complete redesign! *SBOOK 4*

You studied for a year at the MI design school in Norway. Did this experience clarify your career objectives? At the time I didn't really know what I wanted to study and I was considering architecture. But because I didn't have any experience of art and design education I thought I might try the graphics course at MI. I enjoyed the course, but I didn't really understand the aspect of drawing absolutely everything. It seemed like drawing skills were more important than ideas and compositions. I think the first year at Southampton gave me a better base for creative thinking. We were able to experiment with all sorts of materials and we produced more than one piece of final work. Did your degree course at Southampton Solent University influence your decision to become an art director? I didn't make a deliberate choice to become an art director. I knew I wanted to work for a magazine, having had some work experience in newspaper production. I also had friends working as AD assistants in other magazines and I just thought that kind of job would suit me too. I felt it was very important to get into work straight after graduating and the job at Fri Flyt was the first one I found advertised. I thought this would be the perfect magazine for someone like me, because I was genuinely interested in snowboarding and outdoor activities. I knew it would be hard to get this job, considering my lack of experience. But I applied and luckily I convinced them it was a risk worth taking. Can you tell us about your Final Major Project at

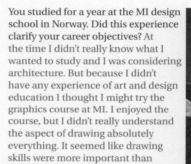

Southampton? The name of the project was, 'Celebrated fabrications', and was kind of a visual journey through a 'micro' celebrity lifestyle. It was created as a book, containing text and imagery from celebrities everyday, but rather odd, lives. It looked at plastic surgery, money/shopping, reality TV and the media hysteria that surrounds them. It's a very strange modern phenomenon. **Has studying overseas been an advantage?** I learned a lot from studying abroad and it made me more independent. The UK is also much more clued up on graphic design than Norway. I came back with international impetus! Employers also feel you are more self-sufficient, and not so afraid of a challenge. **As you've already mentioned you began working as an art director straight after completing your degree course. Did you feel you were qualified for the job?** Well of course I adjusted my application with this particular job in mind. Fortunately my sports background mirrored the content and direction of the magazine. And I was able to show how motivated I was to work in this kind of publication. It wasn't easy and I went through two interviews before I finally landed the job. I like to think I'm a creative designer with my own ideas, as well as being a good project manager. And I think I can create useful systems to keep order, control and improve efficiency. I'm also quick to learn new skills and take on board new information. They understood I really wanted the job, and they knew I would put in the effort required to get it done. I also had that experience from press production through my summer jobs as a typographer. I knew I could work fast, and when it came to layout and composition I was quite confident. Fri

Flyt was also unusual in that it didn't have a permanent art director. They outsourced this to different designers. That meant there wasn't any continuity of design from month to month. Luckily, I had some time to settle into the job and build up the knowledge required to organise things effectively. It was a lot of responsibility, but I enjoyed the learning process and I was very focused. The people at Fri Flyt liked my ideas, and after a couple of months I had more control and could take charge of things independently.

it's rather an advantage. I wouldn't want to be an old, worn out male! I can only talk about my job at Fri Flyt, they might have other routines in other publishing companies. But it's a lot of work, with many late nights and weekends, so being young (meaning; having no kids or family) is almost a necessity. **Do you have any advice for recently qualified design**

How much do you think being a snowboarder helped? I think I might have been able to get the job without being a skier or a snowboarder, but not if you also factored in my lack of experience. It definitely helped! **What were the positive aspects of becoming an art director straight after university?** When you're a student you've got a lot of freedom to solve any given project. And I think the same goes when you are a new graduate. You're not stuck in a certain way of thinking when it comes to applying the design process. And of course getting paid for all the hours you've put into your design work is very rewarding! **Did you experience any problems in being young and female in an industry dominated by men?** I don't find any negative aspects being young or female in a job like this,

EVA CAMILLA BRANDT FRI FLYT

graduates? Find the area you want to work within and then invite yourself for an interview! Be enthusiastic about the job, and show them you really want it. Then make follow-up calls to ensure they don't forget your name! Get experience from producing actual print work. This will become your primary responsibility when you work as a designer. Start with something easy, like designing adverts for your local supermarket, or your dad's office. **What do you think are the major differences between English and Norwegian design?** It's hard for me to define typical Norwegian design, and therefore also hard to compare. Norway lacks publication like Wallpaper and Adrenalin, although it has got a few internationally orientated lifestyle magazines, such as Carl's Cars and Fjords. The layout here is very simple, with lots of white space. The photography is used as the major design element, not the typography. Norwegian design is generally more minimalist than its English counterpart. UK design contains more humour and tends to be more experimental with its use of cropped photos, vector graphics and collages. **And where do you think Norwegian design is heading?** I like the cleanliness of Norwegian design. It seems that traditional Norwegian symbols, produced in a more modern and contemporary sense, is becoming popular. For example the work of Moods of Norway, Norway Says and Bleed. **Fri Flyt differs from other magazines in its distinctive usage of a variety of typefaces for its headings How many different faces do you normally use in an issue?** I couldn't give you an exact number. Many articles have similar looking action photographs, so I think it's important that readers can easily define and separate them. I like to give all the major articles an identity through their headings. The typeface should echo the theme of the heading, or the photograph used on that spread. It should say something about the article, or the feeling I want the readers to achieve from it. **Do you favour a particular typeface?** I haven't got a specific favourite. My taste in typefaces changes all the time. If I've used a characteristic font several times, I get the feeling it's used up, or I get bored of it. If I was forced to use only one face for an entire magazine I would have to use Helvetica. It leaves you with heaps of options, and it has a good appearance. It's also very easy to add design and illustrations to it. **Are there any recent articles you have enjoyed working on?** I had a lot of fun designing the Kashmir article. I had the idea for some time, but it took awhile before I could find a spread where such a design would fit. The article was all about this exotic destination and its photography. I found it perfect for this kind of design. The Shaun White spread was the first one where I felt really happy. It's simple, and contains more white space than I normally have the opportunity to use. The photos are bright and fun, and the heading contrasts nicely with the cleanliness of the rest of the layout. **How often do you think a magazine needs to be redesigned?** That depends entirely on the market and the magazines content. I redesign whenever I get a better idea! But obviously I attempt to bring something fresh to each issue of Fri Flyt. Personally I would rather design a magazine from the start, instead of redesigning an old one. This would give you the freedom to add more of your personal touches. **Where will Fri Flyt be in five years time and do you think you will still be its art director?** Fri Flyt has become a major sport and lifestyle magazine that is now important to a lot of people, and not just in Norway. Fri Flyt has several sister publications, like Terrengsykkel, that follow the same quality and enthusiasm as us. But where I picture myself in five years is hard to say, particularly as I have only worked here for three. I would like to be in a position where I work with several other designers. And I would like to be a creative leader for younger designers working within magazine publications. **Fri Flyt contains some of the very best action photography. Is it difficult to art direct sports photographers?** I know many of the photographers personally, and we give each other regular feedback on our work. The photographers leave me with lots of options and I pick the photographs in cooperation with the editors for covers and spreads. The photos should document the story, and we do not manipulate them. **Clearly you can't join a photographer when they are at the top of a snow capped mountain. Does this cause problems when you come to create the articles?** This doesn't really affect me, because this is the way I've always worked. I take my inspiration from the photography. But this does mean I'm not able to prepare any layout before the actual photos arrive. **Does this mean you need to crop photographs more often than you would like?** Cropping is normally done to adjust it to the layout. The cropping shouldn't change the expression of the photo. Where the rider is coming from is especially important. **Where do you get your inspiration?** Magazines, ski, snowboard, surf and skate graphics are a great source. Also traveling and experiencing the activities that Fri Flyt writes about is inspirational. **Many youth orientated magazines do not seem overly concerned with legibility. Why have you chosen a very clean and legible approach for Fri Flyt?** We have a lot of things to tell our readers, and we know that they read everything we write. To me the major challenge is to combine the creativity of design driven magazines, like Adrenalin, with the legibility of mainstream magazines. We have different kinds of readers. The youngest ones are very concerned about image, looks, stars, tricks and the visual aspects of the sports. Some of our older readers use the magazine as a guide: to travel destinations, and new equipment. The design has to serve both. **Do you think the readers of a magazine like Fri Flyt**

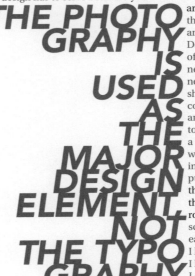

THE PHOTO GRAPHY IS USED AS THE MAJOR DESIGN ELEMENT, NOT THE TYPO GRAPHY

are interested in its design? I think for the dedicated reader the content (text and photos) are the most important. Design should help every issue of the magazine to look fresh and new. I think a good wrapping should never be underestimated. The design should give the impression of being contemporary, then the products and the people in it, will seem like tomorrows 'next big thing'. I receive a lot of e-mails from design students who use Fri Flyt as a source of inspiration, and buy it for that purpose. **Do you still struggle with the construction of an article or has the design process now become fairly routine?** I design each article from scratch. Sometimes the ideas come easily, while other times it's harder. I have a few tricks on hand, so even if I have days when the ideas don't flow I can still design a usable spread. Not one day at the office is the same. There are always new projects and new things to be done. If it's not the magazine, it's the webpage, a book, an advert, a poster or a logo for a new event. **How closely do you adhere to the magazine's grid?** I follow the grid systematically and precisely. I start up with a blank page with the grid, then I treat the text and photos as if I've been given a puzzle to sort out. I normally use a 9 grid system. This is because a page with more than three columns is harder to read, and if I used less the design wouldn't be flexible enough. **What's the best part of art directing Fri Flyt?** It's the design that's closest to my heart and that's what I enjoy the most. The situation I dislike is when I run out of time. When printing is just hours away, and there's just too much work left to get the end result up to the level I want. *SBOOK 4*

ANGHARAD LEWIS, GRAFIK WITH A

You worked with Caroline Roberts on Graphic International. How has the magazine changed since it became Grafik in 2003? The content of the magazine has developed considerably since it changed from Graphics International to Grafik, although the basic structure of the magazine - the editorial skeleton - has remained quite constant. The main development has been in the quality of the magazine's content. In the Graphics International days the magazine had a more corporate profile and was much more trade magazine-like in character. Since changing to Grafik, the magazine has broadened its net and appeals to a much wider audience, which means that we have relationships with a much more exciting range of people. Caroline Roberts and I are on a continuing mission to find new people, work and stories all around the world. How many people work on Grafik Magazine and how is the office structured? The editorial team is the editor, Caroline Roberts and myself, deputy editor. We also have an intern to fuel our intravenous tea drips, as well as getting lots of hands on experience including writing a bit in the mag. Our advertising is headed up by Heather Mead who works closely with us on the editorial team. We all work together in a small, colourful and perpetually cluttered office on Great Portland Street. Our publisher is Alan Lewis, who along with myself and Caroline, owns the magazine. Of course we also have a collective of regular freelance writers whom we commission to write features and reviews. Much of the rest of the magazine is written by us. What was the brief when the magazine was re-launched? The basic brief was to do something different. Graphics International was looking tired and dated. We wanted something that reflected the best of what we were seeing in the contemporary design field in Britain–something that would inspire and excite–something that people would look forward to reading each month rather than a tired old trade mag that people subscribed to just because they felt they ought to. We see Grafik's job as pushing boundaries - it should challenge and motivate its audience, not make them feel comfortable and self-satisfied. Progress comes through shaking things up a bit, not by plodding along with the same old formula. Why Grafik with a K? There's a rather convoluted story behind that 'K'. In the days of Graphics International the magazine was commonly known as 'Graphics'. Initially the idea was just to drop the "International" part of the name. It seemed like a pretty outmoded, cumbersome and unnecessary part of our title. Being "international" isn't something you generally have to point out these days. We always intended the title to simply be 'Graphic'. But between starting our redesign process and actually launching it, a different mag came out with that name. Rather than cause conflict, or, as our then publisher suggested, sue them, we decided to be gracious and take a different name. Grafik with a K was born. There was a little bit of confusion at first but luckily most people are clever enough to notice the difference. Unfortunately a few people out there still have a problem with the spelling and it never fails to rub us up the wrong way. Tip to all those people submitting work - it pays to check the spelling of the mag you're sending it to. Grafik has no art director. Who controls its design direction? The designer is effectively the art director. The design direction is a collaboration between the editorial and design teams. Like any good magazine there is a very close collaboration between the editorial team and the art director. We have to respect each other's territory. Ultimately it's a relationship based on trust

with a healthy dose of honesty. If something's not working from one person's perspective they have to be able to pipe up and make their feelings known. So, there's no one person 'in charge'. It's a collaboration between the editors and the designers. There has been a continual steady evolution in the magazine's content and design over the last few years. The two elements drive each other forward. Just as Grafik's editorial has a distinctive voice, so its design has an equivalent visual personality. Ultimately it's about making the written content and the visual content work together to the best end effect. **How closely does the editor, sub-editor, and deputy editor get involved with the design process?** Caroline and I hand the written and visual content over to the designer at a set deadline each month (approximately two weeks before we go to print) and let him get on with designing the magazine. He then feeds things back to us as they develop. While we might have some suggestions, we try not to interfere. After all, the designer is the designer and we are journalists. Robert Shore's role as sub editor is as a freelance. He basically proofs the words in the mag each month to check for spelling and grammatical errors. Luckily for us he's got an eagle eye. **Do you see the design of Grafik as a holder, like a gallery almost, for other peoples work?** This is one aspect of Grafik. Certainly the Showcases and Talent articles function on this level. They're a chance for us to bring work by talented people to the attention of the industry. We're especially proud of the way our Talent section has helped out people at the beginning of their careers. Most people featured in the Talent pages come back to us with encouraging stories about how being in Grafik has brought them work and contact with other interesting people. Aside from the visual, gallery-like aspect of Grafik, we believe that the words are equally important. What we say about the work is as relevant as the fact that it's featured at all. Some parts of the magazine are quite light-hearted in tone - we want them to be entertaining and easy to read. Other parts, such as the Profiles on studios and the articles in the Special Report look into work and subjects of debate in greater depth. **The spreads all** look very fluid. **How does the structure allow so much flexibility?** Yes, there's a lot of flexibility in the way the pages are designed. This is to allow the visual content to be accommodated in the most suitable way. Watch this space early Autumn 2006 for some developments in our design. You heard it here first… **Do you think experimentation within the layouts should take second place to the work being shown?** The first consideration with layouts is how to show off the work being featured / written about to best effect. The second consideration is how to keep the page visually stimulating. If we're showing work that we claim to be the best and most exciting, then the design of Grafik has also got to hold its own. **Do you think Grafik has influenced the revival in slab serifs and Avant Garde?** Very possibly. **Why have you recently increased the number of pages?** When we bought the magazine and became independent in March 2005 we increased the number of pages to a standard 84 pages per issue. During the time when the magazine was owned by a big publishing company the number of pages was dictated by an advertising / editorial ratio. We weren't happy with this ad-driven approach. We wanted more pages of editorial in order to be able to feature more work and more stories and allow visuals to breath on the page. We also wanted readers to feel they were getting more for their money. In October we'll be increasing the number of pages again to 100 pages. **Do you spot new talent by scouting galleries and degree shows, or do the designers contact you?** A bit of both. A lot comes to us, of varying quality and we also work hard to get out and find the rising stars. We get a lot of e-mails and a good armful of post everyday. The quality ranges from the magnificent to the embarrassing, which pretty much reflects what you see of graphic design in the world around you. But unlike some magazines you won't catch us featuring a piece of work just because there's a gap to fill on the page. What we feature is in the mag because it has merit and an interesting story behind it. We get quite a few very gimmicky items from marketing agencies, which invariably seem to be a waste of money, paper, stamps, brainpower etc. They generally go straight in the 'circular file', i.e. the bin. We recycle all the waste paper. The classic must be the single 'branded' sock we were once sent. Total waste of energy even opening the envelope. **Why do you think graphic designers buy Grafik magazine?** A. To be nosy and find out what other graphic designers are up to. B. Because graphic designers like collecting things. C. To stay engaged with the worlds that neighbour graphic design. D. To feel like they're part of a community. **Do you think their clients buy the magazine?** Certainly advertising agencies subscribe to Grafik. Also larger companies with in house design teams. It is also a resource for people who want to commission design but aren't sure where to begin looking for someone. **What impact do you think magazines like Grafik have on the design industry, and particularly on young designers?** We hope to provide inspiration to young designers and hopefully a bit of encouragement, advice and information. We also aim to show how graphic design relates to the wider world. We're not in the business of trying to shape the design industry, we leave that to institutions like the Design Council. Grafik is there to have a bit more of a hands-on, accessible relationship with designers. Something they can genuinely engage with. **Is Grafik's target audience the design student or the working professional?** About twenty per cent of our readers are students. The rest are professional designers. We don't target our editorial just at one group or the other, but the majority of the work featured is by professionals, although we do feature a bit of work by students.

EX STEN

IT'S A
DESIGNED
OBJECT,
TALKING
ABOUT
DESIGN
FOR A
DESIGN
AUDIENCE
BUT
THAT'S
JUST WHAT
WE ARE. WE
TRY NOT
TO GET
TOO

Would you say design magazines are a fair reflection of the Industry and the experience of a graphic designer? A magazine is only ever a magazine. There are so many experiences and types of work that we could never 'reflect' the entire industry. We're in the business of making magazines that people want to buy, look at and read. If you showed everything, each issue would be an unreadable breeze block of a book with not a great deal worth looking at. It's our job to edit a mass of stuff into something interesting and digestible. A graphic design magazine could be seen as a very self-obsessed product. It can be written by a designer, designed by a designer and then read by one? How do you provide balance and a wider social perspective? Neither Caroline or I are designers and while we often ask designers to write for the magazine, the majority of our writers are professional journalists. So there are other perspectives in the mag. Yes, it's a designed object, talking about design for a design audience but that's just what we are. We try not to get too existentialist. What do you think of phenomena like Magma bookstores? Is it a collection of glamorised business cards or an important way for graphic design to express itself? At the end of the day it's a shop. It reflects the current 'visual junkie' trend, which isn't something I really approve of. It often seems like indiscriminate consumption of visual "stuff" for the sake of it. How do you commission an article.

Do you always start with a working title or do contributors come to you with ideas? A combination. Articles are based around our Special Reports so more often than not we have an idea for an article we want written. We have a great group of regular writers each of whom has different strengths and areas of interest and we commission them according to those. We also send out an e-mail about our upcoming features to contributors and writers so if anyone has an idea or piece of work they want to pitch to us they can. The special reports cover themes like photography, art, fashion, editorial design, music, moving image; all things that designers are interested in and fields in which they often work. Graphic design doesn't happen in a vacuum so we want to reflect that. It would also be a boring magazine if all we ever talked about was graphic design. We also do special reports like Process, where we find 10 projects that use amazing techniques, and Heroes, where top designers write about a person whose work has inspired them. What ways would you like Grafik to grow and how will you keep your audience captive? The good ship Grafik is set to sail in several exciting directions in the next few years. We have some great projects coming up in the next 12 months, including events, exhibitions and books. We already have a flourishing international readership but we hope to expand. The magazine itself is also about to get bigger as we'll be increasing the number of pages again. Also look out for more Grafik products in the future. Keeping our audience captive is a matter of great content. And while there are still people out there making exciting work, Grafik will keep getting better from issue to issue. *SBOOK 4*

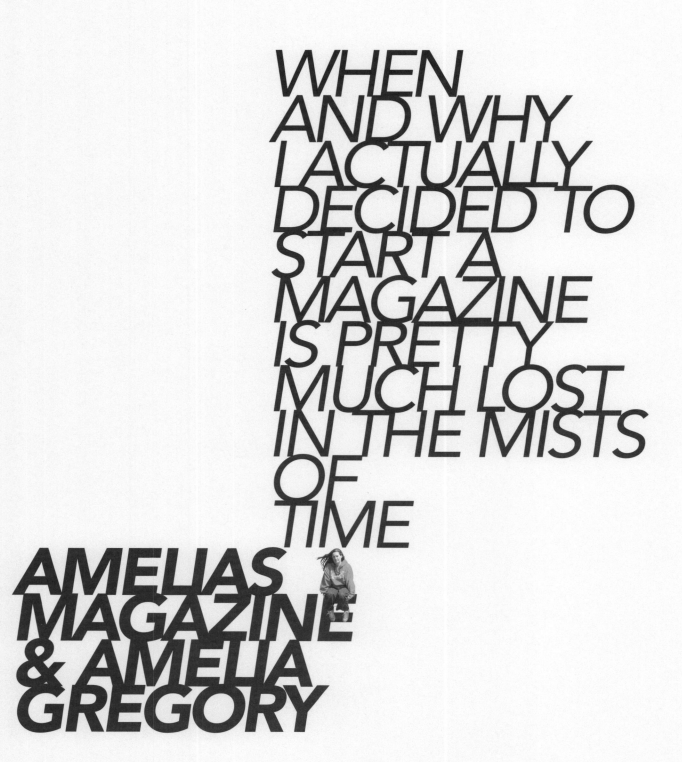

WHEN AND WHY I ACTUALLY DECIDED TO START A MAGAZINE IS PRETTY MUCH LOST IN THE MISTS OF TIME

AMELIAS MAGAZINE & AMELIA GREGORY

Can you explain the concept for Amelia's Magazine? I wanted to produce a magazine that had a very personal feel to it, in that it was entirely honest and unconstrained. I decided to make it highly desirable and collectable through beautifully designed, production and innovative presentation. But I also wanted the content to be really good quality, relevant and highly readable. **Did you have a specific plan for the direction of its design?** I just go with my gut feelings where design is concerned, but I always knew I wanted it to reflect my love of older design, of the type I often find in children's books, records, annuals and magazines from charity shops. **How did you finance the first issue?** I borrowed a couple of grand from my parents, and managed to get some really good sponsorships from my printer and a paper merchant. **How important is advertising?** Advertising is very important in terms of surviving financially. All magazines want to be in the luxury market to attract all the advertisers. An example of that was this magazine called Watch, they had cottoned on to the fact that there were loads of really expensive watch companies. They tried to base a magazine around the advertisements they were hoping to achieve, and I just thought who uses watches anymore, everyone uses mobile phones. You have to keep the advertisers happy that's the way it works in fashion magazines. **Single-handedly starting up your own magazine would appear to be a daunting adventure. Did you have a clear idea of how the industry worked?** Well, I knew how certain aspects of producing a magazine worked, for instance how to produce a fashion shoot, because I had done that for many years, but otherwise I pretty much muddled along and learnt on my own, especially in terms of production, distribution and advertising. **Was the decision to launch the magazine difficult?** When and why I actually decided to start a magazine is pretty much lost in the mists of time. All I remember is that about two years prior to me actually launching it, I had a discussion with my friend Lou Winwood, who was a former fashion editor of Sleaze Nation, about launching our own magazine. She gave up on the idea fairly early on, but I continued to tell people that I was going to do it. After two years of talking about the magazine I was one day going to start, it had become a bit of a case of crying wolf, so I thought 'Right, it's now or never. I had better do it or no one will ever believe what I say again.' It took another six months to put everything together to launch. Actually at the same time I was thinking of starting a knit wear business but that went tits up because I had too many moths, its on a backburner now in my parents office, so now they've got all the moths! **How successful was the launch party?** I had a really great launch party and loads of people came. It was a really memorable night. I remember being in the basement when the music was turned off and it was like a herd of elephants stamping their feet above my head and demanding more. I was just happy that I had actually done it and everybody was having a good time. **You are the publisher, editor and art director. Do you have a system in place to manage the production of the magazine effectively?** Not really. I actually do everything myself except for a few days before each launch when I sometimes get a few work experience people in to help me with the design, but they invariably leave me with lots of bits to clear up. Hence I have been having a lot of very long days and late nights finishing off issue 05 right now. I need to change that situation but it is very hard to put together a team without having the proper resources to do so. **You had previously undertaken work experience at Marie Claire, Arena and The Face. How useful was the knowledge gained when starting up your own magazine?** Those internships were invaluable. In the case of Marie-Claire, which was my first one, I realised the kind of environment I wasn't going to be happy in, i.e. a load of bitchy girls. There were literally catfights in the fashion cupboard. At Arena and The Face I made lots of really good friends through working with some amazing people. Although I was doing really menial jobs for ages, I developed more of a sense of design. I was able to call on all my fantastic contacts when it came to putting together my own magazine, and they trusted me to do something well. I also learnt loads about how the fashion industry works, but not so much about actually producing a magazine. **There are so many magazines available now. What do you think is the key to producing a sustainable magazine?** I think you need to have a really devoted core readership who look forward to every issue. I hope I have that! But I also think it's important to evolve and not become too complacent in what you produce. This is definitely something I need to look into in the future. I would love the magazine to become an absolute bible for all the best creativity I can find, but for that to happen I also need to concentrate on building a team that can help me do it. It is also absolutely crucial to get enough advertising support, because you cannot survive on sales alone. **What part of your magazine production is the most laborious, and what's the most interesting?** A lot of it is extremely laborious and tedious… where do I start? The glamorous element of what I do is actually microscopically small. Trying to keep track of the distribution and chasing invoices, trying to get advertising, co-ordinating all the contributions and then editing everything. Then making sure the magazine is designed properly and prints the way it should. All of these things are pretty unexciting, boring and ultimately very time consuming. But all of that stuff is what makes the good shit happen, and I love finding new talent, encouraging it and bringing it to a wider audience. I love producing something I am proud of and other people find inspiring. **You have never been short of impressive contributors. Why do you think you are so successful in establishing these relationships?** In the first place I approached people who I had worked with before and asked them to do something that I knew would fit into the magazine. But since pretty early on I have had loads of people approach me wanting to contribute, and now I tend to just pick the best. I ask them to come up with concepts and then commission them to do something in the style of something I like. I think I have good relationships with my contributors because I can offer them a great forum to show their work. They know I will always respect their work and show it in the best possible way. **Do you think your 'freebies' are a useful marketing tool?** I think it's dangerous to get too stuck in freebie mode. I enjoy producing something a little different, and I know that sometimes it can make the magazine more collectable. I usually approach a collaborator with an idea, or they will approach me, and then we will work together to come up with something suitable. **How do you develop the content for each issue?** It happens pretty organically. I commission things and find things over a good few months, or remember something that I saw awhile back. Sometimes people need to remind me of their work! Whatever feels right and fits in I guess. I try not to use themes too much, although sometimes they happen almost by accident, as in the current scratch 'n' sniff issue. I think relying on themes is a lazy way to produce a magazine. **How has the distribution of the magazine changed since its launch?** I could go on about the perils of distribution for a long time. But I still do a lot of distribution myself. I have been known to get my mum to drive me around, whilst I jump out with the boxes of magazines and she hovers on a yellow line! And then Comag also does some, to Borders in the UK, and for the next issue globally. It's hard because I don't want to lose control of what is going on at the shop floor level. It takes up a lot of my time and I really don't enjoy it. I would rather be doing something creative. But I do think it is important when you are a small business to understand how all aspects of that business works. **What creates the magazine's collectable appeal?** Hopefully it is collectable because of several reasons. It is limited edition, and produced on high quality paper and printed well, so that it has more of the feel of a book. Hopefully it is also very different to other magazines in terms of what I do with design and giveaways etc. So that helps too. **You trained as a printed textile designer at Brighton, and Amelia's Magazine reflects a love for pattern and texture. For example the cover of issue 3 is printed on a velvet effect flock paper stock. Do you think your affection for textiles and fashion has directly influenced this tactile quality?** I can't believe how much you know about me! Yes, I think that background has probably had a very strong influence on my design sensibilities. I have never had minimal tastes, and although I can appreciate something that is minimally designed, it's not something I could do myself and why bother to try when so many other people do it better? I love pattern and colour and always will! **How do you decide on the clothes you want to feature?** There are different ways that clothing companies lend their clothes to shoots. There are umbrella pr companies who also do marketing for loads of brands, so when you go over to their showrooms there are rails and rails of clothing that you can choose from. Some pr's will do it in house. You never get to keep the clothing, although quite often people do nick it. That's quite hard to do when you're just one person, because they know where its gone! But if you are in a fashion cupboard for a big magazine its quite easy to do… although I would never recommend doing it, because you will lose your job! **The magazine's logo is in the style of a signature, reflecting the concept of your personal project. Did you design it?** That's because it is my signature! So yes, I designed it. I knew from very early on that I wanted to put my name to the magazine. I felt that people who knew me in the fashion industry would be likely to say, "Have you seen Amelia's Magazine?" to each other. I thought I would pre-empt them and call it just that. I also thought it made it totally clear that this was a very personal venture; I am after all the only person behind it. I also wanted to really put myself out there and I didn't want to be able to hide from what I had produced. I knew that by giving the magazine my name I would be unable to do that. And anyway, people name bars and shops after themselves all the time, why not a magazine? **Did you study the structure of other magazines before designing your own?** The magazine's grid structure was organised by my first designer, and has altered very little since then. She didn't come from a background of magazine design and I certainly don't, so we just did what felt right. I've never really looked closely at the structure of other magazines, although having said that I probably will pay closer attention nowadays. **What was your concept for the magazine's typography?** I knew I wanted to have fun with type, whether that be through using some

MAKING SURE THE MAGAZINE IS DESIGNED PROPERLY AND PRINTS THE WAY IT SHOULD. ALL OF THESE THINGS ARE PRETTY UNEXCITING, BORING AND ULTIMATELY VERY TIME CONSUMING

fun typefaces or doing something more handwritten. I got a bit typo obsessed for a while. **What sort of regular problems do you encounter publishing the magazine?** I am constantly coming up against brick walls, whether they are financial or more physical, like computers breaking down at the worst possible time. It's not like I can phone IT support. But I am not someone who admits defeat easily. I just pick myself up and look for a way around a problem as best I can. **There are not many people who can say they have a magazine based purely on themselves and what they like. Did you ever worry about its long term success?** I hope that it doesn't come across as based entirely on myself. Yes it is a collection of things I love, but mostly created by other people. I do have a firm belief in my own creative tastes and I guess I feel they are worth sharing. I know what I like and I think I can express myself well. I sometimes worry about not selling enough magazines, usually just before a launch, but I guess that for the most part my faith in my own creativity has been vindicated, so I don't worry too much. I do worry about never having enough advertising, as that's the only way I can possibly hope to make a financial success of the magazine. I am conscious that I need to raise more advertising revenue in order to survive. Especially as copy numbers increase and production runs become more expensive. My financial expenditure is the most worrying part. It's not fun knowing you are digging your way into huge debt! **You have experience in many creative industries, including photography, writing and fashion. Is there an area you would like to concentrate on in the future?** Well, I definitely like variety, and sometimes it's really nice to sit down and do a good piece of writing instead of running around like a headless chicken with a bag of clothes, but having said that I love taking photos more than anything

else. I just wish I had more time to do it, and make a proper living out of it. **Where do you find your design inspiration?** I'm not very good at questions like these, as there aren't any particular people I idolize. I will like a shoot by a particular photographer, and then not like the next one I see. My inspiration comes from anywhere. I see most of my life as a photo, and I am constantly noting the design of everything. I can't pass a charity shop without entering and finding design inspiration from the books within. **Where do you create the magazine?** I work from a spare room in my house. There's hardly any room for anyone else to join me, which is one reason why I have trouble getting a team together! It is stuffed full of books and bits of paper, as I come from a long line of paper ferrets. It's quite isolated and that's something I need to address. I like working as part of a team and I miss that a lot. **What would you like to improve if more funds were available?** Oh God, loads of things! If I had some investment I would get a proper office and put together a team of people to help me produce the magazine. I would love to start some other related projects. For example, events, exhibitions, albums, possibly even a record label. The possibilities are endless. I am never short of ideas, just resources! **Have you ever wanted to do something, but been restricted by printing?** Nobody has said can't yet. I tend to get ideas from things I've seen before, like the laser cut in issue 2 was by an illustrator called Rob Ryan. I had seen his work with all these fantastic paper cuts, and I thought that would be fantastic for the cover of my magazine. It was really interesting for him and he got loads of work out of it. His profiles gone sky high, because he realised what he could do, for example he got to do invites for Alexander McQueen. **Are you interested in launching another magazine?** One is more than enough for me! *SBOOK 4*

MY FINANCIAL EXPENDITURE IS THE MOST WORRYING PART. IT'S NOT FUN KNOWING YOU ARE DIGGING YOUR WAY INTO HUGE DEBT

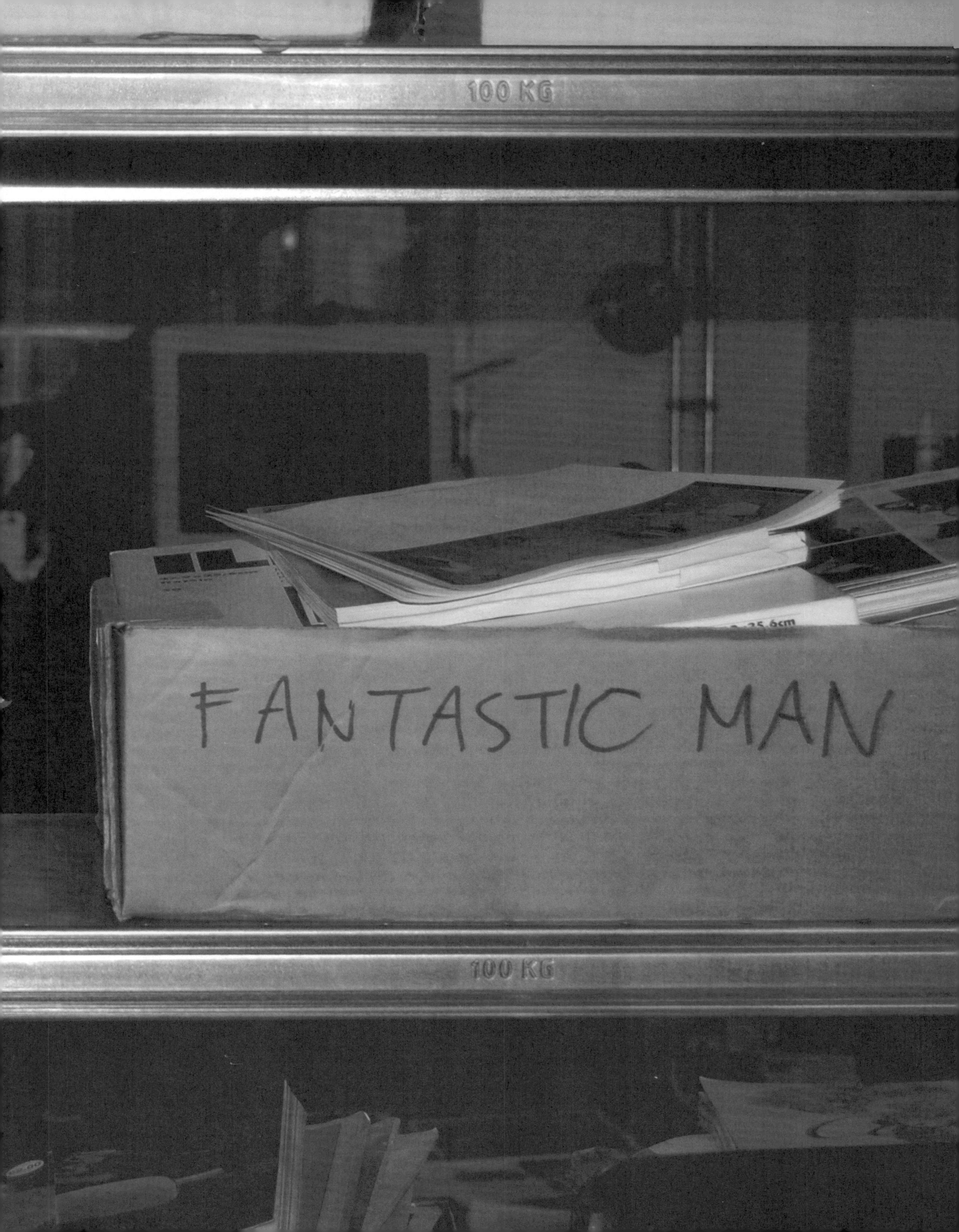
100 KG
FANTASTIC MAN
100 KG

RE, BUTT
FANTASTIC MAN

JOP VAN BENNEKOM

Re-Magazine 12
Hester A magazine about one person
Winter 2004-2005

'Hester
in Sint Anna Parin

DEPRESSE

How long have you been involved in magazine design? I have created magazines since high school, but at that time I didn't realise you could turn it into a career. I produced all sorts of school newspapers, partly because the Netherlands is very democratic, and students tend to organise into groups to ensure they have a voice. Then I discovered design and I went to study at a school for window dressing. And of course I put together a newspaper whilst I was there too. It was really more of a magazine and it looked pretty pretentious, as I'd just discovered the work of 8vo. I started buying all these British mags like ID and Octavo. I also discovered Peter Saville's work at Factory Records. His graphics was a real enigma and I didn't really understand why it looked the way it looked. It was only much later, when I found an article by him, that I could appreciate his intentions behind these strange record covers. I also really admired Vaughan Oliver's atmospheric cover art for 4AD records. After studying all of this fascinating British based work I began to think I should get involved with similar projects. **How do you feel about being a graphic designer who is also his own client?** It took me a very long time to realise I was actually a media person and not really a designer. That sounds a little stupid having had a formal education in design. But if you are ambitious in the Dutch design industries, it mostly means you are working for clients, and not for yourself. When I graduated that perspective seemed rather boring and I thought there was so much more to life than working in this submissive position. I wanted to create my own messages and not communicate someone else's. It means I can generate my own contents and express it in my own way. I had my fair share of commissioned work for clients, but I didn't enjoy it, and that was the reason I started my own magazine. I wanted a different role as a designer. That's when I started RE magazine. **Did your work as Art Director of 'Blvd' and 'Forum'**

I WANTED TO
CREATE MY OWN
MESSAGES
AND NOT
COMMUNICATE
SOMEONE ELSE'S

influence the development of RE? Blvd was the Dutch equivalent of the Face and I was there for a year. It was kind of a deception in the sense that I was under a lot of pressure, with a very limited budget and tight deadlines. That meant things weren't done the way I would have wished. At the time I was also designing and editing the architectural magazine, 'Forum', on a freelance basis. Just two of us produced the entire magazine, but at least it was only a quarterly. I quit Blvd magazine at the age of 29 and that's when things really started to happen. In 1997 I joined the Jan Van Eyck Academy in Maastricht to study on a postgraduate course. I graduated with RE magazine as my final project. The first issue was completed there, and the project expanded into 3 issues just after I graduated. I think it's different now, but in the 90s photography wasn't directly connected to design education, and there wasn't a course in the Netherlands that would teach you how to become an art director, only a designer. I am still an oddity in the Netherlands, because I am a graphic designer and also an art director. What were those early issues like? The original idea was not to do everything myself. However, I still ended up doing the writing, editing, photography and design! Then I had to sell the magazine to the bookstores, sort out the distribution and find ways of financing it all. It was all very clumsy and I don't know how successful issue one was. The print run was just 250 copies and that first RE was really about my friends. I interviewed and filled the whole magazine with them. We talked about interiors and about how space is organized. Looking back it seems like it's from a pot smoker's perspective, as

Re-Magazine 9
John
A magazine about one person
Autumn 2002

RE IS FUNDAMENTALLY ABOUT SELF-–EXPRESSION AND THE EXPLORATION OF SUBJECT, AND IN THAT SENSE IT COULD JUST AS EASILY BE A BOOK, A DOCUMENTARY,' OR A MOVIE. IT JUST HAPPENS TO BE A MAGAZINE

it's really slow, like a cigarette burning in an ashtray. It's got long interviews and I sought to create something that's almost anti-media, something really mundane. I wanted to attain a level of detail that you can't achieve within the structure of normal media. The photography in that issue applied a different rule, and they were effectively snapshots. Aesthetically interesting images showing cables on the ground or the backside of things, but it was still very formalised. Of course with the second issue I had already used all my friends up, so I had to go out and find new people to interview. The third issue was about sex, and I began to collaborate with other writers and photographers. Making magazines is a great way to meet new people and make connections. If you put this interesting thing into a shop, people will contact you and they will want to take part. Each issue of RE magazine follows a narrative, a conceptual idea that shapes the design, down to smallest typographic detail. For this reason each issue is always designed from scratch, so there is no grid structure or template like a conventional magazine. It's a difficult magazine to construct both editorially and by design, because everything is new. That makes it very exciting to create, but also very time consuming and without profit! It's a labour of love and "It comes from the toes up," as we say in Holland. There are no rules in RE magazine and that's why it's appreciated. Every individual element within RE is connected to everything else. That makes it an extremely coherent entity and unconventional, as it doesn't reflect contemporary culture. RE is fundamentally about self-–expression and the exploration of subject. And in that sense it could just as easily be a book, a documentary, or a movie. It just happens to be a

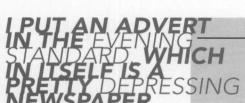

magazine. I'm not sure if that puts us in a difficult position, as it sometimes seems the only people that understand RE are those working in the media itself. **Why did you create the fictional characters 'John, Claudia and Marcel' for issues 9, 10, and 11?** At the time we were working as a 'group' of editors on a collective basis. We thought it might be interesting to give all those voices just one voice and that became the person. The fictional character was designed to 'push' the narrative forward. We started by deciding what subject we wanted to question and then we created those characters around it. The 'John' issue takes an opposing view of the media. It's about hiding, about being out there and escaping everything, like the consequences of hyper individualism. What happens if you drop everything? It's a narrative about a man that leaves all of his commitments, in search of freedom from the responsibilities of life. The 'Claudia' issue is about a 2 metre tall woman who is too big for this world. In some ways it's a metaphor for the inflated image of the media. The story is a fiction but we met this model from Germany who took part in the project. We had almost completed all of the text, when we found her on the Internet. Then we had to rewrite the entire text, because she had such a strong personality. **Dare we ask on what Internet site you found a 2 metre tall woman?** There are a lot of fetish sites of course. At the time I was living in New York,

MARCEL
by: Bela van Lamsweerde/Vinoodh Matadin

– 4 –

and it was impossible to get hold of very tall women, because a lot of them were working in fetish clubs. So we researched for 3 months and found a photographer who was obsessed with photographing tall women. The fictitious 'Claudia' is someone who is extremely tall, extremely happy, extremely beautiful, and extremely intelligent. The character becomes intimidating as a reaction to how the media presents celebrities. In the issue she tells us about herself. The editorial is made up of a fictitious interview, based on our real interviews with successful women, women with IQs over 145, and women who are just plain happy. But it was a very labour intensive issue. 'Marcel' in issue 11 is half fiction and half real. He was a fat guy based on a person that ran an experimental theatre group. They created performances centered on alter egos, and on their own existence. They would step out of their performance and out of their roles. So they were in some ways following a similar path to those issues of RE. We made 'Marcel' a fictional French character and we gave him monologues based on someone who was extremely paranoid about food. The text is about all the contradictions surrounding food, about what's good for you and what isn't? The issue is based around Marcel's philosophy on consumption and diet. **The subject of your next issue was depression. Is this something you have experienced?** In a way it's always about you, but I don't really suffer from depression. Issue 12 was about Hester, a real story and a real woman from London. I was fed up with fiction and Hester suffered from depression. It was a difficult subject, as the more I read about it, the less I understood. I guess I am attracted to miserable things and I thought depression needed some interesting representation in the media. We all know what it's like to be down, but it's hard to imagine the nervous tendencies that make you want to kill yourself. I wanted to do some kind of documentary, but I didn't want it to become too realistic. There are a lot of documentary films that are extremely humanistic, and through their respect for the subject, end up missing some the points. I didn't want to do that. I was travelling around London at the time, and of course it's a perfect place to find depressed people! So I put an advert in the Evening Standard, which in itself is a pretty depressing newspaper, and we received a lot of replies. I wasn't really prepared for that, and I ended up interviewing people all day. We were looking for a woman in her

I PUT AN ADVERT IN THE EVENING STANDARD, WHICH IN ITSELF IS A PRETTY DEPRESSING NEWSPAPER

'BO
'N
'BI

DIALOGUE II
ING

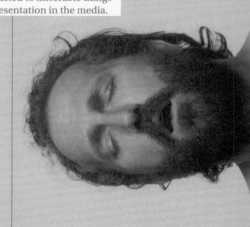

– 20 –

– 21 –

RING'
UROTIC'
TER'

early thirties, as it's the age of disappointment. You should be doing well in your career at this point, but of course most people aren't. It's a cultural thing, especially in England, and it's partly down to the media promising people a life they are unlikely to achieve. The perfect job, the perfect relationship, the perfect children and the perfect home. If you are living in a small one bedroom flat in Islington, that's costing you half of your £1600 a month salary, then life is likely to be hard. That issue dealt with all aspects of the fall out from that kind of a situation. When these women started to talk about their problems, I must admit I began to worry about whether I was exploiting their predicament, just to make an interesting magazine. It was an uncomfortable feeling being part of those casting sessions, but that's how we found Hester. **How do you 'design' depression?** The entire magazine became a therapy. Hester talked about her life, but would never mention her depression. That issue focused on her self image and the assumptions she had about herself. All the interviews with her were reproduced with really big headlines, using words like 'boring', 'neurotic', 'bitter', and 'disappointed'. They were almost like stamps and they helped deconstruct the text. Everything was set in Times and we started out by making the issue very dark. Then I thought that's way too easy. So I began to move in the opposite direction and in the end the issue became glossy yellow, because it was uncomfortable to touch and look at. My work is grid based and I tend to build in repetitive elements to reinforce the design system. That issue was no exception. I also commissioned a number of photographers to shoot Hester and so it became very visual. RE magazine also became much more monochromatic. One issue was very red, one was very grey and another

- 17 -

predominantly white. At first the colour sticks behind your eyes, but after six pages you tend to forget it. **What was your motivation for publishing 'Butt' magazine in 2001?** When I was working at blvd magazine, my partner Gert, was the editor. When we met for the first time he said, "you should be the art director at blvd", and I said, "I agree." So I got the job. He gave me a present at this first meeting, which was an old copy of 'Straight to Hell' from America. It's a gay porn magazine with stories, textual porn. I hadn't seen it before and found the concept very exciting. It was completely 'jerk offable', with some extremely hot text. I was creating an issue of RE about sex at the time, so this magazine was an interesting find. That's where the idea for Butt magazine originated. The two of us thought it would be great to have a gay sex magazine that's reality based. It was liberating to create a magazine about sex that was close to us. That's why we didn't want to include any straight or lesbian action. At that time there were a lot of gay websites and it was just after Big Brother. Reality porn was already in the culture. I didn't want to become a pornographer, because I'm not interested in pornography. At least not on a professional basis! It's much more interesting to talk about tea for half an hour, and then talk about sex. To talk about psychoanalysis, then what you did for Christmas and then finally talk about your last shag, is an unusual way of doing things. This is an integral part of the magazine's personality and obviously it has a humorous side. We developed the concept for the best part of a year. Then we decided to make it interview based and to create a kind of Playboy pin up of our interviewees. **Can you explain how you designed Butt?** First and foremost it is a network of people that didn't exist before Butt existed. Our photographers are creating a kind of gay alternative world that wasn't out there. We already had a cheaply produced black and white magazine, but something was clearly lacking. Then I came up with idea of doing the whole thing in pink. It was totally ridiculous and I don't identify myself with the colour pink. However, I thought it would be hilarious to have a pink gay magazine. There are a lot of older gays that take its 'pinkness' very seriously, but the younger gays don't care. They just think it's cheesy. I am always in contact with maybe 30 people at any one time, usually through email, about ideas for the magazine. Butt works very well because it's a collaboration and there are always people who want to work with us. Butt is very much a magazine made by email. Most of my collaborators are in the UK or in New York and we always have things laying around that can go into any issue. The strict format

I DON'T IDENTIFY MYSELF WITH THE COLOUR PINK. HOWEVER, I THOUGHT IT WOULD BE HILARIOUS TO HAVE A PINK GAY MAGAZINE.

and template sometimes means they don't fit, and they have to go into the next issue. **Butt magazine has been described as a hybrid of, 'Straight to Hell', Andy Warhol's 'Interview', and a photocopied proto-zine decorated with amateur porn. Do you think Butt hits those dirty lows and arty highs?** We didn't set out to continue the tradition of 'Straight to Hell', or reinvent Andy Warhol 'Interview'. Index magazine in New York was trying that at the time and it became very uninteresting. Gert was very well known in the Netherlands for doing excellent one on one interviews, and for producing text that is very close to the here and now. We wanted to make something very 'real', so we started with our influences, not other people's. 'Straight to Hell' and 'Interview' were two brilliant American magazines from the Seventies and therefore I am proud when we are compared favourably to them. Butt sells very well in the USA with 5,000 copies going there, out of a print run of 12,000. **Have you worked out why 'Butt' sells so well in America?** Because it's

I'M NOT INTERESTED IN PORNOGRAPHY. AT LEAST NOT ON A PROFESSIONAL BASIS

in English, in French it wouldn't sell. It's also a very Anglo Saxon magazine, with a bold Dutch irony, which is not necessarily English irony. A lot of people in the USA don't know where Butt originates. They know it's not British, German, or French. Americans understand zines, and they have a big zine alternative culture. Also maybe because Americans are sexually repressed, like you English! Although the Germans are different and Butt is also successful there. **How is Butt different from other forms of gay magazines and media?** That first issue of Butt took a long time to research and get right. Partly because there were no photographers shooting the aesthetic we wanted, so we had to create it. We knew what we didn't want. We didn't want muscle bound bodies. We wanted people that were aware of their physical appearance. I wanted raw! That doesn't mean I wanted men posing with enormous penises, as that's shown in other forms of gay media and tends to be extremely intimidating. That just makes a wallpaper of what men should look like. There are more than enough photographers producing that kind of work, and the rules are very restrictive. We have created a new aesthetic for gay men and it generates its own scene. Right now a lot of girls are reading Butt, especially on the west coast of the USA. Straight people have it on their coffee tables next to Art Forum. **Is Fantastic Man a natural progression from Butt?** It's a progression in the sense that we tend to make magazines about what interests us. And although we are very clumsy in calling the magazine Fantastic Man we make a positive out of our 'bad English'. For instance, all the headlines in Butt are written in less than perfect English, deliberately. We are well aware of the kind of dialect we speak. Butt became too big in a way and through it we met people that worked for other magazines, including those from a fashion background. A number of them were sending us fashion stories we couldn't use for Butt. So, why not use them to create a fashion magazine with a unique approach. I wouldn't describe Fantastic Man as a straight magazine, but it's also not a gay magazine. It's a men's style magazine. It's about clothes and not about fashion. That's a very big distinction. It separates us from every other men's fashion magazine. It's an alternative fashion title, one that's mainly content driven and very personal to us. **How difficult was it to develop the concept?** The first idea was the title. Initially we wanted to make a gay fashion magazine, like Another Man or Dior Homme International. They are bought by gay men and are extremely 'faggy' but aren't gay magazines. We thought why not make a magazine that's deliberately gay, instead of hiding it's gay. But then I felt that was going to be very limiting, as there are men I would like to feature who are not gay. We also found it would be hard to raise advertising revenue without a broader appeal for a fashion magazine. At that stage the working title was Sexy Man, a deliberately ridiculous name, and then we came up with Fantastic Man, which is even more ludicrous. Before I decided on the magazine's graphic language and format, I made a trip to London, to talk and just look at people. I was already working with a number of people from British magazines on Butt, and it was good to get their views on this new concept. We wanted Fantastic Man to be a British magazine. **Did you create a prototype?** We publish it ourselves and a prototype is only really needed if you want to get someone else on board. However, we made a commercial plan, and a dummy using lots of photographs from 70s magazines. I am sure many people thought we were going to make a "Big Butt". But again, with the help of the right photographers, we developed a new aesthetic. Putting the first issue together was really tough because we were covering new ground and trying to work out what it should contain. I think the photography was more successful than some of the early articles. The first issue used Q&A and we have since decided not to do that in Fantastic Man. We don't want to do conventional profiles, just very extensive and extremely good journalism. We want to be the 'New Yorker' of Fashion! **Fantastic Man uses a matt grey recycled paper and is bound with staples. Was this a deliberate rejection of a fashion magazine's 600 glossy pages?** I don't think so, as I have also used glossy paper when I want to distinguish between the advertisers and the editorial content. I needed staples to give the magazine a retro feel. Most fashion magazines are really thick and predominantly made up of advertising. I wanted a slim and quality publication, something you can

LIKE ANOTHER MAN OR POUR HOMME INTERNATIONAL. THEY ARE BOUGHT BY GAY MEN AND ARE EXTREMELY 'FAGGY' BUT AREN'T GAY MAGAZINES.

grasp and that's not intimidating. It's not like the normal magazine experience, where you flick through quickly and never pick it up again. I needed it more intense, compact and physical. I love grey, as it can give a faded 50s atmosphere. Undoubtedly the magazine will evolve and in five years time it will probably be printed on glossy brown paper! Butt was printed on colorado pink paper, so it made sense to print Fantastic Man on colorado grey. **Why did you decide to only use black and white?** It's partly economics. You can do all the scanning easily and we create these things with next to no budget. I was opposed to black and white when I started RE magazine. I thought it was so fictitious, but I don't think that anymore. Every jewellery shop has its merchandise reprinted in full colour and everyone uses colour these days. It's interesting to create a world in black and white. Plus there's a lot of crap colour photography out there. It's much more difficult to make things look good in colour. I guess in the end it all comes down to glamour. It's media retro! **How is the design of Fantastic Man going to evolve?** It's really more about what I want to achieve editorially. All the design decisions come from that, although it's unlikely the simple grid will disappear. The first issue was clumsy, too formal, and the headlines were crappy. I think I lost my nerve and wondered if I could do it anymore. I was afraid I couldn't come up with something that was 'right to the point'. I think this can happen if you work in isolation. In the second issue I changed the design and introduced another typeface. I used Gill Sans, with Times. They were both designed in the same country at the same time and I think that's the reason they work well together. In the third issue we understood more about what we were trying to achieve and it received a very good response. For the fourth issue I want it to evolve again. I like the idea that Butt is a magazine that doesn't change, but I want Fantastic Man to evolve continuously. It needs more advertisers and maybe it needs to be a quarterly. At the moment it runs for the fashion season only. It's also about becoming a little bit more business like, finding finance and possibly a publisher. I'm talking to a British publisher at the moment. **How interested are you in contemporary design?** I hardly know what other people are doing in the design world. I do look at a lot of magazines in the same field, simply because I want to avoid featuring the same people. And obviously I am interested who photographed the interesting spreads, and who art directed what. However, I find a lot of graphic design very cosmetic and I think it's become this way because there's just so much of it. Good design can be copied so easily that it ends up getting devalued. Graphics isn't rocking the design world anymore, and it's not like the 80s when there was an exciting counter-cultural element. I think the design explosion of the 90s has a lot to answer for, and perhaps I am fundamentally anti design. **Gert Jonkers, the editor of Fantastic Man, believes it is a fashion magazine about real people. Is he right in this assertion?** Well we didn't want to use models in Fantastic Man, and unfortunately we haven't managed to achieve this. It's a very difficult thing to do. The idea was to feature people wearing their own clothes, amongst other stories. I didn't want to use models because I'm not interested in the fashion fantasy. I find 14 year olds in designer clothes singularly unappealing and I also don't like the sexualisation of fashion. I'm interested in people who have something to say, who have a story to tell, but might just happen to look good. Someone who can talk for half an hour about the buttons on their jacket could be surprisingly interesting. Or perhaps we might look for people who wear red sweaters. I'm more interested in details and how they are connected to a person. You won't find us featuring 22 year old boy band singers. Its called Fantastic Man for a reason, as we think you need to live a little, before you have a story worth telling. As a magazine we want to represent men over thirty. Obviously their fashion sense has also evolved. They may have looked like skaters five years ago, but maybe now they want something more formal. **Do you think Butt and Fantastic Man has influenced how we view the modern male?** Butt hasn't changed the gay scene. It's just given gay men another place to visit. I believe 99% of things are fixed structures, but a magazine can show people new possibilities. Fashion doesn't have to be designed for twelve year olds reading FHM, and we can all see the rise of the older model. If you buy FHM or Esquire you are buying into a dream world, and for some people that maybe empowering, but for most it's just a way of relieving the boredom. **Is it difficult to make a cover choice?** There is an entire diplomatic world behind that choice! You must realise that everyone who works for Fantastic Man, works for free. Obviously if a famous photographer is giving their time for free, they might reasonably expect to get one of their photographs on the cover. The difficulty occurs if you have other ideas

YOU WON'T FIND US FEATURING 22 YEAR OLD BOY BAND SINGERS. ITS CALLED FANTASTIC MAN FOR A REASON, AS WE THINK YOU NEED TO LIVE A LITTLE BEFORE YOU HAVE A STORY WORTH TELLING.

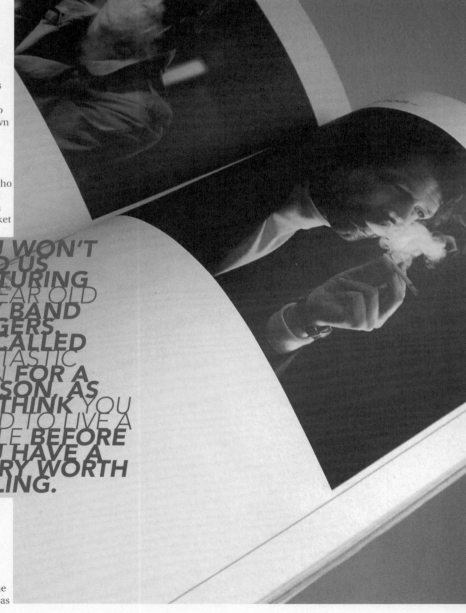

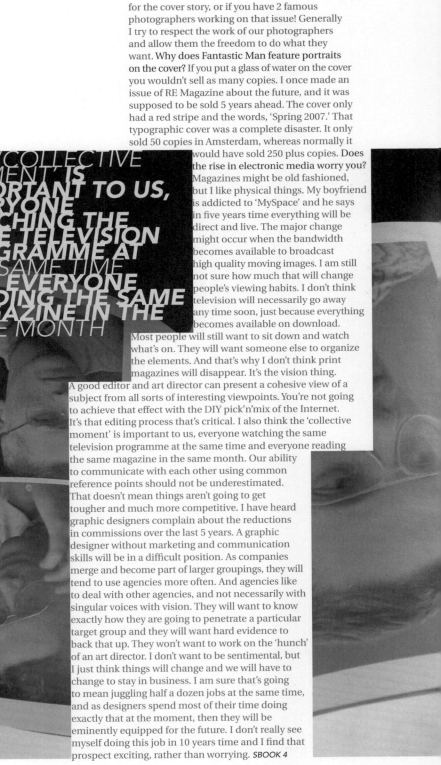

for the cover story, or if you have 2 famous photographers working on that issue! Generally I try to respect the work of our photographers and allow them the freedom to do what they want. **Why does Fantastic Man feature portraits on the cover?** If you put a glass of water on the cover you wouldn't sell as many copies. I once made an issue of RE Magazine about the future, and it was supposed to be sold 5 years ahead. The cover only had a red stripe and the words, 'Spring 2007.' That typographic cover was a complete disaster. It only sold 50 copies in Amsterdam, whereas normally it would have sold 250 plus copies. **Does the rise in electronic media worry you?** Magazines might be old fashioned, but I like physical things. My boyfriend is addicted to 'MySpace' and he says in five years time everything will be direct and live. The major change might occur when the bandwidth becomes available to broadcast high quality moving images. I am still not sure how much that will change people's viewing habits. I don't think television will necessarily go away any time soon, just because everything becomes available on download. Most people will still want to sit down and watch what's on. They will want someone else to organize the elements. And that's why I don't think print magazines will disappear. It's the vision thing. A good editor and art director can present a cohesive view of a subject from all sorts of interesting viewpoints. You're not going to achieve that effect with the DIY pick'n'mix of the Internet. It's that editing process that's critical. I also think the 'collective moment' is important to us, everyone watching the same television programme at the same time and everyone reading the same magazine in the same month. Our ability to communicate with each other using common reference points should not be underestimated. That doesn't mean things aren't going to get tougher and much more competitive. I have heard graphic designers complain about the reductions in commissions over the last 5 years. A graphic designer without marketing and communication skills will be in a difficult position. As companies merge and become part of larger groupings, they will tend to use agencies more often. And agencies like to deal with other agencies, and not necessarily with singular voices with vision. They will want to know exactly how they are going to penetrate a particular target group and they will want hard evidence to back that up. They won't want to work on the 'hunch' of an art director. I don't want to be sentimental, but I just think things will change and we will have to change to stay in business. I am sure that's going to mean juggling half a dozen jobs at the same time, and as designers spend most of their time doing exactly that at the moment, then they will be eminently equipped for the future. I don't really see myself doing this job in 10 years time and I find that prospect exciting, rather than worrying. *SBOOK 4*

THE 'COLLECTIVE MOMENT IS IMPORTANT TO US, EVERYONE WATCHING THE SAME TELEVISION PROGRAMME AT THE *SAME TIME* AND EVERYONE READING THE SAME MAGAZINE IN THE *SAME MONTH*

How did you become involved with Adrenalin Magazine? When I was studying graphic design I spent most of my time designing my Uni magazine instead of doing coursework, because it felt like that was something that could actually get me somewhere. Well, pretty much in the first month we were at Uni, one of our lecturers (a big magazine lover) brought in issue 01 of Adrenalin to show us all how great it was. Sure enough, she was right, so everyone went out and bought a copy. I kept buying it all the way through our first year and by issue 8 I decided it was time to get out in the real world, so I bugged Mickey_Boy_G, the creative director, for some work experience. Mickey gave me a shot, and I did ok, and then I kept in touch and bugged them for more work experience and came down a couple more times in the next year or two. Then, towards the end of my course when everyone was starting to think about the fact that soon they'd be unemployed and, well, basically screwed - I was sat in the Uni magazine office on a Saturday afternoon and Mike Fordham, editor of Adrenalin called me and offered me a job. Needless to say, I was, to use the great cliché, "in the right place at the right time" - or in other words - "a lucky bastard". How do you decide on the subject for each issue of Adrenalin? They seem to decide themselves really, and to be honest I've never really been too concerned about what they are, so long as they aren't too abstract. I preferred "California" to "Speed" for example. Lately we've tried to make them a little more relevant to what's going on in the world, and also the seasons in which they're released. Can you surf, skate or snowboard? Nope - can't do any of those things. I do them all vicariously through the

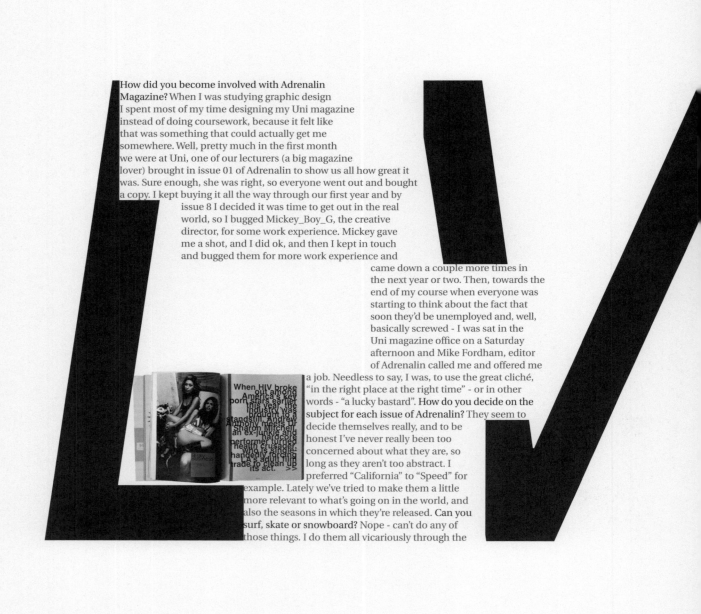

When HIV broke out across America's key porn stars earlier this year, the industry was brought to a standstill. Andrew Anthony meets Mr. Marcus, an ex-junkie and hardcore performer turned health crusader who's single-handedly put the trade to clean up its act. >>

mag, I guess. **Adrenalin has carved out a distinctive style in the marketplace. Where does it draw its influences?** Well I would say that Adrenalin's style was fully created by Mickey_Boy_G, and everything I've done since is just trying to carry on his work. I think Mickey is a very naturally talented, uninfluenced designer. For my part, I draw a lot of influence from the design of The Face, between 1999 and 2002. At that time, I think it was the best-designed mag around. Bold, imaginative and always evolving. **Why do you think Adrenalin has been so successful?** There are many ways in which a mag can be successful. Editorially, visually, commercially. If you were to say, "why do you think Adrenalin is so well received" - I think that the answer would simply be that it is something truly mould breaking within it's own market (board sports) and beyond that, as a magazine in general. I'm not saying that all magazines are not made by people with passion for what they're doing, but it seems to me that the people who started and came to Adrenalin had an enormous desire to make magazines. We're magazine makers through and through. Magazine lovers. And we LOVED Adrenalin, and I think that this was reflected in the magazine itself. **How would you describe your use of typography in Adrenalin?** I think we try to do interesting things with simple fonts, rather than find new fonts and just slap them on a page. Mags like Dazed do this, and it annoys me. We've stuck with Helvetica in Adrenalin from the start, and I think it's a great challenge to keep using it creatively. In general, I'm inclined to keep the magazine very clean and readable, whilst occasionally doing something

completely against the rules. **Do articles or illustrations change as an issue evolves?** Most of the illustrations are commissioned, so we couldn't change them as a mag is being put together. The articles themselves can change a lot though. I think it's very important to have a flatplan on the wall, and keep printing our pages and getting them up there so you can see the progress of the whole magazine at a glance. I really change things a LOT as we make an issue, to keep a good flow through the issue. **Do the articles define the layout?** You know, they ought to, but they don't. The quality of images often defines the layout. If images are good, then I keep layout simple. If they aren't I get into the design a little more to compensate. **How significant is your use of the magazine's grid in creating page structures?** Not hugely important. I've never really been one for grids. So long as there's continuity (of point size, or column width for example) within each individual story in the mag, I'm happy. **Is Little White Lies a logical step on from Adrenalin?** In a way, LWLies is very much borne of Adrenalin, but also it's a very old idea that myself and my friend Matt had many years ago back at school. When Adrenalin moved to a new publishers (between November 2004 and February 2005) I decided to have a crack at publishing an issue, and it just kind of went from there. We knew then that we'd like to make a movie magazine with a difference and Adrenalin showed that themeing issues was a very interesting thing to do. **Was it a conscious decision to carry over the negative leading and typeface usage?** Anything stylistically that the magazines share is a result of whatever I like doing at the moment. I was happy to carry things over, though I wish I could get more time to develop the visuals in LWLies. **Would it be fair to say that both magazines have a down-to-earth philosophy that creates an almost 'everyman' persona?** Absolutely. We have a very 'no bullshit' approach. We try to be very honest and down to earth and unaffected - qualities that I really hope my colleagues and myself possess. **Do you think they appeal to the same readership?** I have no idea! One

THE JARHEAD ISSUE

ISSUE 4

LITTLE

Truth

of the most interesting aspects of LWL is each issue is 'influenced' by the lead film review. How do you decide which film is going to be the lead? We're currently a quarterly, and an issue takes around 2 months to make. For the first month we just sit round arguing about which movie to cover. It can be a very difficult decision, especially for example at the time of my writing this, when we're starting to put together issue 6 and have until recently had no idea which film to base the issue around. There are many things that are important to me about the lead film. That it's good. That it's creative and original. That I like the cast and that it contains someone interesting that we can put on the cover. That it is interesting enough to base a whole magazine around. That is a bit different to the kind of film that might be on the cover of other mags at the time. We're looking to do a cover about The Beastie Boys at the moment, for many reasons including the fact that in a time of the release of massive blockbusters I think it'll be interesting to ignore them completely and do a music related issue. **How do you construct the other 'influenced' chapters?** Our editorial team decides the features list during a number of meetings. We then commission out the words and pictures for these articles accordingly. The back section is very much down to Rob (who designs it) and David Jenkins (who edits it). It's all about how creative they can make it, and fortunately for me and for the magazine, they're super creative people. An excellent magazine called Marmalade, which is well worth checking out, heavily influences the look of the back section. **Who is LWLs target audience?** Anyone at all. We're not targeting anyone in particular, just whoever feels like picking it up. I wouldn't like to pitch it at just one type of person really. **As an independent magazine you must have a limited budget. To what extent does this affect the production?** We basically have a budget of nothing. I'm paid to work on Adrenalin, but so far with LWLies no one has been paid a penny (including myself) to do anything. We have all the tools we need to make the magazines and we're able to gather enough cash together each issue to get it printed and that's all we need for now. I guess that the only way having no money really affects us is that it makes it necessary to find people who'll work for nothing. Luckily, this has proved no problem. *SBOOK 4*

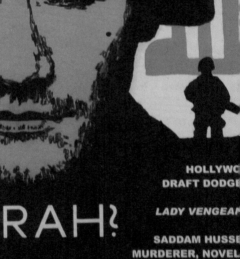

HOLLYWO
DRAFT DODGE

LADY VENGEA

SADDAM HUSSE
MURDERER, NOVEL

-RAH?

THOMAS PERSSON
ACNE PAPER

1s Issue Autumn—03

ACNE PAPER

Acne started as a jeans label in 1996 and has grown into a multifaceted company that now operates across fashion, advertising, film and publishing. The first Issue of Acne Paper was launched in autumn 2005. Why did you feel a magazine was the next step? Creating a magazine was a natural evolution for Acne because we look at all sorts of new opportunities all the time. To be an entrepreneur is very highly regarded here; people with the initiative to start things, and then be helped along the way with the existing infrastructure of the company. I think the idea of doing a magazine was conceived long before I started here and I guess this is because a printed publication belongs in the same creative sphere as Acne's other companies, such as fashion, advertising and film. When Acne approached me they didn't have a set idea and plan for what the purpose of the magazine should be. It was just this joy of creating something they had wanted to do for a long time. I think they were interested in the creative discipline of making a magazine, more so than what exactly the magazine should be about. Since Acne wanted to explore the idea of being a publisher I think a magazine was a good way to start getting an idea of what this is about, in terms of thinking of ideas, producing content, dealing with contributors, art direction, printing and distribution. I think a magazine, if it is done well, is a great tool to make Acne more known internationally - to make people interested in us and

what we do. What did you want the magazine to be about? The first thing I did was to go through several decades of fashion magazines, from about 1930 to1990. This gave me an overall view of what has been, and perhaps what I was missing in the magazine market today. I work very intuitively, so after my week of research I had a big box full of photocopies of things I thought had something interesting in terms of graphic design, editorial angle, a strong article, or just a nice way of doing a photo shoot. Then I sat down with my art director, Moses Voigt, and we decided on a grid based on a few principles we thought strong enough to travel from issue to issue. Would it be fair to say that your first response seemed to be a reaction against youth worship in fashion? First of all my ambition was to try to create a magazine that didn't look or feel like any other magazine today. I wanted to offer something quite different. Secondly, I was personally tired of seeing teenage models dressed in clothes that are way too sophisticated for them – in editorial shoots, in campaigns, at the shows. I am not against the beauty of youth. I like perfection and I guess I want to live forever too, but I think it is a very narrow obsession in fashion today and it is simply getting boring. I see beauty everywhere, not only in youth and luxury products. I mean the world is flooded by beauty, and I wanted to get that across somehow in the magazine. Also, since Acne Paper more than anything is about personal stories I wanted to include all generations as we all have wonderful stories to tell. More often than not the better stories come from people who have lived a little. There are, of course, exceptions. **Is this an Acne philosophy or does it just relate to the magazine?** Everyone at Acne is relatively young and occupied with their own lives and interests, so this is definitely not something we chant about at the office. I don't run around promoting my fascination for history, for instance. Fashion is young and should be young, but fashion doesn't live in isolation. Fashion, the way I see it, belongs to creativity, to culture, to the arts. And everyone at the office is interested in these things, so yes, we are all on the same wavelength - we fulfil each other because we have different strengths. It's all about the excitement of presenting something amazing that may have been forgotten about, or introducing something for the very first time. It's about curiosity and wanting to learn more. **How are you going to balance the need for Acne Paper to be a promotional vehicle for the Acne brand, against its need to be an independent magazine?** We shoot Acne Jeans because it is the company we work for. And we love the clothes! I mean, we are all influencing how the collections look, so Acne Jeans is a very personal thing for all of us. All fashion magazines must include their advertisers in their editorials somehow, to make everyone happy. In every fashion magazine a commissioned stylist is given a list of labels from the fashion editor. With advertisers they must incorporate in their shoot, so I like to put it like this: all magazines survive by their advertisers. Some have tons of them. We have one, for the time being. And it is very exciting to work like this. It makes our shoots different because we base them on the thoughts that have gone into each collection. And we don't have to struggle getting clothes – they are all hanging next to us – and we can focus on the idea, the scenery, the photography, and the

initial ideas behind the clothes. **You say you wanted to create something historical, romantic, personal and human. Can you tell us how you turned this into a usable concept?** There are enough magazines about news, trends, celebrity and consumer culture. Personally I'm not interested in general news, trends, shopping or celebrities. I prefer a good biography to reality TV. I love to listen to a wonderful story at a dinner party. I don't understand the current market and their need to know who's dating who and who is pregnant now. Why are people so obsessed by gossip, rumours and trash? I want the real thing. I mean, why shouldn't one be romantic about people's lives? To be human is something so extraordinary it should never be reduced to triviality. It should be celebrated with dignity. So history, romance, personalities and the human concept came quite naturally. Luckily it translated quite well into a magazine. **Every issue covers just one theme, the first being cities. How does this influence the design process?** We try to put across a mood in each issue so the design is very important as it binds all the elements together. In the first issue, which was about the city, we wanted to present a film noir idea of a city. We wanted black and white photography; the streets of Paris, or an imaginary New York, perhaps seen through the eyes of a child. We looked at a lot of images and books that, in one way or the other, could be translated into romanticism around living the creative life in a city. We wanted the names of the cities to look beautiful: Paris. London. New York. We wanted the text to look like an old newspaper of the sort you can imagine flying around in the streets. So yes, the design is very much inspired by the theme of the issue – it is the tool on which the magazine is designed. **What did you learn from the first issue that you have been able to use in subsequent issues?** To not let stress enter my body. **How do you decide on a theme?** In an abstract way

I get inspired by the things Jonny Johansson, the creative head of Acne Jeans, has thought about while designing his new collection. Then there is always a certain mood, something in the air… Then I narrow this down to something timeless, a theme that doesn't belong to any generation specifically but somehow touches people who work creatively. **Who do you think is the target audience?** When asked this I like to refer to Diana Vreeland's legendary quote when she was asked about her editorship at American Vogue in the 60's: "I want to give people what they never knew they wanted!" In other words, we don't have a target group in mind, and we certainly don't think about what people want to read, or what they expect of us. We want each issue to be a surprise and a treat for everyone interested in culture and aesthetics in general. Age, education, status and cultural background are not remotely relevant. We all have eyes and we all react positively to beauty. **How does this reflect in the design?** It makes us follow our hearts and do what we think looks great. **Did you test to see if there was a market for this kind of magazine?** We don't do tests. We trust our intuition. **Your stated objective was to make Acne Paper more like a beautiful book than a magazine. What do you mean by this?** The world, and life in general, is so fantastically chaotic, every day is stuffed with good and bad impressions. Wherever we turn our heads someone is telling us what to buy, what to see, where to go, and whatever else. But when you open a book and start reading it, and if it's any good, you get drawn into its world completely. I have always liked magazines that have that quality of escape, like we escape into books. As we are lucky enough not having to interrupt the magazine with lots of advertising, we wanted to use this opportunity to create a magazine with a certain atmosphere, perhaps not like a book of fiction but more of a coffee table book. Design-wise we want it to look effortless, simply to use design to communicate the content in an inviting way: like in a book. **What influenced your choice of a large A3 format?** Andy Warhol's Interview magazine. David Bailey's Ritz magazine. Egoïste magazine. Handsome newspapers. **Your degree is in fashion journalism, not design. Was your transition into a creative director at Acne difficult?** I have always been very visually interested but wanted to tell stories rather than taking pictures or doing graphic design, which seemed to be the only options in the trade when I first started out. As a creative director - to be able to decide what the magazine should be about and how it should look - is nothing but a fantastic bonus because writing can be a very lonely occupation. To be able to leave my laptop in the comfort of my home and enter a creative environment where I was allowed to make tough decisions was not difficult at all. It was a dream come true. **Where does the creative directors' job begin and end at Acne?** I conceive an overall idea for each issue – the theme. For number 3, for instance, the theme is education and learning, with a strong focus on the relationship between master and apprentice, mentor and protégé. Then I start thinking about ideas: who to interview, who would be relevant to do a big feature on, what are the diversities of the theme, what should the photo shoots signify and represent. Then I present this to the art director who starts to think about how we can translate this graphically and visually by doing lots of research for himself. Then we get together, exchange ideas and put the magazine together. **Who are you**

working with at the moment? Today
I do the magazine with an art director
called Jonas Jansson who I think
is very, very good - a great eye. And
then I work closely with a stylist called
Mattias Karlsson who is responsible for the
shoots. Mattias is very knowledgeable and
works for other titles too, such as Another
Magazine, Dazed & Confused, 10, and The
New York Times. He has a wonderful way
of casting the right models and creating
visually stimulating images. Mattias
is the one pulling the shoots together.

**Has your work for Self Service magazine
influenced your approach at Acne Paper?** I
started contributing to Self Service directly after
college and I learned a lot from it, especially as a
journalist. Their demands for what an interview
should be are very high. You don't deliver
something mediocre to Self Service. I have
always been very hard on myself and by getting
every single piece I did published by Self Service
I gained enough confidence to finally think: "Ok,
so perhaps I am not such a lousy journalist after
all." It set a certain standard for me. I think I
have learned to reach further, by working for
them. **Who are the magazine designers you
admire?** I love what Alexey
Brodovitch did at Harper's Bazaar in the 30's, 40's and
50's. But there are so many other art directors I love.
I like elegance, intelligence and wit in magazine
design. I think Fabien Baron has done amazing
things. I also think Esquire in the 60's was
breathtaking. If you are talking about magazine
design today I think of Ezra Petronio at Self Service.
He is one of the very few who has a unique style, and
everyone is shamelessly copying his vision. **How do
you choose your photographers and how do you
work with them?** We choose the photographer that is
right for the idea we have in mind. I also think it's
interesting to use photographers differently than the
other magazines that are also commissioning them.
For instance, Benjamin Alexander Huseby, who
shoots for magazines such as British Vogue and
Another Magazine, always has a very light and
romantic quality to his images. But he is also a very
fun boy to party with and he knows everyone worth
knowing on the London fashion scene. So we
commissioned him to take trashy polaroids of a

fashion party crowd having fun at a fabulous drag haloween party in London – a very different Alexander Huseby than people know, but equally good. I always have an idea for each shoot and if I'm lucky the photographers are able to take it to the next level. It's a process of communication and mutual respect. I like the idea of working for a long time with a group of photographers that are all very different, and learn and develop by collaborations with longevity. I am a bit allergic to the trend of jumping on every big hot-shot photographer. It makes all magazines look the same and I want us to look different. **What's the timescale for an Acne photoshoot?** One shoot can take a day, another can take four. And then there's all the meetings, the casting, etc. so this is almost impossible to answer as it varies enormously. **Can you tell us about the storytelling element in Acne Paper?** I have always found it so much more interesting to know what the interviewee has to say rather than getting the journalists opinions. So I have chosen a monologue form for most of the interviews, which means that the subject does all the talking. This does not mean that our journalists are bad, because they are all very good, but I think that if the idea behind each interview is great there is no need for a journalist to be extremely present in the final published text. The real work for a journalist is to have a great idea, to be well prepared and to direct the subject in an interesting, unexpected way. There is nothing worse than reading a badly written feature, or a journalist who wants to be the star. Here in Stockholm it's very correct for a journalist to be extremely opinionated. Unless you are a genius I find that so boring. There are so many angles on things; so many perspectives. There isn't one single truth to anything. Being resolute only shows narrow mindedness. I think, however, one can be very opinionated when searching within ones own personal life. A personal story told well is never bad. We all want stories and I hope that our interviews can live a little longer than the average magazine feature. *SBOOK 4*

ROLLING
STONE

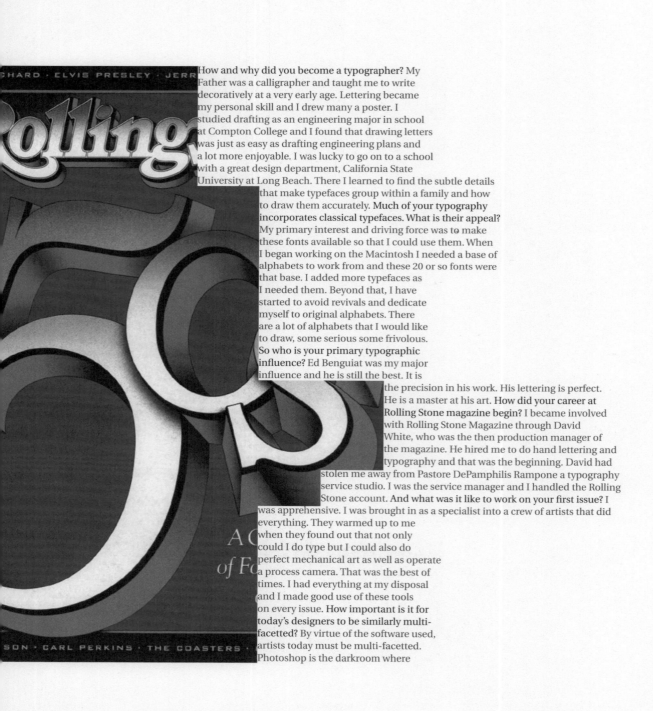

How and why did you become a typographer? My Father was a calligrapher and taught me to write decoratively at a very early age. Lettering became my personal skill and I drew many a poster. I studied drafting as an engineering major in school at Compton College and I found that drawing letters was just as easy as drafting engineering plans and a lot more enjoyable. I was lucky to go on to a school with a great design department, California State University at Long Beach. There I learned to find the subtle details that make typefaces group within a family and how to draw them accurately. **Much of your typography incorporates classical typefaces. What is their appeal?** My primary interest and driving force was to make these fonts available so that I could use them. When I began working on the Macintosh I needed a base of alphabets to work from and these 20 or so fonts were that base. I added more typefaces as I needed them. Beyond that, I have started to avoid revivals and dedicate myself to original alphabets. There are a lot of alphabets that I would like to draw, some serious some frivolous. **So who is your primary typographic influence?** Ed Benguiat was my major influence and he is still the best. It is the precision in his work. His lettering is perfect. He is a master at his art. **How did your career at Rolling Stone magazine begin?** I became involved with Rolling Stone Magazine through David White, who was the then production manager of the magazine. He hired me to do hand lettering and typography and that was the beginning. David had stolen me away from Pastore DePamphilis Rampone a typography service studio. I was the service manager and I handled the Rolling Stone account. **And what was it like to work on your first issue?** I was apprehensive. I was brought in as a specialist into a crew of artists that did everything. They warmed up to me when they found out that not only could I do type but I could also do perfect mechanical art as well as operate a process camera. That was the best of times. I had everything at my disposal and I made good use of these tools on every issue. **How important is it for today's designers to be similarly multi-facetted?** By virtue of the software used, artists today must be multi-facetted. Photoshop is the darkroom where images are modified and Quark and InDesign are the paste-up room. Illustrator, Fontographer and FontLab just round out the mix. I am a rarity, I only do typography and typographic services. **You hand rendered much of the title type for Rolling Stone. How do you decide to approach each article?** Rolling Stone designers were well-known for their meticulous layouts so doing perfect typography to match them was easy. We usually had live copy on the layouts so we read every article before it was done. **Are there particular issues that still stand out for their design content?** Being on tight deadlines kept tabs on perfection. I love the line work that I did on the 50s issue cover but Fred Woodward jobbed out the colour to an airbrush artist. I always do my own airbrush work so I was not too happy about the final cover. Still, the conical logo and type treatment were cool. Other than that, the 20th Anniversary issue was a good cover piece for me but the most inclusive was the Hot Issue with Uma Thurman. I had to do 14 ornamental alphabets for the composition of the titles and subtitles for the entire issue. That was a huge job. **And how tight were the deadlines?** We closed an issue every two weeks or more often for special issues. We didn't work the first

WE CLOSED AN ISSUE EVERY TWO WEEKS OR MORE OFTEN FOR SPECIAL ISSUES. WE DIDN'T WORK THE FIRST FEW DAYS OF THE FIRST WEEK. THE SECOND WEEK WE LIVED AT THE MAGAZINE AND WORKED THROUGH THE NIGHT few days of the first week. The second week we lived at the magazine and worked through the night. They fed us and deadline dinners were catered and usually very tasty. **How much design autonomy did you have?** I was usually given a lot of freedom although the layouts were usually very tight. I never screwed up a cover or a layout so they trusted me to do the best with all things considered. During my first stint with the magazine I would also close the issue as the last person there. That involved reviewing and signing off pages as done and ready for camera. If anything, and I mean anything, was wrong, I made it right. **What was it like to work on John Lennon's 'death' issue?** It was a nightmare. Annie Leibowitz had been with the Lennons the night he was shot and she and most of us were all in shock. We had completely redesigned the issue and this was the first issue using the new format. We had

THE TWENTIETH ANNIVERSARY

ISSUE 512 • NOV. 5TH – DEC. 18TH, 1987 • U.K. £2.75 • $4.95

Rolling Stone

INTERVIEWS *with Bob Dylan, Bruce Springsteen, Paul McCartney, Mick Jagger, George Harrison, Keith Richards, Stevie Wonder, Pete Townshend, Bono, Sting, Tom Wolfe, Hunter Thompson, Edward Kennedy, Walter Cronkite, Jack Nicholson and more*

THE COMPUTER HAS MADE ART DIRECTORS OF SOME PEOPLE WHO WOULD NEVER HAVE HAD THE SKILLS TO DO IT BY HAND. COMPUTERS AND MAGAZINES HAVE MADE DESIGN ACCESSIBLE to throw it all away and redo an entire issue in a matter of days. Everyone worked themselves into the ground to get that issue done and we worked long hours to make it so. In the end John Lennon got his wish and the cover photo was his choice. All things considered, we did pretty okay. **What sort of production problems did you encounter?** Well the biggest problem came on that John Lennon issue what with having to redesign an entire issue overnight, every layout and every page was bad enough normally, but to do it in a matter of days and not two weeks was insane. In the end Jann Wenner had a fit when he saw the classified ads and pulled most of the pages (they were pretty tasteless). That left the magazine with a bunch of blank pages that we wound up filling with memorials. A seamless switch and a good way to close the issue. **Were pages ever 'pulled' due to design problems?** No, pages were never pulled out. If they did people didn't keep their jobs. **How and why did you change the format?** The format of the magazine changed from using centred pages on newsprint to a full bleed on slightly better paper than newsprint. It meant that we could do the same things now that other magazines did and our work would have a longer shelf life than the others. **Why do you think the Rolling Stone logo became so iconic?** You would have to thank Jim Parkinson. He created the look and it has become a classic. I did a total of three logos myself, but they were never meant to replace Jim's logo. **How did your design work develop after Rolling Stone?** My work changed from feature art into logo and typeface design, but I still miss doing feature art sometimes. I loved the geometry of a well-designed page. Making things fit was not that simple in those days. Everything had to be done by hand. Today a complex title is a simple thing in Illustrator. I rarely do feature art anymore. Today I specialize in font and logo assignments so the work tends to be rather basic. I am always on the lookout for font design assignments. **Do you think your skill for hand rendering typography helped ease your transition into the digital creation of type?** Fontographer worked in a very similar fashion to how I drew by hand so it was an easy changeover. I still miss the simplicity of pen and ink but digital media is much faster. I can draw an uppercase font in a matter of hours and it is ready to use. It was a hard climb for many people. Computers were rather alien to many visually creative people and some did not make the change. **How do the design processes for hand rendered and digital type differ?** Drafting a letterform is much more flexible than rendering a letterform digitally. They have yet to include ellipsis guides into font rendering software. Still, the immediacy of digital art is a huge bonus. You have more time to work on your creation. **To what extent did this technology diminish the need for skilled hand rendering of layouts and type?** It is a direct comparison to video killing the radio star. **What do you mean?** Put enough glitz on something and it will outshine itself. **Has the computer improved magazine design or just made them easier and faster to produce?** I would say both because the computer has made art directors of some people who would never have had the skills to do it by hand. Computers and magazines have made design accessible. All you need is good taste and an audience. Make that just an audience. **So is there a more important object a designer could own other than their Mac?** Good taste and a PC, or maybe the next generation of Intel Core Duo Macintosh towers. Apple has yet to outdo Microsoft at making their computers universal. Actually, it's a case of 'virus-envy': PC users hate Mac users. **How easy would it be for young designers to set up their own magazine today?** Print publications still require big cash and crews to depend upon. An online magazine would be a breeze. **Do you think there is a need for students to be taught how to create layouts by hand?** Helpful, yes, but does anyone still do layouts by hand? **And what advice would you give to a young magazine designer?** Hire me to draw for you and revive the days of real typography. Other than that, research, research, research. **Can you tell us about your name Siynn bar-Diyonn?** It means S son of Dion (my father's birth name was Dionisio). Siynn is the phonetic spelling of one of three hebrew S's. I took the name when I converted to Judaism. **As part of your Type Foundry you have designed many Hebrew fonts. How difficult are these to produce?** Hebrew is very modular. I can create a complete Hebrew alef-bayt in a few hours. **You can count the Vatican amongst your clients. What did you do for them and what were they like as a client?** I did the work through an agency so my client contact was minimal. I did a Hebrew typesetting of a Papal speech commemorating the Holocaust. The copy I had to work from was supplied by the Vatican and horribly bad, so I saved the day by calling in a real orthodox Jewish copy editor. **Do you look back at your time on Rolling Stone with a great deal of affection?** We enjoyed our work and worked ridiculously hard but almost every issue had a piece of history attached to it. **Besides, you didn't work at Rolling Stone, you lived there and your entire life revolved around your time there.** I have many memories of parties and just plain fun that we had working there like paper airplane contests from the 22nd floor or the Rolling Stone Christmas party. Jann Wenner was a generous and understanding employer and provided what he could to keep us happy. After all, we had to create perfection to a 1/8 of a point accuracy (I am not kidding. I created a ruler for this purpose that we all used to maintain 1/8 of a point accuracy). I can only imagine what we could have done with a crew of Digital Artists. It would have been cool. *SBOOK 4*

WE HAD TO CREATE PERFECTION TO A 1/8 OF A POINT ACCURACY (I AM NOT KIDDING. I CREATED A RULER FOR THIS PURPOSE THAT WE ALL USED TO MAINTAIN 1/8 OF A POINT ACCURACY)

How did you become Art Director at PPC? When I was at Southampton Institute I sent out about thirty CV's during my second year asking for a summer work placement. Due to lack of funds I was only able to take up a placement in Peterborough, my home town. Emap's headquarters are based in the town, along with many of their automotive, sport and hobby titles. So I sent in a couple of CV's to the Automotive and Active departments. Luckily there was a placement space at Practical Classics, which was the magazine I ended up working at before moving to Practical Performance Car (PPC). Practical Classics was run by the same editor who later left and started PPC. After my placement ended we lost touch, but I went back to interview him when I was working on my dissertation. It was looking at brands and how they influence people on different levels. Classic cars are a good example because, even though they are unreliable and terrible to drive, everybody still loves them- the strength of the brand survives, even in old age! I had just bought an old Jaguar for the commute between home and University. My mother wanted to pass her old Metro on to me. It was yellow with a brown interior; luckily it failed its MOT, fatally. When I went back to see the editor he was more interested in my old Jaguar than my design skills. After that meeting we kept in touch. We had informal meetings regarding possible freelance, but they didn't bear fruit. Then, on the day I was taking down my final major exhibition, I received a call from Will, the editor. He said "I've got a bit of an opportunity for you". We arranged to meet up the next day. When I arrived things seemed different, formal rather than relaxed like before. We all sat down and Will informed me that the Creative Director would be, "making an appearance". I'd heard about this guy before; a couple of people I went to college with had been interviewed by him. When I say interviewed I hear grilled might be a more appropriate word- someone was even reduced to tears! This should have put the fear of God into me, but the adrenaline seemed to be flowing. He gave me quite a grilling, but I seemed to come out of it quite well. He even said my portfolio was impressive. I guess I caught him on a good day. It turned out they had an opening for a designer and I was the only person they interviewed. I started the next week. **Was a career in magazine design your primary goal after completing your graphics degree?** No, I guess is the short answer. It really fell into my lap after the work experience. And in all honesty it was great to get a job straight away, but it wasn't where I saw myself ending up. I've always thought that because many magazines are quite formulaic it would become rather monotonous after a couple of months. But when I started working on them I realised that a magazine is really an ongoing,

STUART HOLMES PRACTICAL PERFORMANCE CAR

THAN IN MY DESIGN SKILLS

THE EDITOR WAS MORE INTERESTED IN MY OLD JAGUAR

continual project. I'm yet to be happy with the month I've just completed and I spend the next month trying to better the last. If you're completely happy with the magazine you've just completed, I think, it's time to move on. **Did you just follow the editor from one magazine to the other?** Not exactly. Will, the editor, had got thrown out of Emap because they realised he was thinking about starting his own magazine. I heard he was a bit down, so I popped around to his house to see how he was doing. He asked how I was getting on at Practical Classics and I said, "It's not great there at the moment and frankly, I'm rather offended you haven't offered me a job yet!" It all went rather quiet and uncomfortable, but it was only a joke! He phoned me up the next day and said, "that comment you made, were you serious?" I said, "I could well be, I could well be!" We had a number of covert meetings before I jumped ship and started working at PPC from the Deputy Editor's converted coal shed. The new HQ came complete with various roof leaks including one strategically positioned above my G4, or rather the large bucket that took pride of place on top of the G4. Just one guy designed the first five issues and he was also putting together three other monthly titles! As you can imagine it looked like everything had been slapped on at the speed of light. It certainly didn't seem to have a grid underneath it. A complete redesign this early was really out of the question so I've changed it gradually, establishing a grid immediately and making changes to the typefaces soon after. **Does the technical nature of the magazine give you much room for experimentation?** This is not a normal car magazine in the sense that we are not dealing with pretty new cars fresh out of the showroom. The readers of PPC build their own cars and we are there to support them. They require complete legibility from the text and the photography, because in many cases they are following a set of engineering procedures. In some ways it's amongst the most difficult of design jobs. If a new car isn't photographed that well, it's a pity, but its not the end of world. If however you're showing readers how to drop half a ton of V8 into an engine bay, and they get lost half way through your instructions, they ring you up and pass on a few well-chosen adjectives. We have quite an intimate relationship with our readers. **Doesn't that restrict your design process?** I rarely get reigned in, but I always have to consider whether the design is clear to the reader. If it isn't they will grumble and it won't matter if you've got a good concept behind the design. Legibility has to be at the forefront of the process. The readership is not design savvy and nor do they want to be. They don't much appreciate white space, as they would view it as a waste of space!

However I've managed to get around this by using full-page images with lots of negative space in the background- big sky design! That way they don't feel like they're paying for blank paper. **Is it easier to design a magazine if you have a personal interest in the subject?** I have better things to do with my weekends than ram large V12 engines into orifices that are clearly too small for them to fit. I am seriously into cars, but that doesn't mean I'm interested in fondling the oily bits. Mind you, it does help having a certain amount of knowledge, if only to know when the photographs are the right way up. **How involved are you in the magazine's production?** It's a small team and I am involved in issue-planning meetings. This will take place whilst we are producing the previous issue, and it's at this point we decide which cars are going to be featured. We look for a good balance of older and newer cars. Front wheel drive cars tend to appeal to a younger audience, where as rear wheel drive usually appeal to older guys. We strive to get a good balance between the features, and the final decision will be made three weeks before we start work on that issue. Everything's commissioned after the planning stage. **Do you need to read the editorial before you design the spreads?** Absolutely. I need to understand the text before I can think about designing the article. I also need to know the essence of a feature before I write the photographic brief or attend the shoot. If the layout is considered in context with the text prior to the shoot, I find, even with the time taken to art direct the shoot, I save time in the long run. The magazine is split into three sections, the glossy front part, the technical section and the buying section. For the technical section, more than any other, it's important to understand the text to help me order the photographs. **Do you need to travel to find stories?** Funnily enough we try to include a travel story every month. It's a kind of action adventure where we might drive to France, break down, spill engine oil everywhere and catch the ferry back. Occasionally we will invite a group of readers and their cars along, just to really upset the locals. I think we call that one a track day. I tend to avoid them, as I can't afford the on the spot fines. **How have you developed the magazine's use of typefaces?** When I started I kept the original typeface, which I think was Paralucent, but I changed to a standard three column grid all the way through the magazine. Any spare time between issues was used to create a redesign. Which was fully implemented in issue 15. The backbone was a three-column grid with a variable margin. I changed the body copy type to a classic serif face to improve ease of readability. For all other applications I chose Jonathan Barnbrook's Priori family. This was chosen in part because it includes an alternate face, which I believe sits well with the magazine's main subject of modifying. The original designer apparently knocked up the masthead in 15 minutes. We felt we weren't in a position to change this completely, so I set about making it more recognisable for news stand viewers. I tightened up the kerning throughout and placed it within a unique shape. I then repeated this shape as a smaller motif across the top of all the pages. The idea is to leave that shape as a subliminal message in peoples' heads. Hopefully they will recognise it again when they scan the news stands. That's the plan anyway. **Are you aiming for an instantly recognisable style?** Obviously the cover is the primary selling device and it's important that people recognise it as ours. The last four or five issues have managed to achieve this, and developed a coherent style of their own. **How much feedback do you get on your art direction?** When we completed the redesign on issue fifteen we received a small, but perfectly formed, positive response. However, we also got a few letters when we started highlighting the text in the technical section. We were trying to get the less knowledgeable reader involved and we were looking for as many ways into the feature as possible. We introduced a step-by-step visual guide at the bottom of the page, as well as highlighted text in the body copy. Some readers didn't like

MAGAZINES ARE AN ONGOING, CONTINUAL PROJECT I SPEND

THE NEXT MONTH TRYING TO BETTER THE LAST

the highlighted text and said, "I had to read that text first because it was just standing out so much". Part of the idea with the highlighted text was that you could just flick through it and decide if you wanted to read the rest.

The highlights were doing the job of pull quotes, but were too visually linked to the text for some readers. **Do you ever become involved in other areas of the magazine?** I just don't have the time to write anymore. I used to do a bit of writing in Practical Classics and when I first joined PPC, but it takes me such a long time to write that I think my time is probably better spent elsewhere. The subject matter of PPC is also hugely technical and I doubt whether our readers would learn anything from my scribbling. They work at quite an advanced level, so a section on how to refill your windscreen washer bottle probably wouldn't cut the mustard. I've started to get quite involved with photography. We have a very small photographic budget, which only stretches to three or so features per issue. This means I often take the openers for features within the technical and buying section. I've even shot the main cover image on a few occasions. **Do you still need to make structural changes to the magazine?** I think I'm quite happy with the basic structure. We are now trying to improve each feature one by one, whilst sticking within our specific style.

PRAC PEREOR
REAL CARS, REAL TUNING, REAL PERF
SUPER SUPERMAR LOTUS
20 TOP WIRING TIPS

The backbone is in place, so it's really about working the features into it. There are some parts that don't really work, like readers cars and readers projects. I've yet to have the time to give them much thought. You have to remember that you are talking to the design office. It's just me! **Do you have to layout all the adverts as well?** I not only layout the adverts I usually have to design some of them too. Small engineering companies don't have access to design groups, so if we want their advertising revenue, we have to put their ads together. There's usually up to twenty adverts in an issue that I make up. The others come in from various sources and I lay them out ready for print. It sounds quite boring but it's quite a cool thing to do at the end of a difficult month. **Do you ever produce features from text and imagery provided by your readership?** Yes, but only for the Readers Cars section and that can cause problems. The digital era is great for small magazine production because it's removed the need to go to a specialist for typesetting and high resolution scans. However it does mean that readers send in pictures that we really can't use- they're only suitable for websites and other low-resolution applications. We probably find the majority of our lead features by looking through E-mails people have sent through, but we always go and visit the owner and re-shoot these. They say they've built something really interesting and in many cases they've done exactly that. **Has there ever been a time when you thought you might not meet a deadline?** I think we're always concerned about scheduling and we are always up against the clock. Occasionally I'll sit there after two weeks and have only one feature in. That only leaves me with seven working days to put the entire editorial content of the magazine together. **Have you studied your competitor's design languages?** I deliberately don't keep any competitors magazines on my desk when I'm working. It would be too easy to subconsciously steal their ideas. Our main rivals are, in appearance, very different from PPC. It's often more difficult to follow the flow of the text throughout a feature. Imagery and pull quotes sometimes cut the flow of the body copy, making if difficult to decipher where to go next. I guess this can be attributed to differing priorities. In general our competitors tend to use far more images than us. These are then often arranged in a montage. I've always found it difficult to make out the individual images rather than simply seeing a large abstract block. Some others show off their photoshop skills by cutting out the sky from the background of a car image and replacing it with a pic of that cars engine. That's maybe how they want to express their creativity; we just try to keep it legible and balanced. *SBOOK 4*

**MAGAZINES, JOURNALS
& NEWSPAPERS**

10 **128**
Acne Paper *122-129*
Adrenalin *118-121*, **8, 92, 93**
Amelias *100-105*, **8,**
Ampersand, D&AD's **28, 29, 34**
And? **12**
Another Magazine **52, 54, 60, 126**
Another Man **38, 54, 114**
Arena **56, 66, 102, 138**
Art Forum **114**
Baseline *76-83*, **8**
Big **28**
Blvd **112, 138, 139**
Butt *112-114*, **9, 39, 115, 117**
Butterfly magazine **29**
Carl's Cars **92**
Colors *114-117*
Cosmo **15**
Crash **42, 43**
Creative Review **80**
Dazed & Confused *50-57*, **8, 30, 38,
39, 43, 56, 71, 119, 126**
Dior Homme **55, 114**
Egoïste **125**
Elle **15, 66, 68**
Esquire **22, 37, 43, 116, 126**
Evening Standard **138**
Eye **9, 28, 79**
Face, the **15, 43, 52, 55, 68, 102,
109, 119**
Fantastic Man *114-117*, **9, 39**
FHM **66, 68, 116**
Financial Times **12, 13**
Fjords **92**
Flaunt **55**
Forbes **8, 88**
Fri Flyt *90-93*
GQ *64-69*, **19, 20, 22, 23, 25, 37, 38**
GQ Style **38**
Grafik *94-99*, **8, 80**
Graphics International **94**
Graphis **42**
Guardian, the **9, 28, 31**
Harpers Bazaar **11**
ID **28, 55, 108**
Independent Magazine **28**
Index **113**

Intersection **36-43**
Interview **7, 11, 52, 113, 125**
Little White Lies **120, 121**
Loaded **9, 22, 68**
Map *32-33*, **8, 34**
Marie Claire **102**
National Geographic **59**
New York Review, the **30**
New York Times, the **35, 126**
Nova **10, 17, 42**
Octavo **82, 108**
Oz **82**
Picture Post **17**
Plastic Rhino *70-75*, **9**
Playboy **27, 112**
Polished T **74, 75**
Pop **55**
Practical Performance Car **134, 137**
Queen **11**
RA *34-35*, **8, 32**
Raygun **28**
RE *108-112*, **9, 39**
Ritz **125**
Rolling Stone *46-49, 130-133*, **28, 83, 85**
Self Service **126**
Sleave Nation **43,101**
Spy *80-89*
Straight to Hell **112, 113**
Sunday Times Magazine **18,19, 25**
Super **55**
Surface **42**
T2 **57**
Tank *10-17*, **7, 38**
Terrengsykkel **92**
Time magazine **27**
Tokion **55**
Vanity Fair **38, 43**
Vogue **17, 26, 30, 52**
   American **124**
   British **15, 126**
   Paris **68**
Wallpaper *18-25*, **7, 30, 68, 92**
Wonderland **38**
Zembla *28-32*, **8, 27, 33, 34**

DEXA

**ART DIRECTORS &
GRAPHIC DESIGNERS**

Alan Fletcher **77, 81**
Alan Kitching **56, 71, 81**
Alex Isley *84-89*, **8**
Alexey Brodovitch **35, 126**
Amelia Gregory *101-105*, **8**
Andy Diprose *64-69*
Andy Warhol **7, 12, 113, 125**
Armin Hoffman **79, 89**
Camilla Eva Brandt *90-93*, **8**
Carlos Mustienes *58-63*, **8**
Danny Miller *118-121*, **8**
Dave Ellis **77**
David Bailey **81, 125**
David Carson **39**
Dennis Ortiz-Lopez *128-133*, **28, 34**
Dominic Lippa **77**
Ed Benguiat **130**
Ed Fella **56**
Erik Spiekermann **77**
Ezra Petronio **128**
Fabien Baron **126**
Gail Anderson *46-49*
Gregoire Basdevant **63**
Hans Dieter Reichert *76-83*, **8**
Harry Peccinotti **43**
Helmut Schmid **76**
Henry Wolf **43**
Herbert Matter **79, 82**
Jan Tschichold **80, 81**
Jean Widmer **81**
Jim Parkinson **132**
Jonas Jansson **126**
Jonathan Barnbrook **137**
Jop Van Bennekom *106-117*, **9, 43**
Josef Muller Brockman **42**
Mark Porter **35, 63**
Masoud Golsorkhi *10-17*, **7, 8**
Matt Willey *26-35*, **8**
Matthew Ball **32**
Moses Voigt **123**
Neville Brody **83**
Nick Logan **52**
Oliviero Toscani **59, 60, 61, 63**
Pastore DePamphilis Rampone **140**
Paul Rand **42**
Paul Ritter **63**
Paula Scher **44**

Pete Saville **108**
Peter Kellett *70-75*, **9**
Peter Stitson *50-57*, **8**
Sigi Odermat **76**
Simon Esterson **34, 35**
Stefan Ruiz **63**
Stephen Coates **29**
Stuart Holmes **134, 137**
Tama Tetsuya **63**
Terry Jones **52**
Thomas Hilland **63**
Thomas Persson *122-129*
Tibor Kalman **9, 59, 60, 63**
Tony Chambers *18-25*, **7, 68**
Trevor Jackson **56**
Vaughan Oliver **29, 108**
Vince Frost **28**
Yorgo Tloupas *36-45*
Zoë Bather **32**

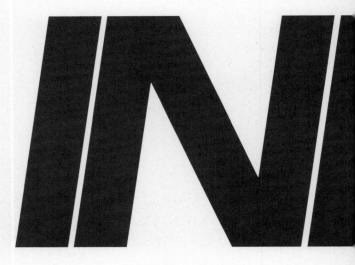

DEXB

**ARTISTS, DESIGN GROUPS,
POPULAR CULTURE, SOFTWARE,
TYPEFACES & MISCELLANEOUS**

4AD Records **108**
8vo *(design group)* **83, 108**
Angharad Lewis **94-99**
Akzidenz *(typeface)* **80**
Alef-bayt *(typeface)* **133**
Alexander McQueen **52,104**
Apple Macintosh **42, 78, 86, 133**
Arete Mono *(typeface)* **32**
Artic Monkeys **72**
Beastie Boys **121**
Big Brother **113**
Bleed *(design group)* **92**
Blur **52**
Bob Geldof **30, 55**
Bodoni *(typeface)* **77**
Bono **56**
Bradbourne Publishing **76**
Chermayeff & Geismer
(design group) **76**
Damien Hirst **52**
Dan Crowe **29**
Dior **30**
E-bay **48**
Emap **52, 134, 135**
Fabrica **61, 62**
Factory records **108**
Fontographer **131, 132**
Fontlab **131**
Franklin Gothic *(typeface)* **28**
Frost Design **28, 33, 34**
Garamond *(typeface)* **80, 85**
Giles Revell **28**
Gill Sans *(typeface)* **115**
GTF *(design group)* **43**
Gridnik *(typeface)* **33**
Gucci **20, 30**
Helvetica *(typeface)* **42, 80, 92, 119**
Hellenica *(typeface)* **40**
Henry Moore **7**
Hoboken *(typeface)* **32**
Ian Rankin **38, 52, 55**
Illustrator, Adobe **48, 60, 86,131, 133**
Indesign, Adobe **63, 72, 131**
Interstate *(typeface)* **54**
Jimi hendrix **30**
Jefferson Hack **52**

Johanna *(typeface)* **40**
John Lennon **131, 132**
Kennedy
    Edward **88**
    John **47**
Letraset **77, 78**
Levi's **30**
London Graphics Centre **78**
Mafia, the **83**
Magma **11, 99**
Manolo Blahnik **30**
Martin Parr **40, 41**
Masturbation **11, 17**
Matty Curtis *(bored)* **142**
Metro *(typeface)* **85**
Moods of Norway *(design group)* **92**
MTV **47, 58**
My Space **117**
Nabokov **29**
Naomi Campbell **40**
New Caledonia *(typeface)* **32**
North *(design group)* **80**
Norway Says *(design group)* **92**
Palatino *(typeface)* **32**
Paralucent *(typeface)* **136**
Paul Smith **30, 79**
Peppered Sprout **71**
Phaidon **76, 77, 78**
Photoshop, Adobe **68, 130, 138**
Picasso **10, 12**
Pixies, the **28**
Prada **12, 20**
Priori family *(typeface)* **137**
QuarkXpress **63, 72, 75, 131**
Radiohead **52**
Red Hot Chilli Peppers **54, 57**
Rockwell *(typeface)* **40**
Rub Down *(typeface)* **55**
Sabon *(typeface)* **80**
Serifa *(typeface)* **40**
Studio8 Design *(design group)* **32**
Suisse *(typeface)* **40**
Tate, The **30**
Tilda Swinton **15, 30**
Times *(typeface)* **111, 115**
Tomato *(design group)* **56**
Uma Thurman **131**
Univers *(typeface)* **80**
WH Smiths **35, 38**
Yeah Yeah Yeah's **54**

DEXC

SBOOK 1
ISBN 1874011745
PUBLISHED AND DISTRIBUTED BY
ART BOOKS INTERNATIONAL

INTERVIEWS WITH GRAPHIC
DESIGNERS FOR GRAPHIC DESIGNERS

Andy Altmann
Sarah Ancalmo
Jonathan Barnbrook
Nick Bell
Hans Bockting
Greg Burne
Bob Cotton
Marion Deuchars
Gert Dumbar
Tim Fendley
David Foldvari
Vince Frost
Jasper Goodall
Jess Goodall
Roya Jakoby
Kalle Lasn
Less Rain
Tracy Oultram
Polimekanos
Nana Rausch
Adrian Shaughnessy
Swifty
Ben Tappenden
Teal Triggs

SBOOK 2
ISBN 1874044600
PUBLISHED AND DISTRIBUTED BY
ART BOOKS INTERNATIONAL

INTERVIEWS WITH GRAPHIC
DESIGNERS WORKING IN AND
AROUND THE MUSIC INDUSTRY

Ian Anderson
Chris Bilheimer
Art Chantry
Daniel Eatock
Fred Deakin
Stanley Donwood
Malcolm Garrett
Kate Gibb
Kim Hiorthøy
Nat Hunter
Karl Hyde
Karlssonwilker
Elisabeth Kopf
Angela Lorenz
Christopher Murphy
Rick Myers
Non-format
Rob O'connor
Nick Robertson
Stefan Sagmeister
Peter Saville
Paula Scher
Adrian Shaughnessy
Storm Thorgerson

SBOOK 3
ISBN 1874011893
PUBLISHED AND DISTRIBUTED BY
ART BOOKS INTERNATIONAL

INTERVIEWS WITH TYPOGRAPHERS

Phil Baines
Ken Barber
Chris Bigg
Halvor Bodin
Catherine Dixon
Alan Dye
Erik Worsøe Eriksen
Alan Fletcher
April Greiman
Richard Kindersley
Max Kisman
Alan Kitching
Rene Knip
Henrik Kubel
Robbie Mahoney
Katherine McCoy
Julian Morey
Bruno Oldani
Angela Pelzl
David Quay
Ewald Spieker
Erik Spiekermann
Wolfgang Weingart

1,2,3

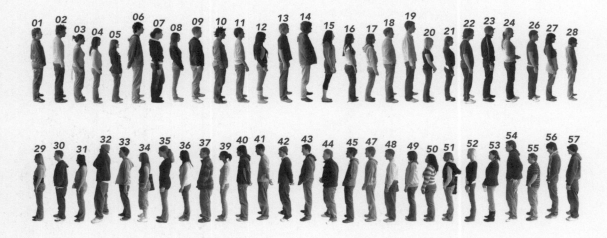

**THE FINAL YEAR STUDENTS ON OUR
BA GRAPHIC DESIGN PROGRAMME 06**

01 Robert **ALLUM** *rza_106@hotmail.com*
02 Peter **ASHBY** *cab_ashby@hotmail.com*
03 Charlotte **ASPERY** *charlotteaspery@yahoo.co.uk*
04 Jennifer **AVIS** *jenny_avis@hotmail.com*
05 Suzanne **BATTENSBY** *family@battmobile1.fsnet.co.uk*
06 Christopher **BELSON** *chrisbelson@hotmail.com*
07 Florije **BLLACAKU** *fbllacaku@hotmail.com*
08 Clair **BREWSTER** *crew_sterrr@hotmail.co.uk*
09 Andrew **CLARK** *flava4raver828@hotmail.com*
10 Peter **COOTE** *petecoote@hotmail.co.uk*
11 Matty **CURTIS** *mcurtis@studio8design.co.uk*
12 Rena **DANIAS** *butterflyatsouthampton@hotmail.com*
13 Alex **DANIEL** *alex_daniel101@yahoo.com*
14 Oliver **DASHWOOD** *oliverdashwood@hotmail.com*
15 Emily **DEAN** *i_am_emlo@hotmail.com*
16 Natalie **DRAPER** *natalie_draper@hotmail.com*
17 Brigitte **EVANS** *brigitte_evans@hotmail.com*
18 Richard **GLEESON** *richard_gleeson365@hotmail.com*
19 Andy **GOODE** *andycgoode@yahoo.co.uk*
20 Emma **HAMMOND** *katiekitten81@hotmail.com*
21 Helene Kjelstrup **HAUG** *helenehaug@gmail.com*
22 Christopher **HEATON** *cheatonc9@aol.com*
23 James **HOPTON** *jameshopton@yahoo.co.uk*
24 Kari **JACOBSEN** *kari_lj82@hotmail.com*
25 Robert **JOHNSTON** *rob@dirtyscience.co.uk*
26 Sachin **KAVIA** *sachin@kaviadesign.co.uk*
27 Hayley **KINGSTON** *hayley_kingston@yahoo.co.uk*

28 Owen **KNIGHT** *owenknight1@hotmail.com*
29 Jemma **LINDLEY** *jemma_lindley@hotmail.com*
30 Thomas **MEDHURST** *medhed84@yahoo.com*
31 Caz **MORRIS** *crazzee84@hotmail.com*
32 BK **MPAMUGO** *bk189@hotmail.com*
33 Luke **NATHAN** *luke@nlrdesign.com*
34 Hayley **NEWELL** *froggy85@hotmail.co.uk*
35 Sissel **NORDAHL** *sissel@sngd.no*
36 Nina **NORDSKOG** *nina_nordskog@hotmail.com*
37 Andrew **PORTER** *andport123@yahoo.co.uk*
38 Alan **RALPH** *spaceman98_98@yahoo.com*
39 Louise **RANGE** *louiserangeis@hotmail.com*
40 Paul **REST** *p_a_u_l_r_e_s_t_ltd@hotmail.com*
41 Steve **REYNOLDS** *safe216@hotmail.com*
42 Daniel **ROMANI** *danromani@hotmail.com*
43 Marc **ROUSSEL** *roussel1983@hotmail.com*
44 James **SMITH** *jsmith1384@yahoo.co.uk*
45 Jonathan **SMITH** *jonathan.s.smith@talk21.com*
46 Paul **SOLOMON** *johnny_toaster@hotmail.com*
47 Matthew **STAPLEFORD** *matstapes90@aol.com*
48 Jamie **STEWART** *jamiedonsimon@hotmail.com*
49 Clare **SZTYPULJAK** *little_sztyp@hotmail.com*
50 Phousa **THIRAPHOUTH** *pa_pooska@hotmail.com*
51 Emilie **TOMANN** *emilie_tomann32@hotmail.com*
52 Gunnhild **VEVATNE** *gunnhild@capilli.no*
53 Anh **VONG** *anh_vong@hotmail.com*
54 Alex **WHITTAKER** *alexwhittaker84@hotmail.com*
55 Darrel **WILLIAMS** *diddy_91@hotmail.com*
56 David **WILLIAMS** *sweatydave@hotmail.co.uk*
57 John **WILLIAMS** *johnajw@hotmail.com*

LEICESTERSHIRE
IN 1777

An edition of John Prior's map of Leicestershire
with an introduction and commentary by members of the Leicestershire Industrial History Society,
edited by J.D. Welding

1st edition 1984
ISBN 0850221722

Published by Leicestershire Libraries and Information Service, Thames Tower, Navigation Street, Leicester LE1 3TZ

Designed by Anna Ward
Typeset in Goudy Old Style by Plyglen Ltd.
Printed by Automedia

CONTENTS

	Page
Introduction	1
Key map	2
Reprint and commentary	3
List of subscribers to the map	51
Bibliography	54
Index of place names on the map	55

Illustrations

All the illustrations selected by the editor to accompany the text are from books and other sources which may be seen in the Leicestershire Collection at the Information Centre, Bishop Street, Leicester.

Acknowledgement

The list of subscribers to Prior's Map is reproduced with permission of the Bodleian Library, Oxford from Richard Gough's manuscript collection for his British Topography. 3rd edition. (Shelfmark – Gough. GEN Top 363-6).

INTRODUCTION

Leicestershire in 1777 was a very different county from the Leicestershire of today. The population, especially of the County Town, was much smaller, there were no railways crossing the landscape, and even canals had only just started to appear. Many landmarks have been built since the time when the map was made, and some have even come and gone in the interim. Successive maps have recorded this process over the last 200 years, especially the Ordnance Survey maps from 1835 onwards, but John Prior's was the first Leicestershire map to be surveyed at a scale sufficient to allow the detailed depiction of features of the landscape. We offer this reprint in the hope that it will encourage the reader to reflect on both the changes and the continuities of the last two centuries.

The research for the commentary has been undertaken by Alan Brittan, Phyl Davies, Peter Neaverson, Michael Tidd and myself. We are all members of the Leicestershire Industrial History Society, and we were drawn to the map by the industrial features on it, but the map has shown us these in the wider context of 18th century life. The inspiration for the project came from the enthusiasm for the map of Dr. Marilyn Palmer, Head of the Department of History at Loughborough University, who is secretary of the Society and tutor in industrial archaeology at Vaughan College, Leicester.

I am very grateful to Mr. Derek Day of the Social Studies Library, Oxford, for transcribing the original list of subscribers from the Bodleian Library. I am also indebted to Dr. Harold Fox of the Department of English Local History, Leicester University, for his valuable comments on the introductory pages. I should also like to thank the Librarian of the Royal Society of Arts, for providing access to the Society's minute books, to Leicestershire County Record Office for access to their collections, and to Simon Harrington of Leicestershire Libraries for undertaking this reprint. The book collections of Leicester University Library I tend to take for granted.

The map is reprinted from the copy held in the Leicestershire Collection, Leicester. Original printings can also be seen at Loughborough Library, at the Leicestershire Record Office in New Walk, Leicester, and in several national collections.

There has been room on our commentary pages for only brief notes about some features of the map which have interested us. The reprint will be of most value for readers who use it as a starting point for further study. It is interesting to compare Prior's map with current and with early Ordnance Survey maps, and with larger scale maps of particular areas. It can lead to the pursuit of much fuller information in historical books, old and new. And it can be taken outdoors into the Leicestershire countryside, to find comparisons between the Leicestershire of 200 years ago and the Leicestershire of today.

David Welding.
Leicester University
Library.
March 1984.

1

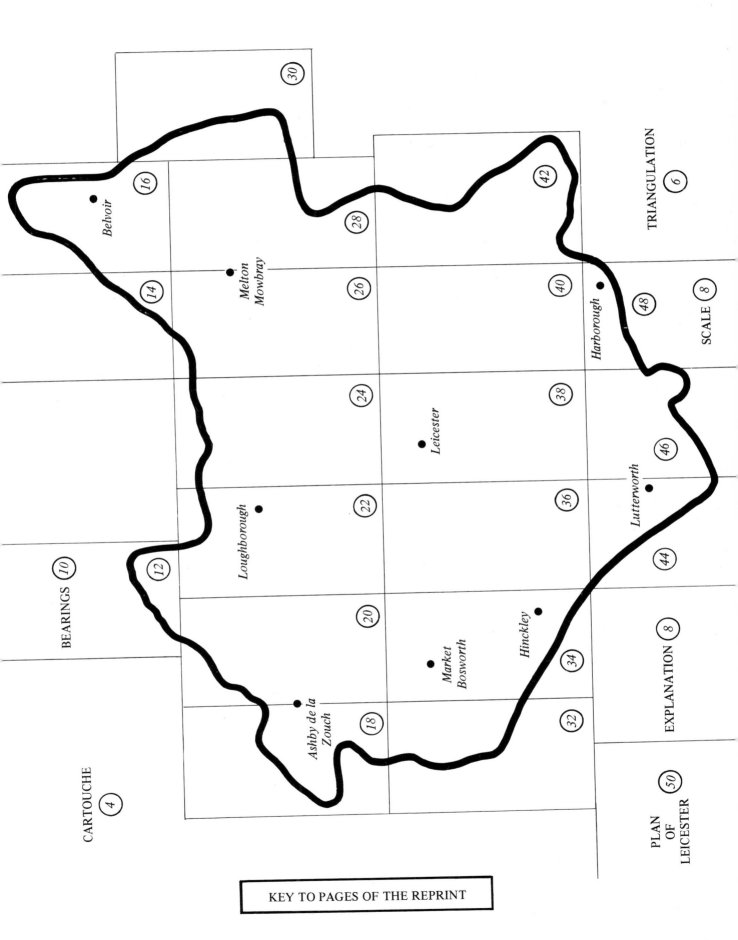

CARTOUCHE ④

BEARINGS ⑩

TRIANGULATION ⑥

SCALE ⑧

EXPLANATION ⑧

PLAN OF LEICESTER ㊿

Belvoir

⑯

⑭

⑫

Melton Mowbray

Loughborough

Ashby de la Zouch

⑱

⑳

㉒

㉔

㉖

㉘

Leicester

Market Bosworth

Hinckley

㉜

㉞

㊱

㊳

㊵

㊷

Harborough

Lutterworth

㊸

㊺

㊹

KEY TO PAGES OF THE REPRINT

2

JOHN PRIOR
1729-1803

John Prior was only incidentally a map maker. By profession he was a schoolmaster and clergyman, for most of his life at Ashby-de-la-Zouch. He was born at Swithland in August 1729, the son of a steward to the Danvers family. He went to school at Woodhouse, and did so well there that at the age of 15 he was appointed master of the same school. He also served as curate of Woodhouse and Quorn from 1755 until 1763, when he was appointed master of the Grammar School at Ashby, where he remained for the next forty years.

In the same year he married a Miss Ann Cox of Quorndon, and they had a son John, who became curate of Willesley, and three daughters, before her death in 1774. Prior took the degree of BD at Emmanuel College, Cambridge in 1772, and in 1782 was presented to the vicarage at Ashby, adding that of Packington in 1792. He taught in the school to within 8 days of his death on October 15th 1803, and his monument is to be found on the North side of Ashby church.

John Prior seems to have been a fine example of an eighteenth century type, the clergyman-schoolmaster who had wide ranging interests and abilities. His professional duties were perhaps not too onerous, for at the time of his death it is recorded that there were only three or four pupils at the school. He was noted particularly for mathematical ability, and it was this that led him to take an interest in surveying methods. He was knowledgeable in musical theory, and was a good performer on the violin. There is a story that when the Earl of Huntingdon described him as a 'poor preacher', one of his friends replied 'but you should hear him fiddle'. His classical scholarship was shown in the publication of an appendix to the Eton Latin Grammar, and he learned Hebrew when past sixty years of age, in order to read the Old Testament in the original language. His obituary in the Gentleman's Magazine describes his 'mild and unassuming temper, perfect freedom from ambition, love of music, and relish for the calm delights of literature, friendship, and domestic society'.

With all his commitments and diverse interests, Prior did not have the time to make a survey of Leicestershire himself. The surveying, which lasted from 1775 to 1777, was carried out by Joseph Whyman. He lived at Aston on Trent in Derbyshire and was a former pupil of Prior the schoolmaster. He had learned his surveying, however, as assistant to Peter P. Burdett, whose map of Derbyshire was published in 1767. Whyman had made at least one Leicestershire estate map under his own name, but the Leicestershire survey was to be his major contribution to cartography. Prior was acquainted with Burdett, and had originally asked him to make the survey of Leicestershire, but Burdett was bound for Germany at the time. So the arrangement was made that Whyman would work under contract to Prior, under his 'direction and inspection', following the principles which they had both learned from Burdett. Prior undertook the financial responsibility, and raised subscriptions from 'several of the first people of the county'. He was obviously worried about not giving Whyman due credit, but in the end felt that he should take the responsibility himself. He explained himself, 'I undertook the business in compliment to the gentlemen of the county (as no other person would do it) and to serve my scholar Mr. Whyman'.

Prior succeeded in obtaining 264 subscribers to his map, some of them taking more than one copy (see list on p.51-53). Local gentry and clergymen are well represented, but there are also lawyers, doctors, and a number of names from outside the county. The most important patron was Francis Earl of Huntingdon, who had already favoured Prior with the appointment to the school at Ashby. When the map was ready the Earl did its author another favour in addressing a letter to Lord Romney at the Society of Arts, on January 20th, 1778.

'My Lord, A map of the county of Leicester, executed by the Revd. Mr. Prior, being to be laid before the Society of Arts etc immediately after the holidays, I take the liberty of troubling your Lordship with my testimony in favour of the author and his work. Mr. Prior is master of a Grammar School at Ashby de la Zouch, where I placed him, and where he has behaved so meritoriously that I intend presenting him to the living, when it becomes vacant. Those parts of the county that are within my knowledge are very exactly delineated and the remainder is universally allowed to be done with equal accuracy. He has a family of children and (as yet) but a small income, and for his learning and good morals deserves reward and encouragement. I have the honour . . .'

Huntingdon

To the Right Honourable,

FRANCIS EARL of HUNTINGDON,

Baron, Hastings, Hungerford, Newmark, Peverel,

Botreaux, Molins, Moels and de Homet.

By His Lordships Permifsion

This MAP of

LEICESTERSHIRE

from an actual Survey,

Begun in the Year 1775, and finished in the Year 1777,

With the utmost Gratitude and Respect

IS DEDICATED,

By His Lordships

most obliged

most obedient and

most humble Servant

John Prior.

Engrav'd by J.Luffman N.º 98 Newgate Street, London.

LEICESTERSHIRE
ACCURATELY SURVEYED

Prior's map of Leicestershire was the 29th of 42 county maps to be published between 1748 and 1797, so it takes its place in a very extensive remapping of the country by private surveyors. It was such 18th century developments as the building of new country houses, the rise of industries, and especially the increase of travel on the new turnpike roads, that gave rise to a demand for maps showing these features.

This development was recognised in, and fostered by, the awards granted by the Society of Arts. The Society, which had been founded in 1754, awarded premiums for developments in a wide variety of different aspects of agriculture, industry and art. One of the enterprises the Society sought to encourage was cartography. A premium for a county map was offered in 1759, then annually between 1762 and 1766. During this time only two premiums were actually awarded, to Benjamin Donn for his Devon in 1765 and to P. P. Burdett for Derbyshire in 1767, and several maps were rejected for what might appear to be technical or capricious reasons. Between 1767 and 1786 the annual premiums were not offered but occasional honorary 'bounties' were made available. One of these was for £50 to Andrew Armstrong for his map of Northumberland in 1769. It was during this period of occasional bounties that Prior's map was prepared, although he did not seem to have been aware until very late that the premiums had been discontinued. On discovering the change of rules he wrote to the Secretary of the Society.

'Now, Sir, as what I principally wish, is the *Honour* of the Encouragement of such a learned and respectable Society, I shall be exceedingly thankful for ever so small a sum.'

The map was accordingly sent from Ashby to London 'by the diligence' in January 1778. It must then have been in a manuscript version, for the Secretary was requested, after the Society had finished with it, to send it to Mr. Dawson, Bookseller in Pater-Noster Row, who would get it engraved. The Society's Committee of Polite Arts considered the map on February 6th, 1778, but deferred a decision. This same Committee, but with an entirely different membership, met again on February 20th, and took into account both the testimonial from the Earl of Huntingdon, and a letter from Mr. Hodgkinson, one of their members, who gave evidence 'That he has examined some of the principle angles given by Mr. Prior in his Survey of Leicestershire and that the same appear to be planned with accuracy'. The Committee 'Resolved that this map is neatly executed' and 'Resolved to recommend to the Society to give twenty guineas and the silver medal to the Reverend Mr. Prior for his Survey of Leicestershire'. This recommendation went to a meeting of the Society on 25th March. There a motion was put that the word *silver* be omitted and the word *gold* be inserted, but this was overruled; we shall never know who made the proposal or why he was voted down. However the Society did agree that the inscription on the silver medal should read 'Leicestershire accurately surveyed' and this must have given Prior a great deal of satisfaction.

Careful study shows, however, that the map is not an entirely accurate record of Leicestershire topography in 1777. The most glaring inaccuracy is the reversal of the villages of Kibworth Harcourt and Kibworth Beauchamp. The placing of watermills can be a mile or two up or down stream, and the extent of parks and woodlands can be a little arbitrary. Nevertheless Prior's map represented an enormous advance in the cartography of the county. The last full Leicestershire map to be founded on any significant fieldwork was Christopher Saxton's of 1576, and between Saxton and Prior all the other county maps were derivative. Prior's map represents two or three years' work on the part of Joseph Whyman, using 18th century instruments and techniques, and at a scale of almost 1″ to the mile. The triangulation on which the map was based is reproduced 'for a testimony of the accuracy of this work', and it was independent confirmation of the accuracy of the angles which obtained the approval of the Society of Arts. The prospectus lays even more emphasis on the calculations of latitude and longitude, also reproduced on the map, which it claims give 'an exactness not to be found in any other MAP whatever.' But while for the contemporary it was the accuracy of positioning of the major settlements, and the network of roads between them, that was important, for the historian the interest lies principally in the detail, the picture it gives of a rural Leicestershire, on the eve of its industrial expansion.

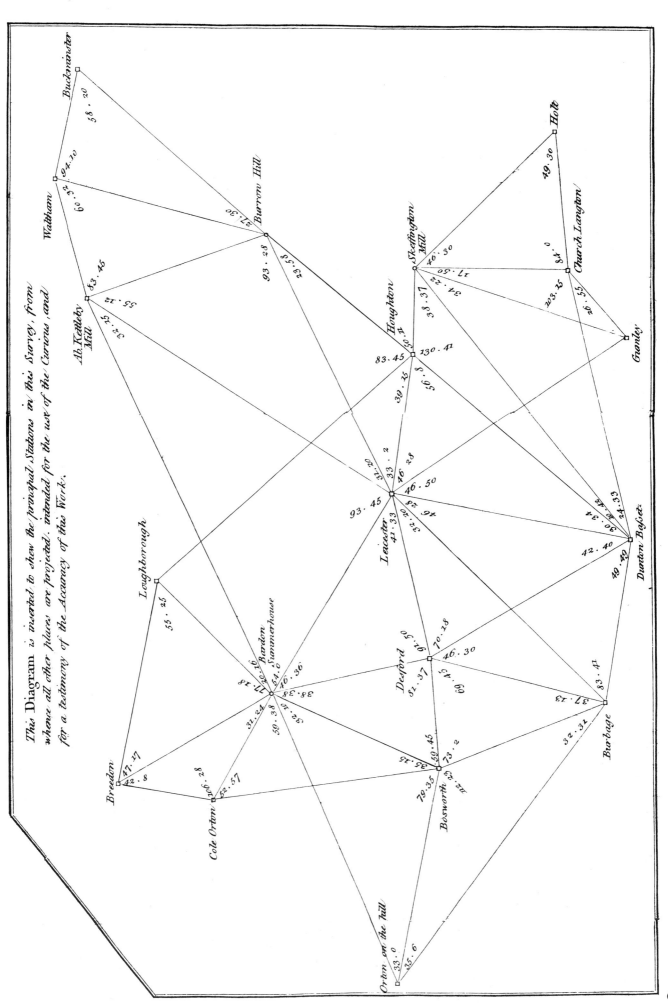

This Diagram is inserted to shew the principal Stations in this Survey, from whence all other places are projected, intended for the use of the Curious, and for a testimony of the Accuracy of this Work.

6

LEICESTERSHIRE IN 1777

'Leicestershire has not many gentlemen's houses of note in it, and not many matters of curiosity, but has much rich pasture, and feeds great numbers of cattle and sheep.'

So observed William Bray on his journey through Leicestershire in 1777, the year that the survey for Prior's map was completed. The cattle and sheep are of course not visible on the map, but the county does present a pleasantly rural aspect with its small settlements, open spaces, abundance of mills and scattered patches of woodland. Although there are not many houses 'of note' there are evident quite a number of houses of the minor variety, the houses in many cases of the gentlemen who subscribed to Mr. Prior's survey. (Unlike some cartographers, Prior resists the temptation to write the name of each gentleman beside his house.)

The population of Leicestershire in 1777 would have been between the 98,000 of 1750 and the 130,000 of 1801 (for comparison, in 1981 it was over 800,000). Therefore we should not be surprised at the comparative smallness of the towns and even the city. The map provides symbols to distinguish market towns from ordinary villages, and also shows seats (ie. country houses) and isolated farmhouses. Each village shows an individual shape, and certainly gives the impression that its layout has been accurately represented.

The hundreds, ancient administrative units, are shown, with a dotted line to mark their boundaries. The Leicestershire hundreds are Guthlaxton, Sparkenhoe, Gartree, East Goscote, West Goscote and Framland.

Prior's map captures a Leicestershire in which the process of enclosure, which had been in progress for over two centuries, was drawing close to completion. Sixty percent of the county had been enclosed by 1760, and a large number of Acts for Enclosure were passed each year during the 1760's and 1770's. Enclosure had an effect on the landscape Prior depicted, but, like most contemporary surveyors at this scale, Prior did not attempt to show field boundaries, hedges or fences, and so the map does not show the difference between enclosed and unenclosed parishes. The purpose of enclosure was particularly for the development of pasture to accommodate the 'great numbers of cattle and sheep', and it gradually gave rise to the building of farmhouses at the centres of the enclosed farms. It also made easier the development of country parks, sometimes replacing a deserted village or alongside a village very much reduced in size. Apart from the wastes of Charnwood Forest, virtually all the county was under cultivation by 1777, making Leicestershire one of the most heavily cultivated counties in England.

The map is particularly detailed in its indication of roads, both the turnpikes and the network of minor lanes which criss-crossed even remote areas of the county. The takeover of major roads by turnpike trusts had begun in the county in 1726, with the main London road through Harborough via Leicester to Loughborough. In 1753-4 the roads from Hinckley, Coventry, Uppingham, Narborough and Ashby were turnpiked, and a number of other roads were added in the 1760's. The map indicates not only the milestones along the roads, but also the positions of the tollbars at which the finance for the maintenance of the roads was collected from travellers.

Only one stretch of canal is shown, taking the River Soar from the North about one and a half miles into Loughborough, and there is also the new cut at Zouch Mills on the Soar. In including these the map is very up-to-date, for it had only just been cut by the time the map was published. The main development of the canal system in Leicestershire had to wait for the 1790's.

There are considerable signs of mineral exploitation, particularly in the north west of the county. Several coal pits are shown, and a number of 'fire engines' are mentioned. These would have been steam driven pumping engines, or 'engines for raising water by fire'. A lead mine is marked, and several lime works are shown, although established quarries such as the one at Swithland do not appear. The activity which the map conceals, because it was purely domestic, was the growing industry of framework knitting. There were over 1,000 frames in Leicester alone, and many of the villages were also involved. The distinction between the industrial villages of the West and the purely agricultural ones of the east of the county was beginning to appear.

Windmills and watermills are the industrial features most clearly shown on the map. There are ninety-two watermill symbols, but some mills which did exist were certainly omitted. Most were devoted to grinding corn, both for bread and for animal food, but some others, such as a papermill, are mentioned. Eighty-one windmills are marked, the majority in the east of the county. They would have been mostly post mills, so vulnerable to fire, and capable of being removed from one site to another. The number of mills does indicate how much grain was still grown in a county renowned for its pastoral economy.

EXPLANATION

Plans of
{
  Market Towns . . . .
  Villages . . . .
  Seats . . . .
  Farmhouses . . . .
}

Churches and Chapels . . . .

Wind Mills . . . .

Water Mills . . . .

Coal Pits . . . .

Lime Works . . . .

Turnpike Roads with Tollbars and Milestones

Cross Roads . . . .

Boundaries of the Hundreds . . . .

Roman Stations . . . .

Furlongs   Statute Miles
1 2 3 4 5 6 7 8 1   2   3   4   5   6

Geographic Miles
1   2   3   4   5

THIS DAY IS PUBLISHED

After the Society of Arts had sat in judgement on the map, there was still a year to elapse before publication was achieved. The next stage was for Dawson the bookseller to get the map engraved, and the engraver he chose was J. Luffman, whose name appears on the finished product. Publication was finally heralded in the Leicester and Nottingham Journal on Saturday, 20th March 1779, in the announcement reproduced below. The map could be bought in sheets for one guinea, or pasted on canvas with rollers, and the turnpike roads coloured, for one guinea and a half. It could be obtained from Mr. Dawson in London, Mr. Gregory in Leicester, or Mr. Prior himself, 'those, who have not already paid, sending their subscriptions.' The final size of the map was 48″×44″. A reduced size edition was published in 1787, without the cartouche, triangulation, or plan of Leicester, and omitting features such as mills, industry, and Roman stations. A second edition was published by W. Faden in 1804, the year after Prior's death.

THIS DAY IS PUBLISHED,
A MAP of the COUNTY of LEICESTER;
From an ACTUAL SURVEY:
By Mr. JOSEPH WHYMAN:
Under the Direction of the Rev. J. PRIOR, B. D.
of ASHBY-DE-LA-ZOUCH.

Price in Sheets, One Guinea; or pasted on Canvas, with Rollers, and the Turnpike-Roads, &c. coloured, One Guinea and an Half.

For the Convenience of the SUBSCRIBERS, the MAP will be delivered by Mr. DAWSON, No. 7, Pater-noster-Row, London; Mr. GREGORY, in Leicester; or the Rev. Mr. PRIOR, in Ashby-de-la-Zouch; those who have not already paid, sending their Subscriptions.

⁎ Mr. PRIOR takes this Opportunity of returning his most respectful Thanks to those NOBLEMEN and GENTLEMEN, who have honoured him with their SUBSCRIPTIONS; to the Society for the Encouragement of Arts, Manufactures, and Commerce, for the Premium they were pleased to assign him, and the Medal they have honoured him with; he also acknowledges his Obligations to many of his Friends for their kind Assistance in carrying on the Work.—Mr. PRIOR also begs Leave to acquaint the Public, that the Position of the Meridian was determined by Astronomical Observations, and not, as usual, by the *Magnetic Needle* only, and the Scale of Longitude and Latitude from some curious and accurate Calculations, of which an Account is given in the MAP; and he ventures to affirm, that the Latitude of any Place in the County may be found to half a Minute of a Degree, and the Difference of its Meridian from that of *Greenwich* to two or three Seconds of Time;—an Exactness not to be found in any other MAP whatever.

Leicester and Nottingham Journal, 20th March 1779
(Leicestershire Libraries)

The Latitude of S.t Martin's church in Leicester is 52.38. See Phil. Trans. 1775.
The difference between the Meridians of S.t Martin's in Leicester and the Observatory
at Greenwich is 4 minutes and 35 seconds of time to the West. See Phil. Trans. 1778.
The Measure of a Degree on the Meridian in Lat. 52,38 is 57122,56 Toises, or
69,1803 Miles. See De la Lande's Astronomy article 2651 &c.
A Degree of Longitude, measured on the Parallel of 52,38 is 34885 Toises, or
42,2488 Miles. See De la Lande's Ast. art. 2698.

St. Martin's Church, Leicester from Nichols, J. History and Antiquities of the County of Leicester. Vol. I.

This section of the map follows the county boundary along the rivers Trent and Soar. The river Trent had been used for navigation as far as Burton since 1699. Its use for transport was already ending with the opening of the Trent and Mersey Canal in several stages between 1770 and 1777. The Derwent joining the Trent was navigable to Derby. Attempts to make the Soar navigable had begun with the letters patent granted to Thomas Skipworth in 1634, but funds were insufficient and it was not till 1778 that the river was made navigable to Loughborough. At Red Hill on this sheet there was a staunch (a kind of lock) where the Soar joined the Trent.

The Ashby-Nottingham and Loughborough-Derby turnpikes crossed in this section, but there was no settlement at the crossroads. The Loughborough-Derby turnpike crossed the Trent at Cavendish Bridge, which had been erected in the middle of the century to replace a ferry, and which survived until 1947. Kegworth Bridge over the Soar had been rebuilt in 1758, as a five-arched bridge to replace a 14th century construction.

Castle Donington was the largest settlement in this area, with a population of around 1,800. The site of the ruined 12th century castle is marked. Kegworth had a population of about 1,000, in 250 houses. Lockington had been enclosed since the beginning of the 17th century and had a population of only about 200 in 1,700 acres. The hall there was the seat of the Bainbridge family until 1797. Hemington had about 300 people in 1,400 acres, and was not enclosed until 1789. The church marked there had been ruined since the 16th century, and the village was in Lockington parish.

The most important house was that in Donington Park, which was the residence of Francis Earl of Huntingdon, the map's dedicatee. In the mid eighteenth century it had been visited by John Wesley on several occasions, for Selina Countess of Huntingdon was a firm supporter of the Methodists, but her son Francis as a deist was strongly opposed to their doctrines. The Tudor house of 1595 only survived until 1793, when it was demolished and the present Hall built.

Kings Mills on the Trent were Crown property from 1400 to 1609, the site having been used since Domesday for cornmilling, but also during the 17th century for forging and cloth fulling, and during the 18th century for papermaking. Kegworth Mill on the Soar had been in use since the 14th century.

Cavendish Bridge on the River Trent, from Nichols, J. The History and Antiquities of the County of Leicester. Vol. III.

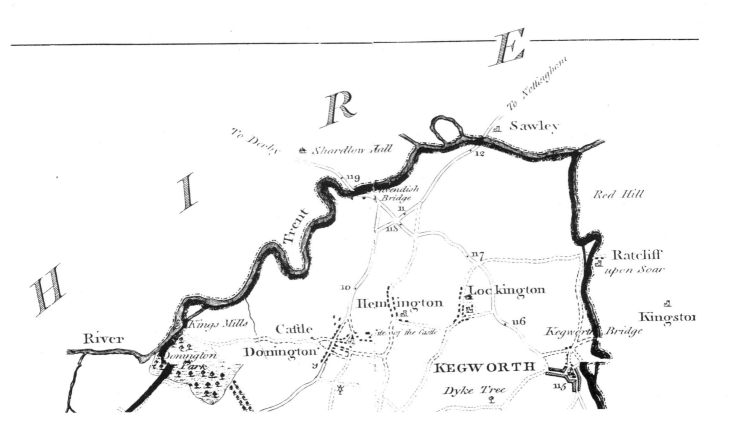

H I R E

To Derby

To Nottingham

Sawley

Shardlow Hall

12

119

Cavendish
Bridge

11

Red Hill

118

Trent

117

Ratcliff
upon Soar

10

Lockington

Hemington

116

Kingstor

River

Kings Mills

Castle

Site of the Castle

Kegworth Bridge

Donnington
Park

Donington

9

KEGWORTH

115

Dyke Tree

There is very little to comment on in this small corner of the Vale of Belvoir bordering Nottinghamshire. It had to wait another 200 years before becoming the centre of attention during the planning enquiry concerning mining in the Vale.

The manor of Long Clawson passed into the possession of the Earl of Rutland early in the 17th century. In Prior's time there were over 500 people in the village. Enclosure here took place in the year the map was published. The ironstone church dates mainly from the 14th century. The churches of Harby and Hose are also of ironstone, and have its characteristic warm colour.

Hose came into the Earl of Rutland's possession in the 16th century. Half the land was old enclosure, but half remained in open fields until 1791. Hose in 1790 contained 256 inhabitants. Hose Grange Nichols

described as a 'large old house, which formerly belonged to the family of Dashwood, and is now a farmhouse'. Piper Hole to the south of Hose was an overgrown, secret spot. It was reputed to have been a place where the Parliamentary forces concealed their plunder in the Civil War, but its contemporary usefulness was as a cover for foxes.

Harby came into the ownership of the Earl of Rutland in the 17th century. There were about 300 people in the village at the time of the survey for the map. Enclosure did not take place until 1790, and a good number of freeholders remained in the village, to work their own land. They took their grain for grinding to the local post mill, which continued in use for another hundred years. Another post mill appears just over the Nottinghamshire border at Hickling. This fell into ruin and was blown down well before 1820, when a brick tower mill was built.

Long 'Claxton' Church, from Nichols J. The History and Antiquities of the County of Leicester. *Vol. II.*

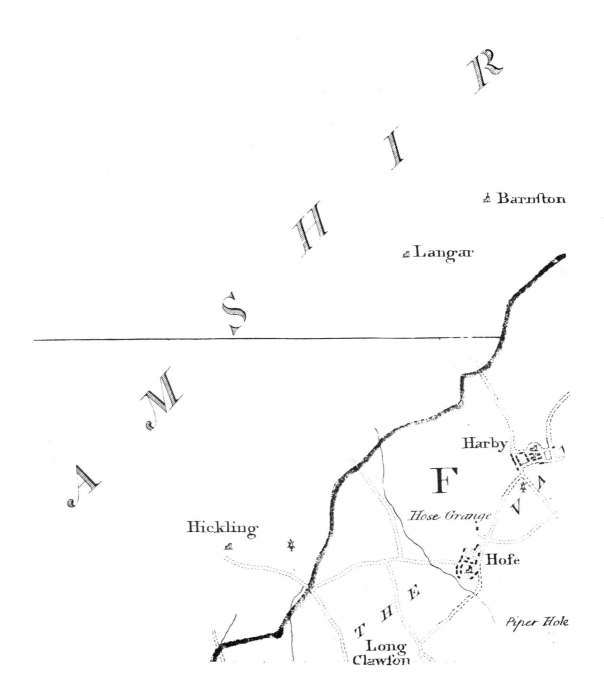

A M S H I R

⌂ Barnſton

⌂ Langar

Harby

F

Hose Grange

V

Hickling

Hofe

Piper Hole

T H E

Long
Clawſon

This northern part of Leicestershire was dominated by the presence of Belvoir Castle. There had been two successive castles on the site before the house Prior saw, which was completed in 1668. It was a large plain rectangular mansion, with an east front eighty-four yards long. The imitation medieval castle which we know today was not built until 1800-1830. Lords of the Manor were the Manners family, Earls of Rutland until 1703 when they were created Dukes. In Prior's time the Lord was John the Third Duke of Rutland. He made some improvements to the castle such as the addition of a picture room and cellars, and the enhancement of the plantations on the slopes around the castle. The Third Duke died in 1779, and the Fourth Duke who succeeded him was known for extravagant expenditure during his short career. Part of this expenditure was on paintings, and he added to the collection fine examples by Rubens, Van Dyck, Frans Hals, and Sir Joshua Reynolds.

Belvoir Castle dominated the area not only physically but also economically. The Duke of Rutland could look out upon 'two and twenty manors of his own paternal inheritance.' His income from property was given as £20,000 a year, and he was patron of twenty churches. No framework knitting was permitted in the Vale of Belvoir, so an influx of poor workers was prevented. The first outside intrusion into the Vale came with the Grantham Canal, which was opened in 1793. The relationship of the villagers to their Lord is illustrated by the fact that every Thursday morning at the castle there was a distribution of fifty-six penny loaves to the poor of nine parishes; Woolsthorpe received five, Knipton nine, Plungar three, Barkston six, Redmile six, Bottesford eighteen, Muston six, Braunston five, and Croxton eight.

Croxton Park was a hunting lodge of the Dukes of Rutland. The house itself (see p.28) was built in 1730 by the Third Duke. The park covered 800 acres and was formerly the site of Croxton Abbey.

Bottesford church is dominated by the tombs of the Manners family of Belvoir, but also contains the finest monumental brass in the county. This was the largest village in the area, with over 800 inhabitants. There was a

Bede House or men's hospital which was founded in 1590, and this was extended in 1786. Its occupants were predictably former employees on the Belvoir estate. Normanton, the most northerly village in the county, contained just under 100 inhabitants.

Woolsthorpe was actually in Lincolnshire, though only a mile due east of Belvoir Castle. The map is not precise in defining the county boundary at this point. The inhabitants in 1775 numbered 333. The Manners family were Lords of the Manor and had built the school here. Redmile was a comparatively large village, with 250 inhabitants. The Duke of Rutland owned three-quarters of the village lands, the rest being divided between twenty freeholders. There had once been an attempt at coalmining at Redmile. A shaft was sunk to a depth of sixty feet, before severe flooding prevented further exploitation. The ironstone was also dug, mainly as a freestone for building, rather than for commercial use.

At the small village of Eastwell there was only one freeholder who could vote at the general election of 1778, and he was also the churchwarden and constable. The leading family here were the Eyres, who were Catholics, and there were more Catholic families in the village. The hall where the Eyres lived had been built in 1634. Twenty years after Prior's map this estate too passed into the ownership of the Dukes of Rutland. At the time of the sale the estate was described as in fine sporting country, in the territory of the Meynell, the Rutland, and the Lowther hunts. The neighbouring village of Eaton was the home of Thomas Wright, who described himself as 'grazier, astronomer, mathematician, and professor of astrology', and whose chief claim to fame was the authorship in the 1770's and 80's of the original Moore's Almanack.

The mills on the Devon at Bottesford and at Knipton were Domesday sites. The latter lost its water rights with the building of the reservoir for the Grantham Canal. Of the six post mills, the one at Stathern worked until 1892, and that at Eaton until 1908.

Belvoir Castle, from Throsby, J. Select views in Leicestershire from original drawings. *1789.*

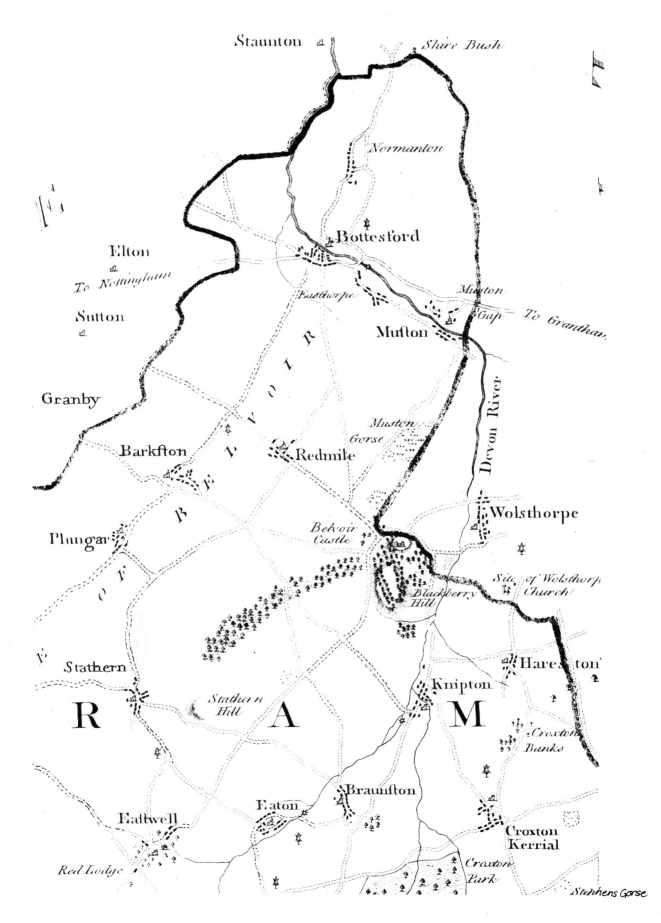

Staunton

Shire Bush

Normanton

Elton

To Nottingham

Sutton

Granby

Bottesford

Eastthorpe

Muston

Muston

Gap

To Grantham

Barkston

Redmile

Muston
Gorse

Devon River

Plungar

Belvoir
Castle

Wolsthorpe

Site of Wolsthorpe
Church

Blackberry
Hill

Stathern

Hareston

R

Stathern
Hill

A

Knipton

M

Croxton
Banks

Eattwell

Eaton

Braunston

Croxton
Kerrial

Red Lodge

Croxton
Park

Stephens Gorse

16

The central band of this section of the map, including Measham and the coal mining area surrounding it, were part of Derbyshire in the 18th century. In black and white the county boundary is a little difficult to trace. From south to north it runs from No Mans Heath to the River Mease, which it follows to Measham Field. It then runs above Measham to encircle Willesley, skirts the bottom of Ashby Woulds, and rejoins the Mease at Stretton in the Fields.

Coal mining had already begun around Measham and Oakthorpe. A steam pumping engine, marked F. engine, which was installed in 1729, is shown with the mines between these villages. The entrepreneur exploiting these reserves was Joseph Wilkes, who was also prominent in the cotton trade, and was one of the subscribers to the map.

The northern section of the Leicestershire part was dominated by the wastes of Ashby Woulds, which were not enclosed until 1800, and several large areas of woodland. Coal mining and iron working did not begin on Ashby Woulds until 1804, and the Ashby Canal was developed soon afterwards to take the coal to market. The area was well served by roads but sparsely populated. The main settlements were Blackfordby, Boothorpe, Nether Seal and Over Seal, but these parishes together totalled less than 1,500 in population.

Prestop Park had belonged to the manor of Ashby-de-la-Zouch since the 15th century.

The southern section, crossed by the Ashby/Tamworth and Tamworth/Burton turnpikes, had three principal settlements: Appleby Magna, Appleby Parva, and Snarestone, with some 1,300 people in all.

The School at Appleby Parva had been built in the 1690's, to a design by Sir Christopher Wren, although modified by a Leicester architect, Sir William Wilson. The School was founded by Sir John Moore, a grocer and Lord Mayor of London. The church at Snarestone had been rebuilt in brick in 1733. The parish also possessed a free school (not marked on the map) donated in 1717 by Thomas Chamells who also founded a library for the villagers' use.

There are three mills shown on the Mease. The one near Measham was to become the property of Joseph Wilkes who bought the parish of Measham in 1783 following his profitable operations on the Trent Navigation. The mill was later used as a tape mill then as a bleach mill. Although it was disused in 1883, buildings remain on this site. Stretton Mill was a Domesday site. The mill standing today was built in 1633 and worked until 1938. Barrat Pool had a windmill and watermill together, and the pool was reputed to be well stocked with fish.

Appleby School, Appleby Parva, from Nichols, J. The History and Antiquities of the County of Leicester. Vol. IV.

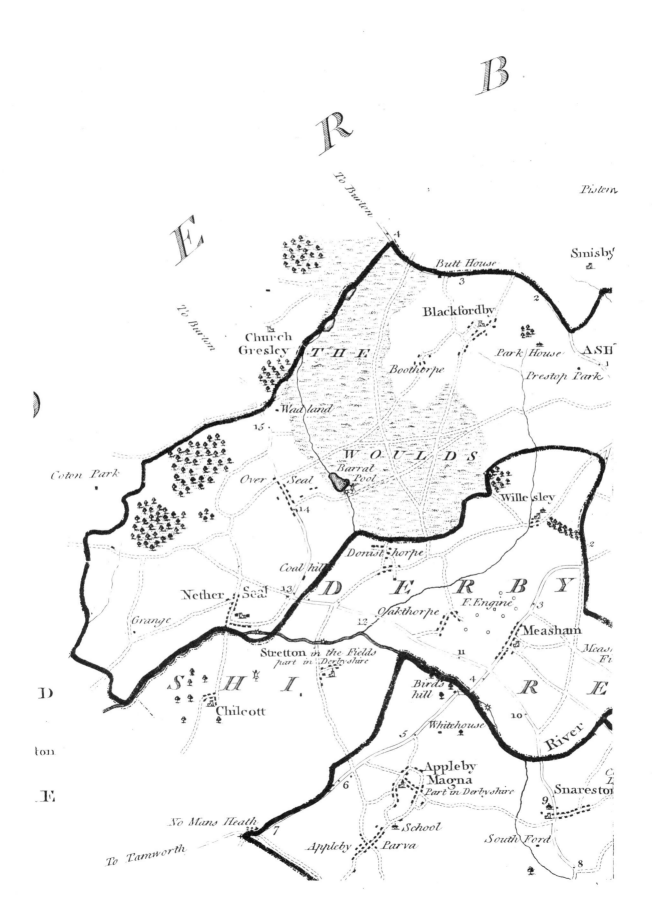

E   R   B

To Burton

Pistern

To Burton

Butt House   Smisby

3

Blackfordby   2

Church
Gresley   THE   Park House   ASH

Boothorpe   Prestop Park

Wadland

15   W O U L D S

Coton Park   Barral   Willesley
                              Pool
Over   Seal

14   Donisthorpe   2

Coal hill

Nether   Seal   13   D   E   R   B   Y

Grange   Oakthorpe   F. Engine   3

12   Measham

Stretton in the Fields   11   Meas.
part in Derbyshire   F.

D   Birds   4   R   E
                                         hill
S   H   I.   10

Chilcott   Whitehouse   River

ton   5

E   6   Appleby
                              Magna   Snareston
                              Part in Derbyshire   9

No Mans Heath   7   School   South Ford

To Tamworth   Appleby Parva   8

18

This sheet is well filled with a large number of settlements, wooded and waste land, a well established road network, and much evidence of the kind of industrial activity which had an effect on the landscape.

The largest settlement was Ashby-de-la-Zouch, with some 2,500 people. Coleorton, Ibstock, Thringstone, Whitwick and Worthington had under 1,000 people each, Belton, Breedon, Diseworth, Hugglescote, Packington and Swannington had populations of under 500. Missing from its modern position on the sheet is the town of Coalville, which was not established until 1833, but Long Lane, along which Coalville grew, is shown.

Ashby-de-la-Zouch was a large parish, some 7,400 acres, with a market established in 1260. The castle is marked on the map as 'in ruins' as it is today. The town had three schools, the Grammar School founded in 1567 being that at which John Prior was master. The town's development as a spa did not begin until the following century.

The Ferrers family lived at Staunton Hall, where rebuilding of the house by Washington 5th Earl Ferrers had begun in 1760 and was still in progress. It was set in a 150 acre park, part of the much larger estate acquired by the Shirley family in 1423 by marriage with the Stauntons. Formal avenues of trees, as well as the house and the famous Commonwealth church, are marked.

At Ravenstone the Hall was built in 1725. Breedon lay in another great park which had been divided into farms by Henry Shirley in 1623. Coleorton lay in a 3,000 acre medieval park, which had been disparked in 1641. The house had been demolished in 1683. Calke Park, shown on this section of the map, was always in Derbyshire. It had been built in 1703 by Sir John Harpur.

There was an established road network across the area, with turnpikes from Ashby to Nottingham, Hathern, Loughborough and Leicester, and the Hinckley to Melbourne road. These roads provided the only means of transport for the expanding mineral extraction industries.

Limestone workings are shown at Osgathorpe and at Barrow Hill, although those at Breedon are omitted. Widespread coal pits occur at Lount, Newbold, Coleorton and Swannington, where mining had been recorded since the 13th century. No coal workings are shown in the southern part of the area, although they were recorded at Heather in 1638. 'Fire engines' are marked at Lount, Newbold and at Alton Grange: it is likely that there were several more. A lead mine is marked near Staunton Harold. This was known as Earl Ferrers mine, and a cupola for smelting lead had been built there by the end of the 18th century. The mine was later used to extract ironstone.

There are five mills on the Gilwiskaw Brook (or River Mease). Packington Mill, a Domesday site, still survives, though derelict since the 1940's. Clock Mill near Swepstone dates from the 16th century and was used until 1967. Of the mills marked on the Sence only Heather Mill now remains. Belton Mill on the Gracedieu Brook belonged to the monks at Gracedieu at one time. Wilson Mill dates from 1240, and Worthington from 1660.

Of the five windmills only two were mapped in 1835. Ashby post mill was sold and removed in 1844. The tower mill in the north-east corner of the section had been newly built in 1773, and survived until the 1940's.

Market Place, Ashby-de-la-Zouch, from A Descriptive and historical guide to Ashby-de-la-Zouch. *T. Wayte. 1831.*

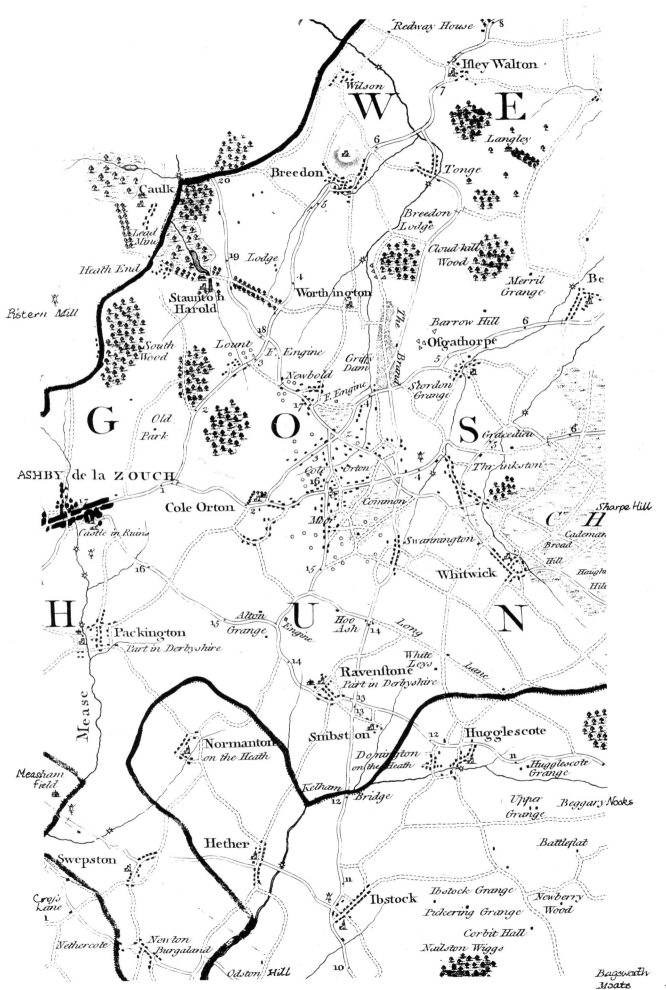

Redway House 8

Ifley Walton

W   E

Wilson   7

Langley

6

Breedon   Tonge

Caulk   Breedon
                              Lodge

20   Cloud hill
                           Wood

Lead Mine   Merril
                                       Grange   Be

Heath End   Barrow Hill   6

Pistern Mill   Staunton   19 Lodge   4   Worthington
                    Harold   Ofgathorpe

South   Lount   F. Engine   Griff   5
Wood   18   Dam
                           Newbold   F. Engine   Stordon
                    3   Grange

G   17
                    Old   2   F. Engine
                    Park   S   Gracedieu
O   3
ASHBY de la ZOUCH   Cole Orton   4   Thrinkston

Castle in Ruins   Cole Orton   2   Common   C H   Sharpe Hill
                                 16   Cademan
                           Moor   Swannington   Broad
                    16   15   Hill   Haigh
                                                   Whitwick   Hill

H   15 Alton   Hoo   N
        Packington   Grange U Engine Ash 14 Long
        Part in Derbyshire   14   Lane
                           14   White
                                      Leys
                    Ravenstone
Mease   Part in Derbyshire
                                 13
                                 13
                    Normanton   12   Hugglescote
                    on the Heath Snibston 12
Measham   Donington   11   Hugglescote
Field   on the Heath   Grange

                    Ketham   12 Bridge   Upper   Beggary Nooks
                                          Grange
                    Hether   Battleflat
Swepston

Cross   11
Lane   Ibstock Ibstock Grange Newbery
Nethercote   Newton   Pickering Grange Wood
             Burgaland   Corbit Hall
             Odston Hill   10   Nailston Wiggs
                                                   Bagsworth
                                                   Moats   20

This section of the map centres around Charnwood Forest. By the mid 18th century there was very little woodland left in the central area of the Forest, and large areas were covered with gorse, fern and grass. There were well managed woodlands on the fringes of the Forest. Oakley Wood with 172 acres was a prime example, but woodland was continuing to be cut down and not replaced. With the exception of some ancient enclosures, the Forest was a free common for the inhabitants of surrounding towns and villages, and was used as sheep pasture by them. The Enclosure Act was not passed until 1808. Until after the passing of this Act the meeting house at Bardon was the only religious building in the Forest. The map shows no evidence of the slate workings which were productive around Swithland at the time.

The population of the area was concentrated in Loughborough, a town of about 4,000 inhabitants. With the opening of the canal to join the Soar Loughborough was on the eve of its industrial expansion. Wool combing and framework knitting were already practised, but the appearance of the town at this time was far from prosperous, according to Thomas Pochin writing in 1770.

Much more prosperous was the nearby agricultural area of Dishley Grange, where the celebrated Robert Bakewell was carrying on his programme of agricultural improvements. He was nationally famous for his work in stock breeding to improve the ratio of meat to bone of both cattle and sheep. He had converted much arable land to pasture to feed his animals, and had devised methods of irrigating the land to produce the richest crop. And all this was not as owner of the land but as a tenant farmer of the Garendon estate.

Shepshed was a large village of about half the size of Loughborough, and a large number of its inhabitants were engaged in framework knitting. Hathern, which had over 1,000 people, was another industrial village. To the south of Charnwood, Anstey was also engaged in framework knitting, but with a population of only five or six hundred.

The hill above Bradgate is labelled Old John, but although the windmill seems to have gone from this site the tower was not erected until 1786. Bradgate House had been abandoned by its owners the Stamfords and left to go to ruin in 1739, but the finest mansion on this page was Garendon. It was designed by Sir Ambrose Phillipps and built by his brother Samuel in the mid 18th century, much altered in the 19th century, and now demolished. Beaumanor was another house of Prior's century, built in 1726 on the site of a much older hall, but replaced in the 19th century by a Jacobean style house. The hall at Long Whatton was the original one in the village, about to be replaced by a new building near the turnpike road.

The area is crossed by turnpikes north-south and east-west on the edge of the Forest, but the turnpike from Loughborough to Ashby was 'not much used'. Perhaps more significant because so carefully mapped is the network of tracks which crossed the Forest.

The Domesday mill sites of Shepshed and Dishley on the Blackbrook worked into the 20th century. Whatton Mill was built in 1773 on a site used from the 15th century, while Zouch Mill on the Soar along with the mill on the Wood Brook at Loughborough were scenes of early 19th century steam powered hosiery machine experiments.

The post mill on Markfield Hill survived until after 1863, the site eventually being quarried away.

Loughborough, from the Midland Counties Railway Companion. *R. Allen. 1840.*

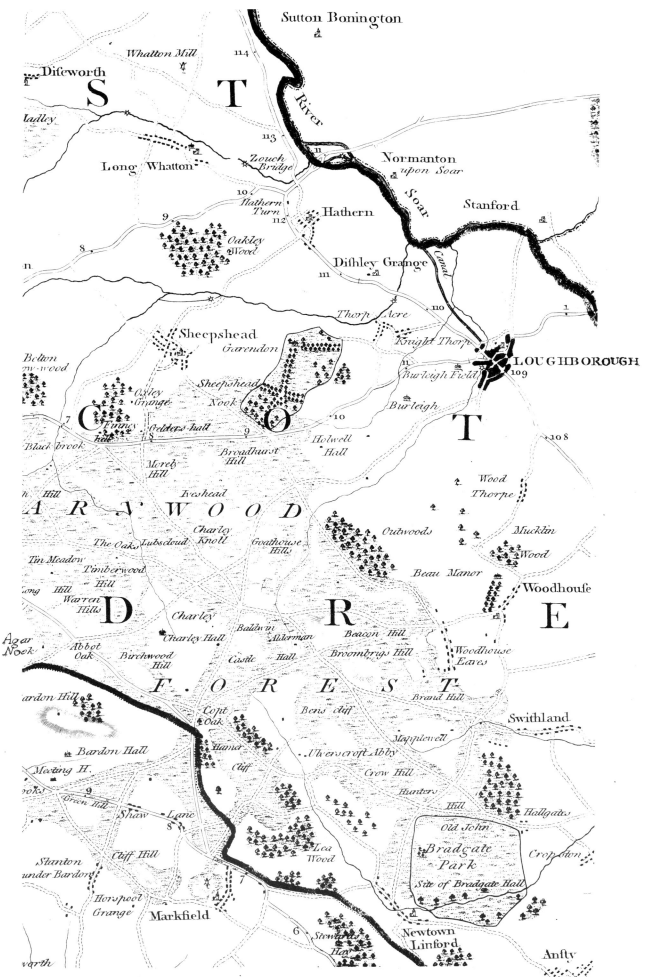

Sutton Bonington

Diſeworth

Whatton Mill

114

S · · · T

adley

113

Long Whatton

Zouch Bridge

11

River

Normanton
upon Soar

Soar

Stanford

10

Hathern Turn

112

Hathern

9

8

Oakley Wood

Diſhley Grange

111

Canal

110

Thorp Acre

Knight Thorp

1

Sheepshead

Garendon

Loughborough

Belton new-wood

Oxley Grange

Sheepshead Nook

Burleigh Field

109

Burleigh

C · · · O · · T

7

Funns Hill

Geldas hall

9

10

108

Black brook

8

Holwell Hall

Wood Thorpe

Morely Hill

Broadhurst Hill

A R Y W O O D

Iveshead

Muckling Wood

Outwoods

Charley Knoll

The Oaks

Lubscloud

Goathouse Hills

Beau Manor

Tin Meadow

Timberwood Hill

Long Hill

D

Woodhouse

Warren Hills

Charley

Baldwin

Beacon Hill

E

Agar Nook

Abbot Oak

Charley Hall

Alderman

Broombrigs Hill

Woodhouse Eaves

Birchwood Hill

Castle Hall

F · O · R · E · S · T

ardon Hill

Bens cliff

Brand Hill

Bardon Hall

Copt Oak

Mapplewell

Swithland

Meeting H.

Hamer

Ulverscroft Abby

oks

9

Cliff

Crow Hill

Green Hill

Shaw Lane

8

Hunters Hill

Hallgates

Cliff Hill

Lea Wood

Old John

Bradgate Park

Cropſton

Stanton under Bardon

7

Horspool Grange

Markfield

6

Stewards Hay

Newtown Linford

Site of Bradgate Hall

worth

Anſty

22

Population in this area was concentrated in the southern section of the sheet. Mountsorrel was the largest centre, adding together the north and south ends, for Mountsorrel at this time was a divided town. The north end was situated in the parish of Barrow on Soar, while the south end was part of the domain of the Earls of Leicester within the peculiar of Rothley. The enclosure award covering both halves of the town was passed in 1782. There had been a weekly market since 1292, but the existing round market cross was not built until the 1790's. William Bray found Mountsorrel to be 'A long, ill-paved town . . . It stands at the foot of a remarkable hill, or rather rock, the stone in many places stands out bare, and is of such hardness as to resist all tools when it has been exposed to the air. Such pieces as can be got from underground are broken with a sledge, and used in buildings in the shape in which they are broken.'

Of the other villages, Quorn would have had about 1,200 people, Syston 1,100, Barrow and Sileby, 1,000 each, Wymeswold and Thurmaston over 500. Nichols commented on Thurmaston that 'Many respectable people have houses here. The village at present contains about 150 houses.' In Sileby the chief occupation would have been framework knitting.

The lime workings shown in three groups around Barrow were noted by Bray, who observed that much of the lime was exported to Holland. He describes the lime burning . . . 'Both sorts are dug out, piled up in the form of a cone, and burnt. The burning of one of these heaps takes up to two days and three nights.' Lime from Barrow had been used for the building of Leicester Castle as early as the 13th century.

The Fosse Way runs directly northwards, but it is the road to Melton that is turnpiked. There is also the Derby turnpike running through Birstall, Wanlip, Mountsorrel and Quorn.

One of Prior's 'Roman stations' appears marked at 'Sex or Segs Hill', the modern Six Hills on the Fosse Way. This was thought to be the site of the Roman Verometum, but it is now known that this site was further up the Fosse, closer to Willoughby.

Stanford Hall, just over the Nottinghamshire border, had views over Charnwood. It was built in brick in 1771-74 by Charles Vere Dashwood. The house marked at Quorndon is Quorn Hall, originally of 1680, and the home in the 18th century of Hugo Meynell, founder of the Quorn Hunt. Rothley Temple was the house with the longest history, having been founded by the Knights Templar in 1231, and turned into a private residence by the Babington family in the 16th century. Prestwold was a very new seat, dating from about 1770, although the hall and its park were both greatly enlarged in the mid 19th century, displacing the few remaining houses.

Of the isolated farmhouses, Quebec House is dated by its name to shortly after Wolfe's famous victory in the Battle of Quebec in 1759.

The potential of the main river, the Soar, was well exploited with ten watermills, eight of which survived for many years. Cotes Upper Mill was destroyed for flood prevention in 1898. Cossington had been used since the 13th century for corn milling, cloth fulling and paper making. Sileby and Birstall became leather board mills.

Six windmills are shown. Mountsorrel post mill, built in 1764, survived until 1874 when quarrying took over. Wymeswold post mill worked until 1914.

Mountsorrel, from An illustrated handbook to Charnwood Forest. *R. Allen. 1857.*

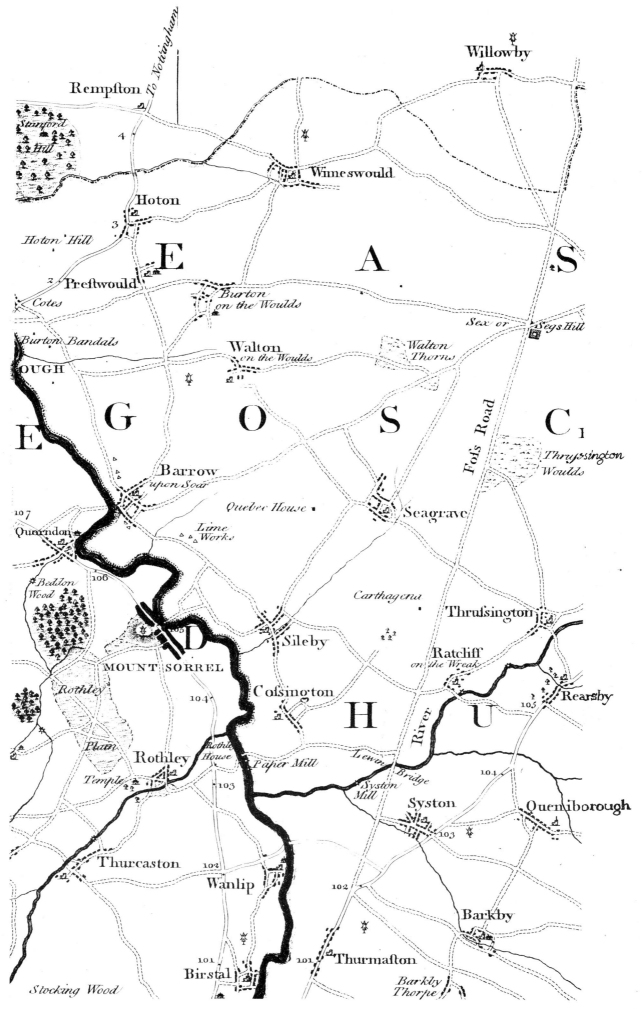

Willowby

Rempfton

To Nottingham

Stanford
Hill

4

Wimeswould

Hoton

3

Hoton Hill

E

A

S

2 Preftwould

Cotes

Burton
on the Woulds

Sex or Segs Hill

Burton Bandals

OUGH

Walton
on the Woulds

Walton
Thorns

Fofs Road

C 1

E

G

O

S

Thrufsington
Woulds

Barrow
upon Soar

Quebec House

Seagrave

107

Lime
Works

Querndon

106

Beddon
Wood

Carthagena

Thrufsington

MOUNT SORREL

Sileby

Ratcliff
on the Wreak

Rearsby

105

Rothley

Cofsington

104

H

U

Plain

River

Rothley

Rothley
House

Paper Mill

Leways Bridge

104

Temple

103

Syston
Mill

Syston

Queniborough

103

Thurcaston

102

Wanlip

Syston

Barkby

102

Stocking Wood

101

101

Thurmafton

Birstal

Barkly
Thorpe

24

The population of this area has trebled since the time of Prior's map, when it would have been about 6,000 in total. Much of the increase has been concentrated in the town of Melton Mowbray. The villages have grown to a lesser extent, and the Wreake Valley was perhaps better populated then than now. Shoby, Saxelby, Welby and Eye Kettleby are all examples of Leicestershire's depopulated villages.

In Prior's time Melton Mowbray was not the important hunting metropolis it became in the 19th century. Hugo Meynell still lived in Quorndon and his brother-in-law Thomas Boothby in Tooley Park, north of Earl Shilton. But the Quorn pack of hounds which they founded in the 1750's hunted almost the whole of Leicestershire at that time. The seats or lodges built in Melton and most of the villages with their tremendous social life were still to come. But the land was kept as pasture and the hedges were maintained at a suitable height for horses to jump. There was some Stilton cheese making in the area, at a scale large enough for exporting to other counties. In the southern villages such as Rotherby some framework knitting was practised. The working of ironstone in the area around Melton did not start until the 19th century.

Holwell Mouth enjoyed a reputation during the 17th and 18th centuries as a medicinal spring. In those days it had a stone surround and seats had been built for the sufferers who visited it.

The 1760's turnpike road is measured at 113 miles from London to Melton via Leicester. Prior would see it still going into the village of Frisby on the Wreake, with coaches calling at the inn, the Black Horse, and then climbing out again up Chalk Pool Hill. A straight piece of road between Rotherby and Chalk Pool Hill was made in 1810 – one of the earliest by-passes in the county. From Melton another turnpike proceeded northwards to Nottingham.

The hall at Ragdale had belonged to the Shirleys of Staunton Harold, but in Prior's time belonged to the Ferrers family, and was let to a farmer. It was built in 1629-30 as an extension to an earlier half-timbered house. Unfortunately in later years it fell into a state of neglect and was demolished in 1958. The present hall was built on a different site in 1785 and altered in the 19th century. Baggrave Hall, built in the mid 18th century, is a surprising omission from the area near Street Hill on Prior's map.

The name of the river is changed on the map from Wreake to Eye above Kirby Bellars, whereas the latter name should probably have been reserved for the stretch above Melton. The watermills on this river were all shortly to be affected by the navigation, and bypass locks were built to preserve the heads of water to drive their wheels. Of the ten windmills, half survived to 1835, and both Ab Kettleby and Barsby post mills worked until the 1880's. At Nether Broughton a windmill worked from 1675 to 1890.

'Rakedale' (Ragdale) Old Hall, from E. S. Palmer, Sketches in Leicestershire. 1846.

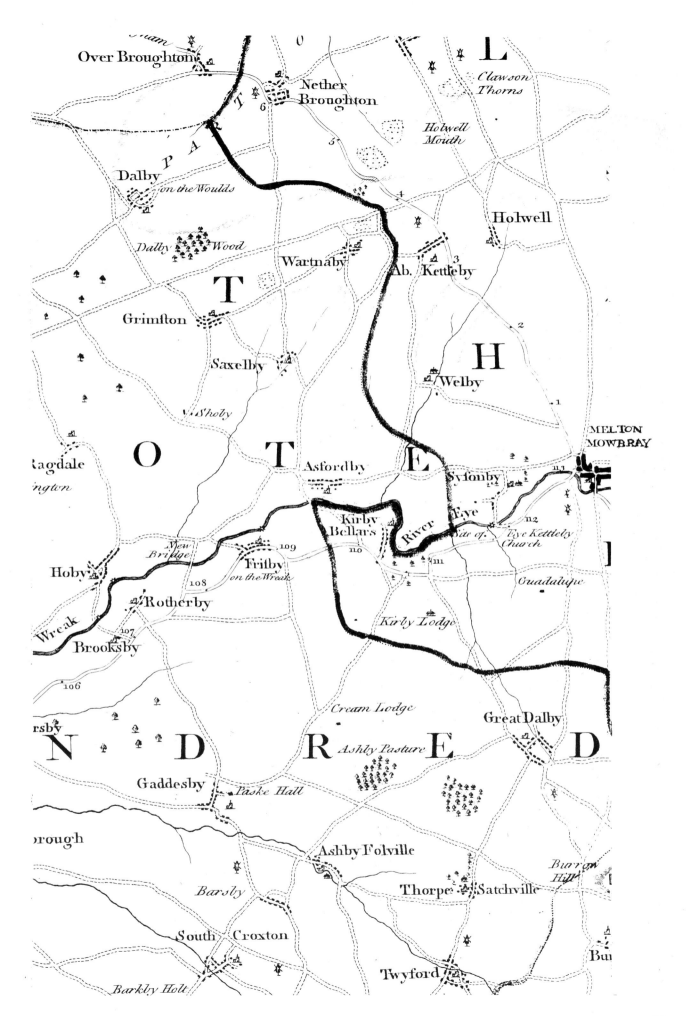

Over Broughton

Nether Broughton

Clawson Thorns

L

Dalby on the Woulds

PART

Holwell Mouth

Holwell

Dalby Wood

Wartnaby

Ab. Kettleby

T

Grimston

H

Saxelby

Welby

Shoby

MELTON MOWBRAY

Ragdale

O

T

Asfordby

E

Sysonby

Kirby Bellars

River

Eye

Site of Eye Kettleby Church

Hoby

New Bridge

Frisby on the Wreak

Rotherby

Guadalupe

Wreak

Brooksby

Kirby Lodge

Cream Lodge

Great Dalby

N

D

R

Ashly Pasture

E

D

Gaddesby

Paske Hall

Ashby Folville

Barsby

Thorpe Satchville

South Croxton

Twyford

Barkby Holt

This area was sparsely populated in Prior's time as it is now. Besides the small villages, a number of isolated houses, presumably farms, are shown – White Lodge, Goldsmith Grange, Spinney House, Jericho. The deserted village of Bescoby is represented by a single dot, below the plantation of Croxton Park, itself containing no more than a hunting seat. Around the River Eye the villages of Stapleford, Brentingby and Wiverby (or Wyfordby) clung to a tenuous existence. The little villages of Caldwell and Wikeham have had their names reversed on the map.

Much of the land had been enclosed early to be used for pasture. It was a well watered area, and nourished the cattle whose milk was good for Stilton Cheese making. Cobbett however commented that good wheat was grown in the Wreak Valley. At this side of the county there was scarcely a stocking frame to be found, but Burton Lazars church has a memorial to a weaver who died in 1780. Several of the manors in the northern part of this sheet were under the ownership of the Dukes of Rutland.

The turnpike from Melton to Oakham dating from the 1750's crosses the map. At Leicesterford Bridge a railway bridge was built in the following century.

'Burrow Hill' has Prior's 'Roman station' symbol which he used for antiquities in general, and was in fact an iron age hill fort. Prior no doubt knew of its use on a Whit Monday by villagers from as far away as Melton for a vast fair, featuring dancing, wrestling and feasting.

Two seats, Cold Overton Hall and Wymondham Hall,

which were certainly there in Prior's day, are not marked on the map. Of the ones that are marked, Stapleford is undoubtedly the most important. Here the 4th Earl of Harborough had been busy in the 1770's with rebuilding and redecorating operations, and had replaced a seven arched bridge over the river in his grounds with a single span. The way in which the river was diverted through the grounds to form a water garden is well shown on the map. The church was rebuilt on a site next to the hall in 1783.

Goadby Marwood church has the tomb of Francis Peck the antiquarian who started the vast collection of information which John Nichols used to write his history of Leicestershire. Peck died in 1742 and his historical collection went to Sir Thomas Cave, of Stanford, who wanted, but never managed, to write the history. Historians of Leicestershire are thankful that Nichols completed what Peck had begun.

Burton Lazars takes its name from the leper hospital built here in 1150. This became the richest leper house in England, and lasted until the dissolution of the monasteries. More contemporary with Prior was the revival of the medicinal springs, because the new Bath House was built in the middle of the 18th century. Several of these springs were exploited in Leicestershire, and it is surprising that the map does not draw attention to them.

The windmill sites marked by Prior were not recorded on a map of 1835, which was also the year that Somerby post mill was burned down.

Stapleford Park, from Throsby, J. Select views in Leicestershire from original drawings. 1789.

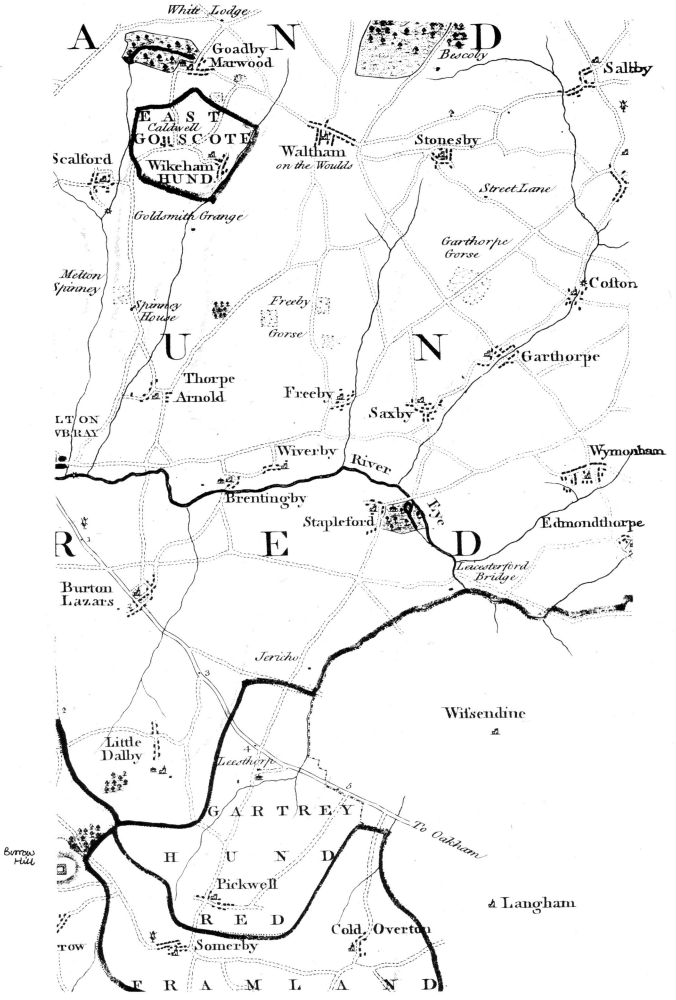

A N D

White Lodge

Goadby
Marwood

Bescoby

Salby

E A S T
Caldwell
GO SCOTE

Scalford

Wikeham
HUND

Waltham
on the Woulds

Stonesby

Street Lane

Goldsmith Grange

Garthorpe
Gorse

Melton
Spinney

Spinney
House

Freeby
Gorse

Cofton

U N

Garthorpe

Thorpe
Arnold

Freeby

Saxby

LT ON
VB RAY

Wiverby

River

Wymonham

Brentingby

Stapleford

Eye

Edmondthorpe

R

E

D

Leicesterford
Bridge

Burton
Lazars

Jericho

Witsendine

Little
Dalby

Leesthorpe

G A R T R E Y

To Oakham

Burrow
Hill

H U N D

Pickwell

Langham

R E D

Cold Overton

row

Somerby

F R A M L A N D

The county boundary here is on the line of a prehistoric track. It remained as a green lane and was one of the routes the Danes used to travel into the Midlands from the area round the Wash. It has been variously called in Leicestershire Sewstern Lane, The Drift, or Sewstern Drift. It was not a Roman road, Ermine Street being about three miles east of it in this area. In Prior's time it would have been a wide road with grass verges and hedges (Buckminster was enclosed before 1600) and good enough for the Dukes of Rutland to use on journeys to London in preference to the Great North Road. Now it is a straight metalled road because it was cleared for the removal of ironstone in the 20th century, and the company made it good after they had lowered the ground level about nine feet.

19th and 20th century ironstone workings had a considerable effect on the landscape Joseph Whyman would have seen from his triangulation point at Buckminster. The lowering and levelling of the land has taken away the small features of the landscape around here, where enclosure for sheep pasture came in the 16th century. Looking out eastwards from Buckminster the fields are very smooth and flat, merging into the Lincolnshire Fens.

At Thistleton Gap Leicestershire, Lincolnshire and Rutland met. Prior does not mark the streams which have gathered from the higher ground to form the River Witham which flows through the Gap. In later times the gap was used for the Melton Mowbray/Bourne Railway line, now disused.

The number of people in the area was under 900, and the population remains small. The one hall, Edmondthorpe, is now ruined, and since Prior's day Buckminster Hall has come and gone, leaving only an impressive stable block. Crown Point Farm still exists as Blue Point Farm. The three churches have survived externally much as Whyman saw them. Sproxton post mill was demolished in 1949, after a rebuild in 1889.

Sewstern Lane, or the Drift, near Buckminster. Looking north towards the Vale of Belvoir from Hoskins W. G. The Heritage of Leicestershire. 1950.

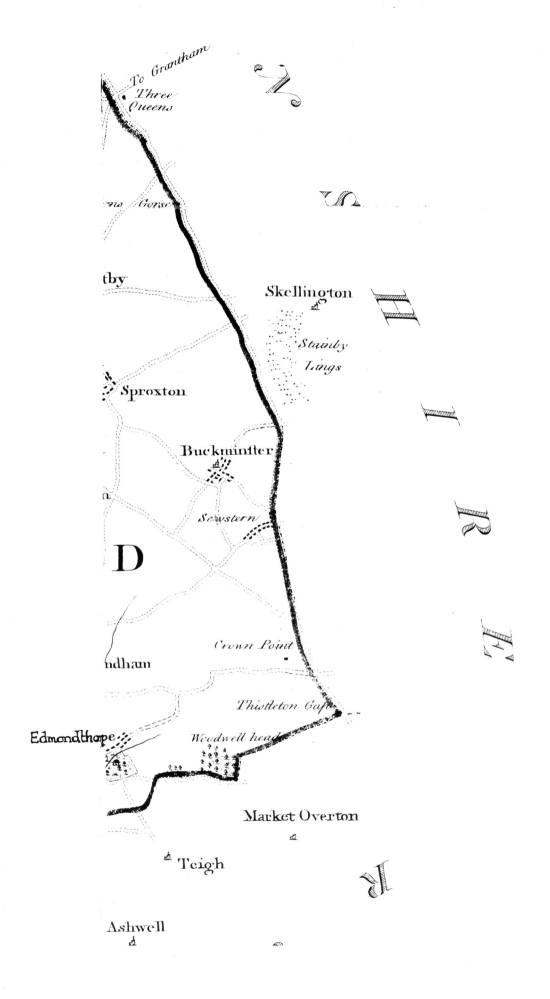

To Grantham

Three
Queens

Skellington

Stainby
Lings

tby

Sproxton

Buckminster

Sewstern

D

Crown Point

ndham

Thistleton Gate

Edmondthorpe

Woodwell head

Market Overton

Teigh

Ashwell

S H I R E R

30

Just visible in the north east corner of this page, although the house actually appears on the page following, is Gopsall Park, which dominated this part of Leicestershire in the 18th century. It was built about 1750 for Charles Jennens, grandson of a wealthy Birmingham ironmaster. Jennens was nicknamed 'Solyman the Magnificent', and the house was built on a lavish scale at a cost of over £100,000. The park was laid out with pleasure grounds of lawns, groves and temples. Jennens was reputed to be 'as benevolent as he was rich', and was a man of very cultivated tastes in the arts. He was a friend and patron of Handel, and was said to have selected the Bible passages for the oratorio *The Messiah*. Charles Jennens died in 1773 unmarried and without issue, and the house was bequeathed to Penn-Asheton Curzon. Gopsall Hall survived for 200 years, but was demolished in 1950.

Charles Jennens was recorded as lord of the manor of Norton at its enclosure in 1749, and the church clock in this village was given by him in 1756. At Twycross a charity school for the use of the poor was established by Jennens' will.

At Mancetter a Roman station is marked, the site of Manuessedum. It straddled Watling Street, part in Leicestershire and part in Warwickshire. It lay within the parish of Witherley, where the church has a tall slender spire still visible from the A5. Nearby Fenny Drayton was the birthplace in 1624 of George Fox, founder of the Quakers. The hall at Fenny Drayton was built in 1701.

The hall which is marked at Orton was demolished in 1786 and a new house built in the Georgian style. Orton Gorse provided good cover for foxes, even when after the enclosure in 1782 its size was reduced from 120 acres to 36. Orton Parva had three houses when described by Nichols, and three houses are shown on the map – a rare concurrence. The isolated farms of Preston Pans and Culloden are dated by their names to the years 1745/6, commemorating battles in the second Jacobite rebellion, when the Young Pretender was defeated. The granges Pinwall Grange and Ley Grange were formerly monastic properties of the Abbey of Merevale. Pinwall was in the occupation of William Wheatley, and Ley belonged to the Dixie family of Market Bosworth.

Fielden Bridge over the River Anker had existed since the 14th century. It was maintained jointly by the counties of Leicestershire and Warwickshire, and was rebuilt by them in 1786.

Sheepy Parva mill on the Sence became a very large concern in the 19th century, with water turbines and roller machinery. Witherley post mill survived until the 1890s.

Gopshull Hall, from Throsby, J. Select views in Leicestershire from original drawings. *1789.*

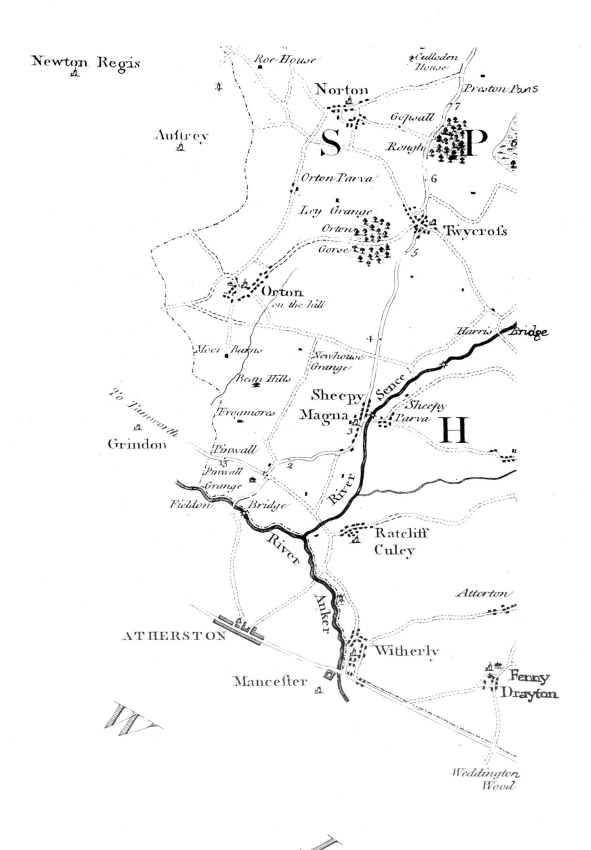

Newton Regis

Roe House

Culloden House

Norton

Preston Pans

S

Aultrey

Gopsall

P

Rough

7

Orton Parva

6

6

Ley Grange

Twycrofs

Orton

Gorse

5

Orton
on the hill

Harris Bridge

Moor Barns

Newhouse
Grange

4

Bean Hills

Sheepy
Magna

Sence

Sheepy
Parva

H

To Tamworth

Frogmores

3

Grindon

Pinwall

River

2

13

Pinwall
Grange

Ratcliff
Culey

Fielden

Bridge

River

Atterton

Anker

ATHERSTON

Witherly

Mancefter

Fenny
Drayton

W

Weddington
Wood

I

32

This section of the map is unusual in having two market towns. Market Bosworth's market dates from 1285, whereas Hinckley's although not documented until 1311, may actually predate the Norman Conquest. Hinckley in 1777 had about 4,500 people compared to under 2,000 in Market Bosworth, and was a bigger town even than Loughborough. It had about 750 houses, many of them grouped in yards rather than with street frontages. In 1778 there were 864 stocking frames employed in the town. These gave employment to 2,150 people, consisting of 1,000 framework knitters, 250 seamers, 50 woolcombers, 28 framesmiths, and 822 spinners, doublers and twisters – the last group would have been women and children. Surrounding villages were also engaged in the same trade. Poverty was beginning to affect the framework knitters, and one in every three inhabitants who died was classed as a pauper. The affairs of the Church of England were in a rather unsatisfactory state in the town, and several nonconformist congregations had sprung up. The first Presbyterian meeting house was erected in 1722. An Independent (Congregational) church was established in 1767, and the first Baptist meeting house was built in 1768. There was also a small Catholic revival between 1765 and 1800. It was however in the Anglican church that the historian John Nichols married his second wife in 1778.

Market Bosworth Hall was built about 1680 as the seat of the Dixie family, though it was much altered in the late 19th century. In the first half of the 18th century Bosworth had been a fashionable place of resort for the county gentry, who assembled for sporting pursuits such as hunting and bowls. It also had a long established grammar school, founded in the 17th century. But by the time Prior's map was surveyed Bosworth had declined to a remarkable extent. The market had few stalls and few customers, the roads were poor, the church neglected, the people reported to be churlish and unfriendly, and the

school was seriously mismanaged. Much of this decline is attributed to the Lord of the Manor, Sir Wolstan Dixie, who became 5th Baronet in 1764, and was certified insane in 1783.

Near Sutton Cheney is marked the only battlefield on the map, where on August 22nd, 1485 Richard III was killed and his army defeated by Henry Earl of Richmond, who thus became King Henry VII. The battlefield by the late 18th century was much altered by the fences and roads resulting from enclosure. It was the scene of some antiquarian interest, as recorded by Nichols, but he had to say that 'no pillar is erected to commemorate the event'. This omission has fortunately now been remedied.

The small (population c.150) village of Barton in the Beans had a contemporary significance greater than its size would warrant. In 1771 Samuel Deacon had set up his clock making and repair workshop there. His work ranged from small watches to church clocks, and there are several examples of his work in Leicester Museums. The Museum also has his amazingly preserved workshop from Barton reassembled in a building in Castle View, Leicester. But Deacon's contemporary significance was as a founder member and leader of the General Baptists, a denomination which spread from Barton into the towns and villages of Leicestershire and all the neighbouring counties during the last third of the 18th century.

The River Soar is seen rising below Barwell, and at the place marked Soar Stone there was a large stone which was used to cross the water 'in floody weather'.

Four mills are marked on the Sence, all extant. Help Out Mill at Odstone was the last Leicestershire mill to make flour commercially by water power, which it did until 1970. The three Hinckley windmills had all disappeared by the 1880's, in the expansion of the town.

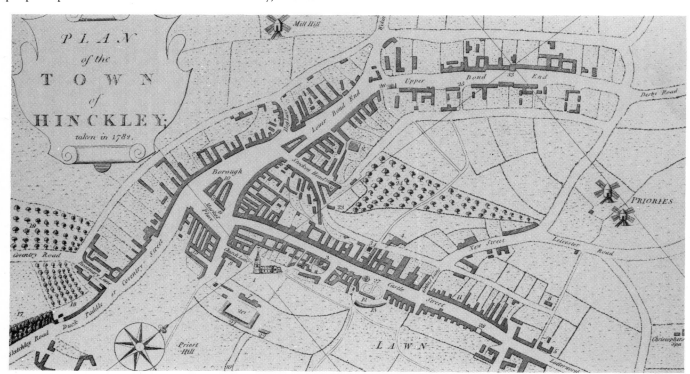

Plan of the Town of Hinckley, 1782, from Nichols, J. History and Antiquities of the County of Leicester. Vol. IV.

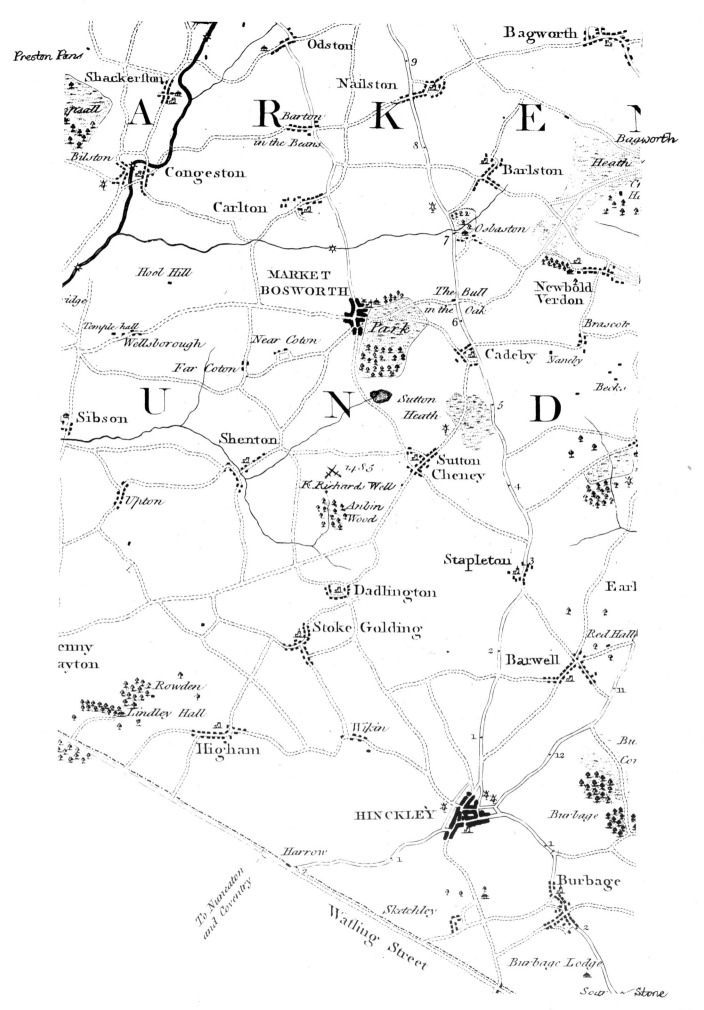

Preston Pans

Shackerston

Bilston

A Congeston

Carlton

Odston

Barton
in the Beans

Nailston

9

8

R

K

Bagworth

Bagworth

Heath

Barlston

Osbaston

7

E

Newbold
Verdon

Brascote

Hool Hill

Temple hall

Wellsborough

Far Coton

Near Coton

MARKET
BOSWORTH

Park

The Bull
in the Oak

6

Cadeby

Naneby

5

D

Becks

ridge

U Sibson

Shenton

Upton

Sutton
Heath

1485
K. Richard's Well

Ambin
Wood

N

Sutton
Cheney

4

Stapleton 3

Earl

enny
ayton

Rowden

Lindley Hall

Dadlington

Stoke Golding

Higham

Wikin

2

Barwell

11

Red Hall

1

12

Bu
Co

HINCKLEY

Harrow

To Nuneaton
and Coventry

1

2

Watling Street

Sketchley

Burbage Lodge

Soar Stone

Burbage

2

Birbage

34

The area from Glenfield to Desford, down to Earl Shilton and across to Narborough, was known as Leicester Forest since the Middle Ages. It had been a royal hunting forest and contained much valuable woodland. Leicester Forest was enclosed and sold by the Crown in 1628 to a number of different purchasers. Several forest landmarks are noted on the map. The part known as Kings Stand had been set aside in 1612 for King James to shoot at deer as they were driven past him, but it was very little used. The Red Cow had been established from the 1650's, originally as a small inn as part of a row of cottages. Barn Park was recorded in 1560. Frith Park in 1571 was referred to as 'The new park of Byrdsnest'. Even in Nichols' time Frith Hall could be described as 'in pleasant open country, about three miles from Leicester'.

Some of the most ancient buildings in this section were not recorded by Prior at all. He did not mark the remains of Kirby Muxloe Castle, the Hastings' moated brick house of 1474-84, which must have been impressive even in its overgrown state. At Groby he did not show either the site of the castle or the 16th century manor house, but he did mark the 'neat modern house' belonging to the Earl of Stamford beside Groby Pool. Nor did he mark the moated site at Old Heys, where the house itself had been rebuilt.

Further into the Forest, Newal (New Hall) Park was built by Richard Turville, of Normanton Turville, in the 14th century. This was a moated house, part of which survived until Prior's day, built of timber and plaster on a stone base. Normanton Turville took its name from the same family, but in Prior's time belonged to Edward-Rooe Yeo. In 1796 it was purchased by Richard Arkwright, the cotton mill owner of Cromford. Enderby Hall, set in a well wooded park, was the home of a famous sporting squire, Charles Lorraine Smith, a life-long friend of Hugo Meynell and one of the famous personalities of the Quorn Hunt. He weighed over fourteen stone and rode the most powerful of horses. Tooley Park belonged to the Boothbys, one of the original fox hunting families of the county, but a little later it was sold and most of its timber cut down.

This section of the map is full of villages and settlements, but there is no major town. Earl Shilton was the largest village, growing towards its 1801 census total of over 1200 people. Thornton had over 900 people at the census, Desford over 600, Narborough, Cosby, Sapcote and Enderby over 500 each. In the larger villages and particularly Earl Shilton many more people were employed in trade than in agriculture, and trade meant mainly framework knitting, controlled by hosiers from Leicester and from Hinckley. At Sapcote the enclosure took place in 1778, and the Lord of the Manor (Rev. Thomas Frewin Turner) took special care that nobody should be displaced from his normal means of providing for his family. There were exactly 100 houses in the village in 1779, containing 450 people. Eighty-five stocking frames were constantly employed, so very few houses were without one, and the women and children were engaged in seaming the hose and in spinning. The parish also produced 20-30 tons of cheese annually. Aston Flamville was also noted for its cheese, which fetched a superior price at Leicester market. But as well as the prosperous villages there were also the depopulated ones, such as Elmesthorpe, which was already deserted when King Richard stopped there on the way to Bosworth. The church here was ruined when Prior saw it, but the chancel was rebuilt in 1868.

Three turnpikes cross this section of the map. The Leicester/Hinckley turnpike won contemporary praise for its use of gravel and the roundness of its contour, but where the road passed through Earl Shilton it was a different matter — 'The material large stones; the form hollow — a rough irregular pavement; the state such as suggests the idea that it was under the direction of a wheelwright or a surgeon.'

Six of the seven windmills survived beyond 1835. Sharnford post mill, struck by lightning in 1783, was rebuilt and worked until about 1912. On the Rothley Brook, Glenfield watermill is probably a Domesday site, Desford dates from the 12th century, Thornton from the 13th and Anstey from the 14th, and all these are extant. At the Domesday site of Broughton Astley animal feed is still ground, though not by water power.

Groby Pool, from Nichols, J. The History and Antiquities of the County of Leicester. *Vol. IV.*

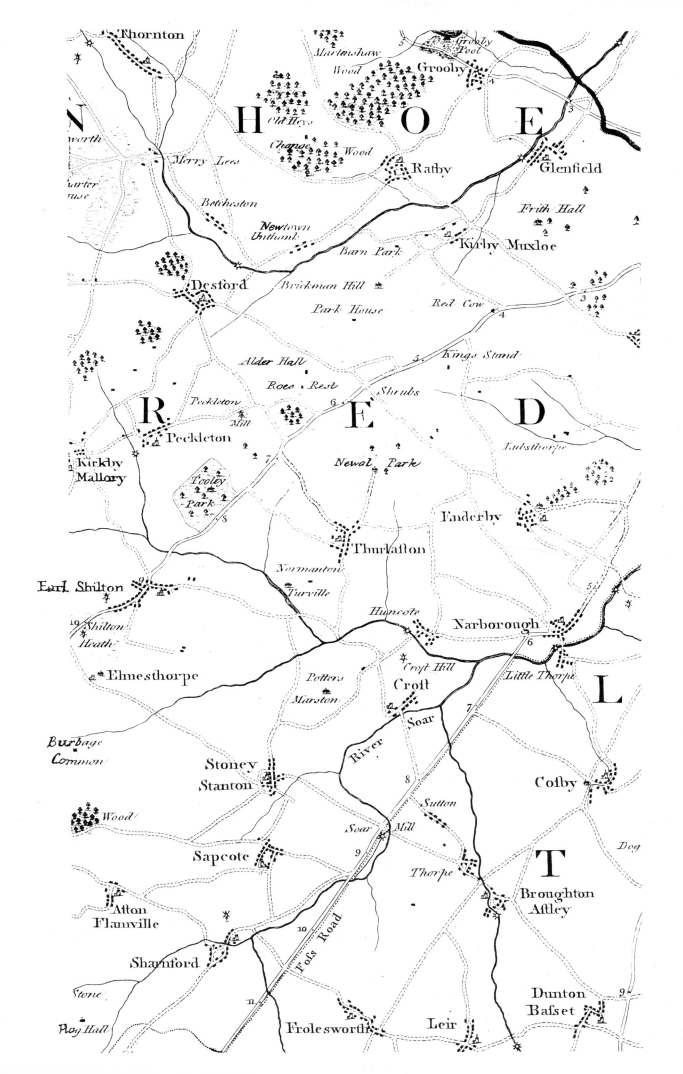

Thornton

Martinshaw
Wood

Grooby
Pool

Grooby

Old Heys

Change   Wood

Merry Lees

Botcheston

Newtown
Unthank

Barn Park

N   H   O   E

Ratby

Glenfield

Frith Hall

Kirby Muxloe

Red Cow

Brickman Hill

Park House

Desford

worth

uarter
ouse

Alder Hall

Roes Rest

Kings Stand

Shrubs

Lubsthorpe

R

Peckleton
Mill

Peckleton

E

Newal Park

D

Enderby

Kirkby
Mallory

Tooley
Park

Thurlaston

Normanton

Turville

Earl Shilton

Huncote

Narborough

Shilton
Heath

Elmesthorpe

Croft Hill

Potters
Marston

Croft

Little Thorpe

L

Soar

River

Burbage
Common

Stoney
Stanton

Cosby

Wood

Sutton

Soar   Mill

Deg

Sapcote

Thorpe

T

Broughton
Aftley

Atton
Flamville

Shamford

Fofs Road

Stone

Dunton
Bafset

Flay Hall

Frolesworth

Leir

36

The most striking feature of this sheet is the comparatively small size of Leicester, and the separation from it of all those areas such as Westcotes, Woodgate, Knighton, Stoneygate, Belgrave, Beaumont Leys etc. which are now heavily built up. Nevertheless with a population approaching 16,000 Leicester was by far the biggest town in the county, and was already beginning to exert a magnetic influence. It was evidently the hub of communications, with the turnpike from London going through to Loughborough and Melton, and the turnpikes to Welford, Lutterworth, Hinckley and Ashby radiating from the town. Further comment on Leicester will be reserved for page 49, facing Prior's plan of the town.

Outside Leicester, Wigston Magna was much the largest village in 1801 with 1,600 inhabitants, but perhaps some of this number was added in the two decades after Prior. Framework knitting was the major employment, occupying over 1,000 people. Belgrave, Oadby, Blaby and Countesthorpe would each have had around 500 people, Aylestone even less and Evington under 200. The deserted village of Hambleton (Hamilton) is represented by one building, while Foston has just a few more beside the church. The village of Whetstone is shown, to the west of Blaby, but its name is not marked.

West Cotes was close enough to the town to be included by Susanna Watts in her *Walk through Leicester* in 1804. She describes the view from here in picturesque terms.

"The churches and buildings of the town, broken by the intermediate trees of the paddock, and the long line of distance varied by villages, scattered dwellings and cornmills, unite in a rich and pleasant prospect."

West Cotes was the Ruding family seat, with an 18th century frontage of about 1730. Nearby was Dannet Hall, described by Nichols as a 'neat little dwelling, which standing upon a small eminence near Leicester, commands an almost bird's eye view of that place. The situation is pleasant and airy, and convenient for an intercourse with a large and populous town.' Just a little further out was Braunston Hall, very newly built in 1775 to replace an old family mansion of Clement Winstanley. About 1750 there was some prospecting for coal in the grounds, but after a fortnight's work the borehole was sabotaged and the attempt was abandoned.

To the north of the city Leicester abbey is marked as a site, i.e. a ruin. Belgrave Hall, built early in the 18th century, and Belgrave House, of 1776, are not shown as seats, but they are perhaps marked as buildings. South of the town, Knighton Hall is also omitted. To the west, the early 18th century building of Scraptoft Hall is shown. Stretton Hall, a brick house of 1715, on the map matches Nichols' description, 'almost surrounded with groves of trees.' The Wistow Hall which Prior saw was Jacobean, and was altered about 1810. The village was depopulated, leaving only the hall and church. On the Ashby road, Sharman's Lodge was named after its builder and dated from the late 17th or early 18th century. Stoneygate House, on the present Toller Road, cannot have been built very long before the map was surveyed.

The tribulations of the outworkers in Wigston, who had to trudge to Leicester to collect raw materials and deliver completed work, are graphically recorded in a passage quoted by Nichols.

"There are a few difficulties the poor of Wigston and of other towns labour under, which, if remedied, would add greatly to their health, one of which is, the stiles between it and Leicester are inconsiderately made, that people with loads, or carrying their work to and from Leicester, cannot get over them, so they are obliged to keep to the turnpike road all winter, by which they are wet, both coming and going, in their feet: and this I take to be another great occasion of the agues and fever the poorer people are so much afflicted with."

The rural character of Leicester is accentuated by the high number of windmills to the south of the town. Two in the south fields had been there in 1710, but one was removed in 1813 and the other before 1835. The three mills near the London Road had gone by 1874. The mill near Welford Road, established in 1316, was removed in 1848 when the Cemetery was opened.

Crow Mill on the Sence at Wigston dates from the 14th century. Belgrave Mill, a Domesday site, was purchased and demolished by the City Council at the end of the 19th century.

Belgrave Mill, from Throsby, J. Select views in Leicestershire from original drawings. 1789.

Oadby Village and Church, from Britton J. and Brayley G. W. The beauties of England and Wales, Vol. IX. Leicestershire, 1807.

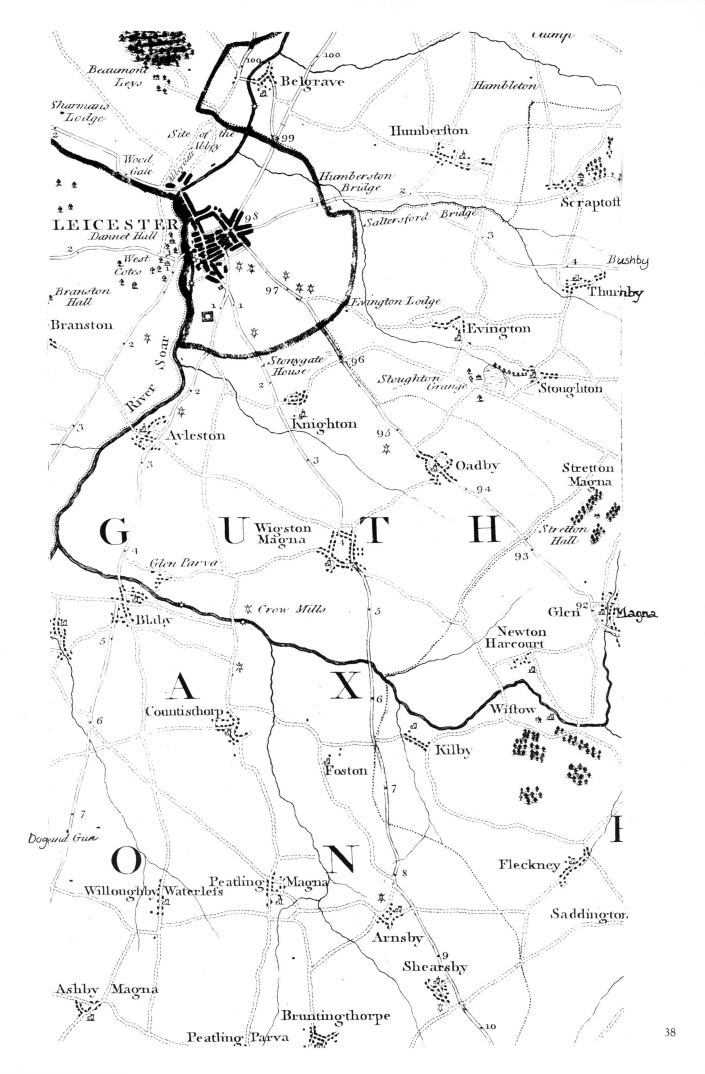

Beaumont Leys

Sharmans Lodge

Wood Gate

Site of the Abbey

Belgrave

Hambleton

Humberston

Humberston Bridge

Scraptoft

LEICESTER

Dannet Hall

West Cotes

Saltersford Bridge

Bushby

Thurnby

Branston Hall

Branston

River Soar

Evington Lodge

Evington

Stoughton Grange

Stoughton

Stonygate House

Knighton

Ayleston

Oadby

Stretton Magna

G U T H

Stretton Hall

Wigston Magna

Glen Parva

Glen Magna

Blaby

Crow Mills

Newton Harcourt

A X O N I

Countisthorp

Wistow

Kilby

Foston

Dog and Gun

Flecknev

Willoughby Waterless

Peatling Magna

Saddington

Arnsby

Ashby Magna

Shearsby

Brunting thorpe

Peatling Parva

The total population of the numerous villages on this sheet would have been around 9,000. Much of the land had been enclosed for sheep pasture before the time of the map.

One glaring error on this section of the map is that the names of the villages of Kibworth Beauchamp and Kibworth Harcourt are reversed. Perhaps this error was introduced by the engraver, who as a London man may have been confused by the unfamiliar Leicestershire names. However the passage of the turnpike road through Kibworth is correctly shown: the modern line which by-passes the old village was not laid out until 1810. The Leicester-Uppingham turnpike crosses through Houghton, Billesdon and Skeffington. Between these, the direct line of the Roman Gartree Road is clearly visible from Stretton to Glooston.

Some of the villages had framework knitting in them during the 18th century, but another widespread domestic industry was clock and watch making. By the mid century many of the villages had a clock maker. Kibworth's was Nathaniel Kirk, and one of his long case clocks made about 1785 is now in a Leicester Museum.

An unusual enterprise centred around the Langton villages, where the Rev. William Hanbury, Rector of Church Langton, had engaged in a vast tree planting operation. The objective was to sell the wood, and also saplings and plants, and to use the money to endow charities in the Langton villages. The charities did eventually provide modest improvements to the church and the village, but these benefits fell far short of the grandiose schemes which William Hanbury envisaged.

Gumley Hall, newly built by Joseph Cradock of Leicester in 1764, seems to be omitted from the map, although the plantations of trees are to some extent represented. Facing opposition in his home villages, Hanbury had carried out much of his planting at Gumley. These 'groves' Joseph Cradock purchased as the site for his mansion, and they became a fashionable resort for visitors from Leicester and the neighbourhood. Gumley was also the site of another of Leicestershire's mineral water springs.

Perhaps the most distinguished church in this part of Leicestershire is that of Norton by Gumley, now Kings Norton, which had been rebuilt between 1757 and 1775. Prior would have seen it with the tower surmounted by a tall spire, which was destroyed by lightning in 1850.

West Langton, another of the bases for the Quorn Hunt, is a hall with neither church nor village. So too is Quenby, still to be seen as Prior would have seen it and as it had already existed for over a century before. Other depopulated villages cluster in the north of this sheet. Ingarsby is represented by a single house, (Cold) Newton by a handful of dwellings, Lowesby by the hall which displaced the village.

Two Domesday mills are marked on the map; Great Glen and Stonton Wyville. They worked until 1885 and 1863 respectively. Six windmills are shown on the sheet, but it is rather ironical that Kibworth, Leicestershire's only surviving post mill, is not marked on the map although it dates from no later than 1711.

Gumbley Groves, from Throsby, J. Select views in Leicestershire from original drawings. *1789.*

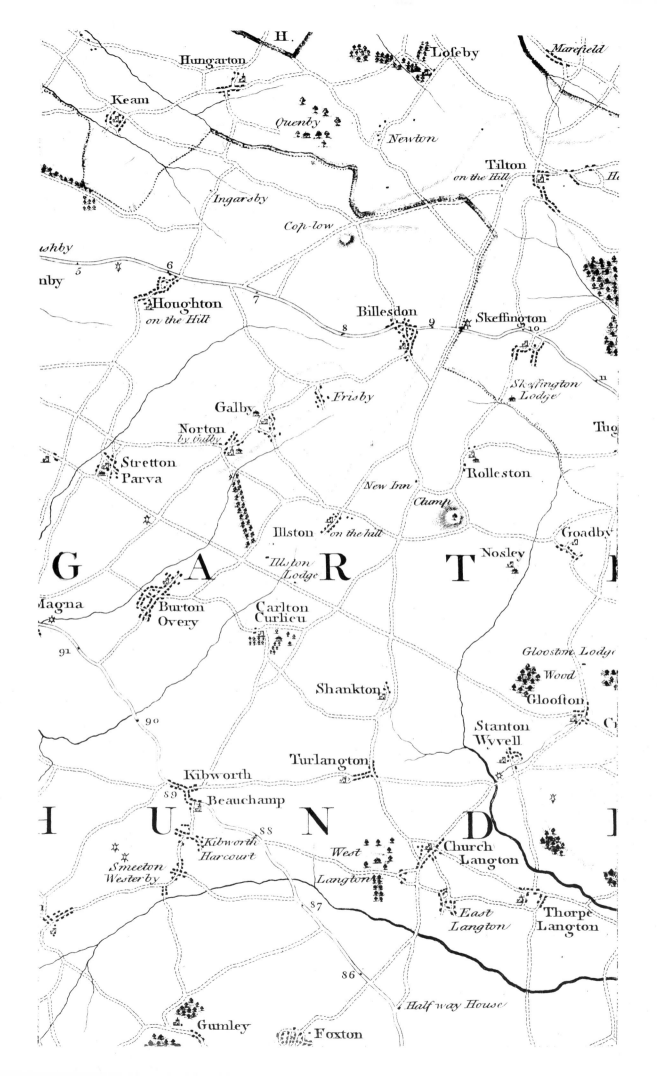

H.

Hungarton

Loseby

Marefield

Keam

Quenby

Newton

Tilton
on the Hill

H.

Ingarsby

Cop-low

shby

nby

5

6

7

Houghton
on the Hill

8

Billesdon

9

Skeffington

10

11

Skeffington
Lodge

Frisby

Galby

Norton
by Galby

Stretton
Parva

Rolleston

Tug

New Inn

Clump

Goadby

Illston

on the hill

G

A

Illston
Lodge

R

T

Nosley

Magna

Burton
Overy

Carlton
Curlieu

91

Gloostn Lodge

Wood

Shankton

Gloofton

90

Stanton
Wyvell

Turlangton

Kibworth

89

Beauchamp

H

U

88

N

D

Kibworth
Harcourt

West

Langton

Church
Langton

Smeeton
Westerby

87

East
Langton

Thorpe
Langton

86

Halfway House

Gumley

Foxton

This peaceful area of East Leicestershire appears well wooded, with woodlands remaining from the days of royal hunting forests. There are high rounded hills – Woodbarrow (now Whatborough) and Robin a Tiptoe – in the northern part and the valleys of the Eye Brook and the Welland in the southern. The Eye Brook (not to be confused with the River Eye) bordering Rutland has now become the Eye Brook Reservoir. From Hallaton northwards the land was enclosed early for pasture. The Medbourne area was not enclosed until 1844, and was still an arable agricultural area in Prior's time. Visitors commented on the wonderful crops. Apart from forestry and agriculture, the occupations of the 3000 inhabitants of the area included wool combing and tammy weaving (weaving of worsted cloth).

The site of Sanvey Castle, between Withcote and Launde, was entirely omitted by Prior. It had been used by King John for hunting, and although it had been abandoned since the 14th century it must have been visible as mounds and earthworks. Woodbarrow had had a settlement on it from very early times, but after enclosure at the end of the 15th century it quickly disappeared. Withcote lost its houses in Tudor times, and consists among the trees of an early 18th century hall and private chapel whose interior was restored in the 18th century. Launde also stands alone but here the late 17th century house replaced not a village but a priory.

Hallaton is shown as a market town in the southern section of the sheet. It had no manor house, but several houses of Prior's century and earlier have survived to the present. Medbourne had confirmed its antiquity in the 18th century by the discovery of a Roman villa there. This village is not shown as a market town, although it was granted a weekly market in 1266. From Medbourne an avenue of trees leads to Nevill Holt, the hall and church standing alone. Further east, the village named as Bradley should be labelled Holyoak. The latter settlement consisted of only a house or two, but Bradley had been a mile or two west and had been completely depopulated by Prior's time.

In his chapter on Slawston, Nichols has a useful description of agriculture before and after enclosure. The farmers had a 'course of husbandry' over three years; first wheat or barley, second beans, third fallow manuring with sheep dung, then wheat or barley again. This had been done since time immemorial. Since the enclosure three quarters of the land had gone down to pasture sown with red and white clovers. Those parts which were still arable often grew turnips or coleworts for winter keeping of sheep. Sometimes they would plough up the oldest greensward, burn the turf, spread the ashes and after ploughing grow oats, a process which was supposed to kill off all the grubs. No doubt this account of one village was typical of agricultural practices in the area.

Allexton and Loddington on the Eye Brook were Domesday mill sites. The former worked until 1912 and the latter until the 1890's. The two Hallaton windmills had gone by 1824, and Tugby post mill was sold and removed around 1842. Medbourne, a smock mill, dating from the 16th century, was demolished in 1902. Slawston post mill first recorded in 1637 survived through two rebuilds until 1947.

Laund Abbey, from Nichols, J. The History and Antiquities of the County of Leicester. Vol. III.

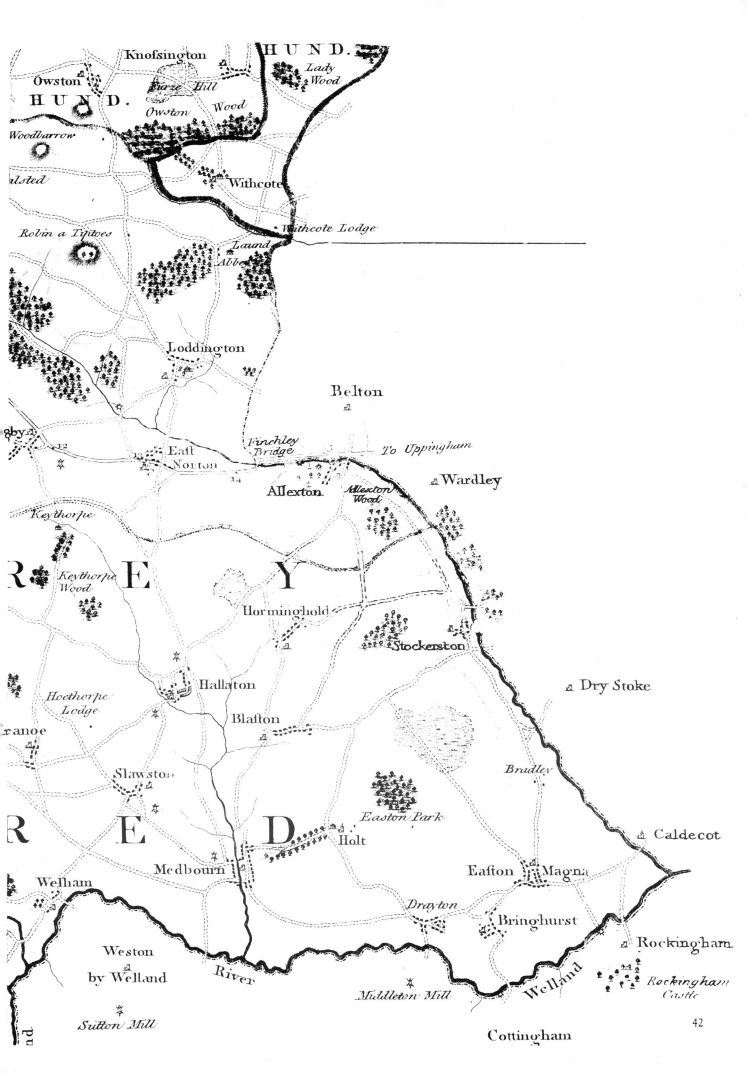

H U N D.

Knofsington

Owston

H U N D.

Lady Wood

Braze Hill

Owston Wood

Woodbarrow

alsted

Withcote

Robin a Tiptoes

Withcote Lodge

Laund Abbey

Loddington

Belton

sby

12

East Norton

Finchley Bridge

To Uppingham

Wardley

13

14

Allexton

Allexton Wood

Keythorpe

R

E

Y

Keythorpe Wood

Horminghold

Stockerston

Dry Stoke

Hallaton

Hoethorpe Lodge

Blaston

ranoe

Bradley

Slawston

Easton Park

R

E

D

Holt

Caldecot

Medbourn

Easton Magna

Welham

Drayton

Bringhurst

Weston by Welland

Rockingham

River

Welland

Middleton Mill

Rockingham Castle

Sutton Mill

Cottingham

42

This is a comparatively low lying area drained by the source streams of the Soar to the north and the Swift and Avon to the south. The land had been enclosed in all the parishes except Lutterworth and Bitteswell before 1775, some parts by private agreement before 1700.

The only market town was Lutterworth with a population of approximately 1500, in 350 houses, followed by the large villages of Ullesthorpe, with approx. 500 people, Bitteswell with 400, Nether Claybrook with 300 and the remainder with under 150 each. The working population was employed mainly in agriculture and its support trades, although in Lutterworth and the larger villages the worsted stocking trade had been established.

The area was well served by roads, the Roman Watling Street forming the county boundary with bridges over the Avon at Dee Bridge and over the Swift at Bensford Bridge. The Foss Way crossed Watling Street (which was not turnpiked) at High Cross. Here in 1712 a monument was set up to commemorate the junction of these major Roman roads. In translation part of the inscription read:

"If traveller you seek for the footsteps of the ancient Romans, here you may behold them, for here their most celebrated ways, crossing each other, extend to the utmost boundaries of Britain."

This monument was struck by lightning and ruined beyond repair in 1791. Lutterworth lay on the road from Leicester to Rugby, turnpiked in 1764, and the road to Hinckley was turnpiked in 1762.

The largest church was St. Mary's at Lutterworth, whose spire had fallen down in a gale in 1703. John Wycliff was Rector at Lutterworth from 1375-1384, during which time he survived accusations of heresy, and worked on translating the Bible into English. A vicar of Bitteswell, Joseph Lee, wrote a treatise in 1656 advocating the advantages of enclosure. Closer to Prior's time, a vicar of Ashby Parva, John Dyer, achieved notoriety through his execution at Tyburn in 1716 for high treason.

The manor house at Shawell was built about 1707. The avenue of trees here Nichols describes as 'some few lime trees standing, which denote that they once ornamented a rich man's domain.'

The three watermills on the Soar streams were Claybrook, Dunton Basset and Leire. Claybrook is probably a Domesday site, the mill building dating from 1675. Dunton mill existed in the 13th century, while the buildings at Leire were very new, dating from 1773. The two mills on the Swift were Spital Mill at Lutterworth and the Lodge or Lord's Mill near Watling Street. Only in 1758 following lengthy litigation were the local farmers able to break the feudal monopoly which from medieval times had obliged them to take their corn for grinding to the Lord's mill.

High Cross, from Nichols, J. The History and Antiquities of the County of Leicester. Vol. IV.

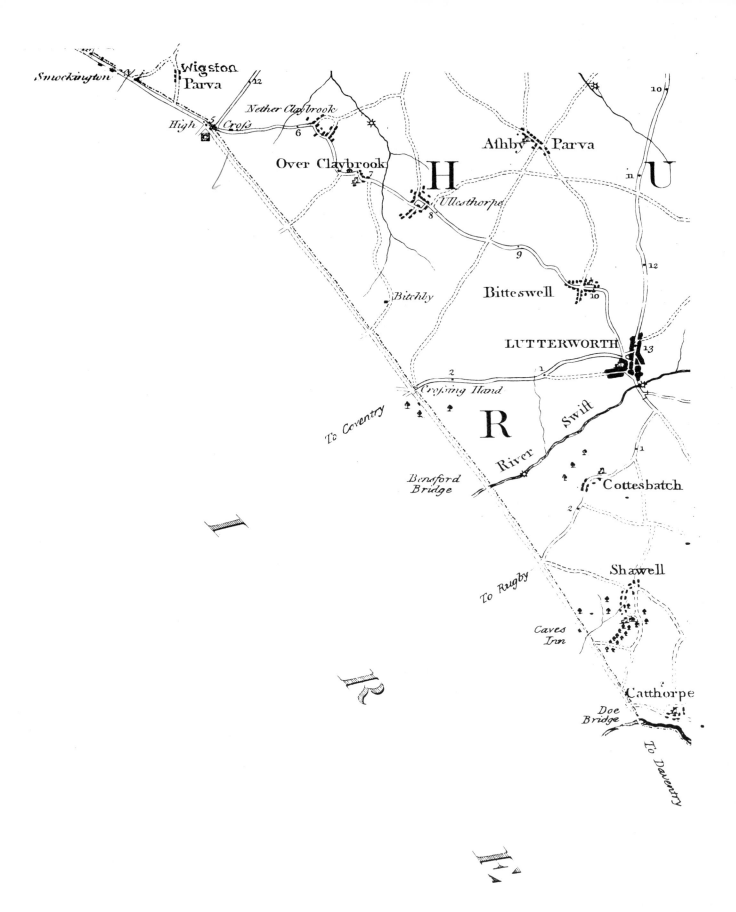

Smockington

Wigston
Parva

12

Nether Claybrook

High 5 Cross

6

Over Claybrook

7

H

Ullesthorpe

8

Ashby Parva

n U

9

12

Bitchly

Bitteswell

10

LUTTERWORTH

13

2

1

Crofsing Hand

R

Swift

To Coventry

River

1

Benford
Bridge

Cottesbatch

2

I

To Rugby

Shawell

Caves
Inn

R

Catthorpe

Doe
Bridge

To Daventry

H

44

Here we find an undulating pastoral landscape levelling to the Avon, which forms the southern boundary. There was a scattered population of about 2,500, Husbands Bosworth being the largest village with around 600 people. The smallest village is Knaptoft, the single dot perhaps representing the hall which was falling into ruin, while the church ruins are not indicated at all. Cotes Deval was another deserted site, where some evidence would remain of the moated house with a drawbridge. Within the parish of Misterton, Poultney is represented by a single farmhouse close to the River Swift, and Walcote by its name only.

Enclosure took place during the 1760's and 1770's in most of the parishes in this area. Employment for the working population was almost exclusively agricultural.

The principal roads, the Leicester to Welford turnpike of 1765 and the Lutterworth to Harborough road turnpiked in 1755, crossed at Husbands Bosworth. They made the village an important centre, though not a market town. The hall here had passed to the Catholic Turville family in 1763 from the Fortescues who had been Lords of the Manor since before 1600.

Stanford Hall, the home of the Cave family since 1430, had been rebuilt on the Leicetershire side of the Avon in 1697-1700 to replace an earlier house on the Northamptonshire side. The adjacent stables and courtyard were completed in the 1730's by Sir Roger Cave, the second Baronet. The beech avenue towards and beyond the road to South Kilworth stands out clearly on the map. The church and village remained entirely within Northamptonshire.

There are three watermills shown on the Avon – Bosworth, North Kilworth and Stanford, the first two being probably Domesday sites. Of the three windmills shown, the Gilmorton site had been used since 1601. There are two windmills marked near Walton, both of which lasted until the 1830's.

Stanford Hall, from Throsby, J. Select views in Leicestershire from original drawings. *1789.*

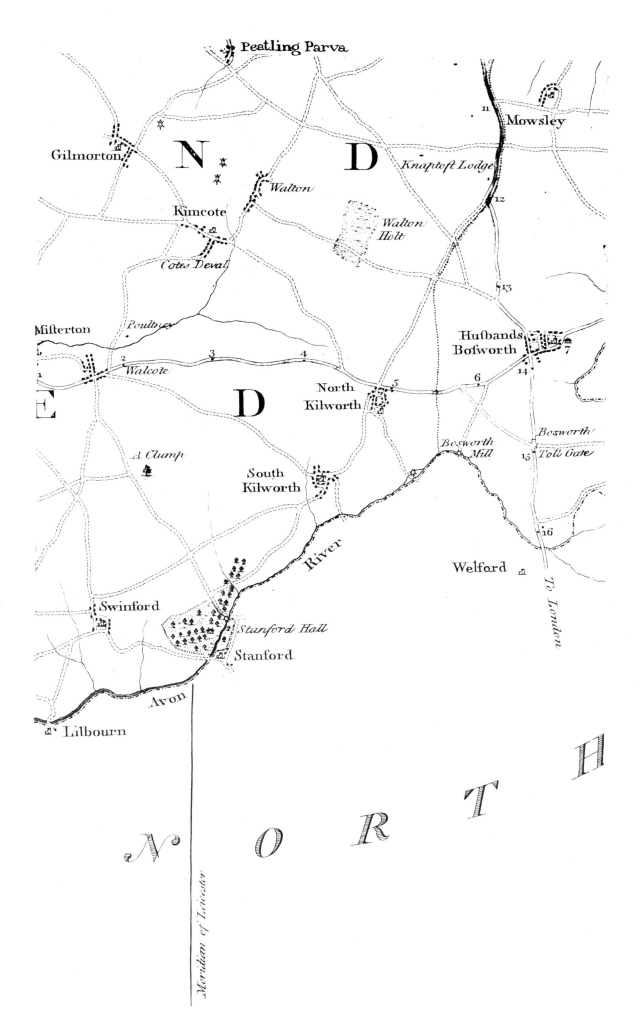

Peatling Parva

Mowsley

N

Gilmorton

Walton

Kimcote

D

Knaptoft Lodge

11

12

Cotes Deval

Walton Holt

13

Misterton

Poultney

Hufbands Bofworth

7

2

3

4

Walcote

D

North Kilworth

5

6

14

E

Bosworth Toll Gate

A Clump

South Kilworth

Bosworth Mill

15

16

River

Welford

Swinford

To London

Stanford Hall

Stanford

Avon

Lilbourn

N O R T H

Meridian of Leicester

This section bounded by the Welland to the south was then as now renowned for its excellent pasture for cattle. Population was concentrated in Harborough and Great Bowden, totalling almost 2,000 in these communities.

Harborough was established in the 12th century as a chapel of Great Bowden at the Welland crossing. It had grown to be a busy town, and an important staging post on the coaching route from north to south. By the late 18th century a variety of textile trades were established, as well as trades supporting local agriculture and the local market, and above all the coaching trade. The Leicester to Harborough road was turnpiked in 1726 and the road south to Kettering in 1751. The Union Canal with its locks at Foxton had not yet been built.

There is no sign on the map of St. Dionysius church, within the town of Market Harborough, despite the fact that it dates from the 14th century and its spire presented

then as now a splendid landmark. St. Mary's church on the Bowden road is marked. This had been rebuilt at the end of the 17th century, although as is evident from the map the population had migrated, and the church again became ruined.

The only seat shown on this section was Pampilion (Papillon) Hall near Lubenham, built in 1622-24 by David Papillon, a Hugenot. The hall was octagonal in shape, with only one entrance. During the 18th century the hall was let to a farmer, and later became a hunting lodge. The house was rebuilt by Lutyens in 1903 but was demolished in 1951.

The two watermills on the Welland near Theddingworth were Domesday sites. There had been a windmill at Foxton since the 12th century, but that at Lubenham was much later. The two sites near Harborough probably dated from the 17th century.

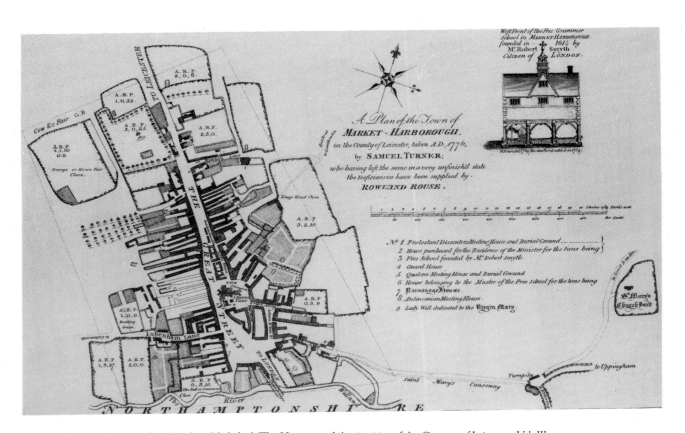

A plan of Market Harborough, 1776, from Nichols, J. The History and Antiquities of the County of Leicester. *Vol. III.*

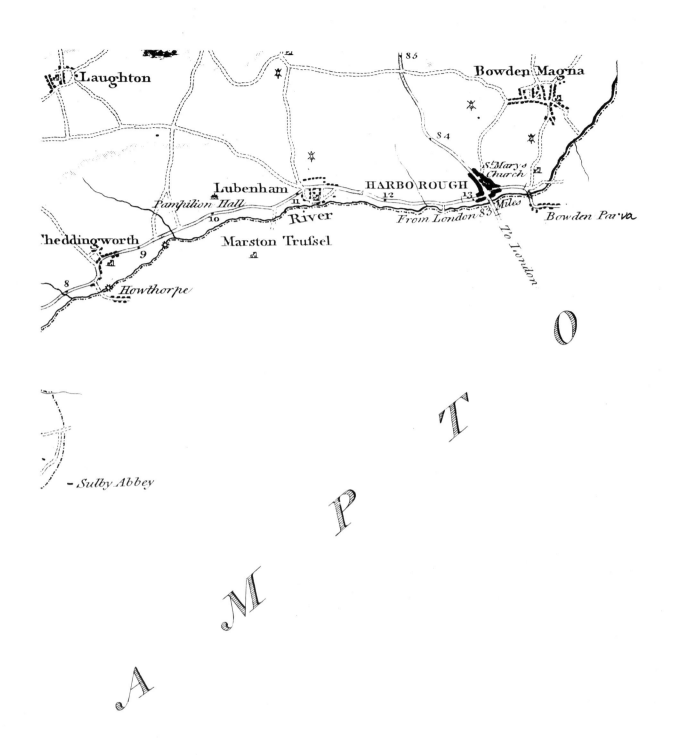

Laughton

Bowden Magna

85

84

St Mary's
Church

Lubenham

HARBOROUGH

Pampilion Hall

10

11

12

13

Miles

River

From London 83

Bowden Parva

Cheddingworth

Marston Trufsel

To London

9

Howthorpe

8

O

T

Sulby Abbey

P

M

A

"Leicester is a place of great extent, being near a mile square, but the entrance from every quarter is disgraced by dirty mud walls. The maket place however is large and spacious, with a handsome building in it belonging to the corporation . . . The town hall is mean, and in an obscure situation."

So wrote William Bray in his account of his travels in 1777. His description reminds us that Leicester was still a square, walled town. In fact the town gates had only been removed in 1773, when they were sold for scrap. The site occupied by the town was still in its medieval location, slightly north-west of today's city centre. The walls and gates had long caused inconvenience to wheeled traffic, which was tending to bypass the town by using Belgrave Gate and Gallowtree Gate. This was in part the reason why the Harborough rather than the Welford Road became the main route to London in the 17th century. Since the 15th century the eastern wall of the town had been largely made up of buildings which had access to Churchgate or Gallowtree Gate at the front and to the inner town at the back. But Churchgate also carried the town ditch, and Gallowtree Gate had an open stream which carried into the ditch all the refuse from the market and from the households alongside. Some improvements were however being attempted in Prior's decade. In 1774-75 Belgrave Gate and Gallowtree Gate were being paved with stone from Mountsorrel, and Gallowtree Gate was illuminated by oil lamps in 1768.

It is unlikely that Whyman made a new survey of Leicester for his plan of the town, and it is difficult to say whether there was new building which the map does not show. The shape of the town much resembles that shown in the rather more picturesque plan by Thomas Roberts, published in 1744 but probably originally drawn in 1712 (reprint produced by Leicestershire Museums). On the other hand the maps in Throsby's *Leicester* and in Susanna Watts' *Walk through Leicester* show the same layout a few years later than Prior. We know that the gardens between Churchgate and Highcross Street remained beyond the end of the century. The South Fields were not enclosed until the first decade of the 19th century, and New Walk was laid out in 1785 but not built along until the 1820's. The expanding population of the 18th century was accommodated in new development along Humberstone Gate and Belgrave Gate, in new tenements built in brick to replace Tudor houses, and by the simple device of multiple occupancy.

Of the buildings shown on Prior's map, five are the ancient churches still standing today. The Castle site would have been seen in much its present state. Bray's 'mean' town hall, (the Guildhall) is not even shown – perhaps it was too mean to mention. The 'handsome building belonging to the corporation' – the Exchange in the Market Place, was built in 1746, and was replaced by the present Corn Exchange in 1851-55. The Assembly Rooms in the Haymarket were built about 1750, with shops below and a hall for theatre, dancing and meetings above. They were superseded by the building now known as the County Rooms in Hotel Street at the end of the 18th century. The Infirmary had been recently built, in 1771, so in that respect Prior's map is up to date with contemporary development. However the Unitarian Great Meeting, built on Churchgate in 1708, does not appear.

The main occupation of the people was undoubtedly the woollen stocking trade, not only as employment for the poor, but as capitalist enterprise with outworkers in the towns and villages. But the plan shows that Leicester was a market town, and its markets were increasing in importance. The present Market Place was the home of the Saturday Market. The renowned horse markets were held outside the town, near the present Horsefair Street, and the cattle and sheep markets were also held on this site. The Haymarket area was the site of the grain market, another trade that required more space than was available in the old walled town.

Three ancient mill sites are shown on the Soar. Castle Mill was possibly a Domesday site, and functioned until the 1870's. Swan's Mill dated from 1301, and worked until 1893. North Mill lasted until 1905, for the last few years grinding by steam power. The endurance of water mills within the city area is a final reminder of the agricultural basis of Leicestershire's history.

The plan of Leicester has been slightly reduced in size for this reprint, to ensure that all the town can be seen on a single page.

The old Town Hall, Leicester, from Flower, J. Views of ancient buildings in the Town and County of Leicester.

A
PLAN
OF
LEICESTER.

A. St Margarets . . . .
B. All Saints . . . .
C. St Nicholas's . . . .
D. St Martins . . . .
E. St Marys . . . .
F. The Castle . . . .
G. Exchange . . . .
H. Assembly Room . . . .
I. Infirmary . . . .

A Scale of Yards

LIST OF SUBSCRIBERS TO THE MAP

Duke of Leeds
Duke of Rutland
Duke of Portland, two copies
Marquis of Rockingham, two copies
Marquis of Granby
Earl of Huntingdon
Earl of Denbigh
Earl of Stamford, 5 copies
Earl Ferrers, deceased
Earl Ferrers
Earl of Harborough, 2 copies
Earl of Warwick
Lord Richard Cavendish
Lord George Cavendish
Lord Frederick Cavendish
Lord George Sutton
Lord Viscount Wentworth
Lord Grey
Honourable John Grey
Honourable Robert Manners
Right Rev. the Lord Bishop of Litchfield
    and Coventry, 2 copies
Honourable Booth Grey
Honourable Colonel Harvey
Right Honourable Sir Thomas Parker, Knt
Sir Robert Burdett, Bart
Sir Thomas Cave, Bart, deceased
Sir Thomas Cave, Bart
Sir Charles Halford, Bart
Sir John Palmer, Bart
Sir Henry Manwaring, Bart
Sir George Robinson, Bart
Sir John Danvers, Bart
Sir Harry Fetherston, Bart
Sir Joseph Mawbey, Bart
Right Hon. Sir Will. Gordon, K.B.
Thomas Abney, Esq
Robert Abney, Esq
Edward Abney, Esq
Thomas Hussey Apreece, Esq, Washingley,
    Huntingdonshire
Shuckburgh Ashby, Esq
J. Ayre, Esq. junior
Dr Ash, Birmingham
Captain Astle
Mr Aspinshaw, Ashby-de-la-Zouch
Mr Avarne, Thringston
Rev. Mr Alleyne, Fellow of University College, Oxford
Rev. Mr Allen, late senior Fellow of Trinity College,
    Cambridge
Rev. Mr Allsop, vicar of Sheepshead
Mrs Babington, of Rothley Temple
Robert Bakewell, Esq
Richard Barber, Esq
Charles Barwell, Esq
John Beaumont, Esq
Lovett Blackborne, Esq
Joseph Boultbee, Esq
Abraham Bracebridge, Esq. senior
Abraham Bracebridge, Esq. junior
John Brogden, Esq., London

John Cave Brown, Esq
Joseph Bunney, Esq
Francis Burges, Esq
William Burleton, Esq
William Burslem, Esq
Mr William Basset, Countesthorpe
Mr Dudley Baxter, Attor. Atherston
Mr Barry, Leicester
Mr Bishop, Leicester
Mr Blunt, Attorney, Loughborough
Mr Simeon Brewin, Leicester
Mr Samuel Brentnall, Odston
Rev. Dr Bickham, Archdeacon of Leicester
Rev. Mr Francis Bacon, rector of Muston, 2 copies
Rev. Mr Barnard, rector of Costock in Nottinghamshire
Rev. Mr Babington, rector of Cossington
Rev. Mr Bakewell, Derby
Rev. Mr Beasley, vicar of Welham
Rev. Mr Belcher, rector of Hether
Rev. Mr Billio, rector of Swepston
Rev. Mr Brown, rector of Hoby
Rev. Dr Burnaby, vicar of Greenwich
Rev. Mr Robt. Burnaby, Prebendary of Lincoln
Nicholas Charnel, Esq
Edward Cheselden, Esq
Richard Cheslyn, Esq
George Clarke, Esq
John Coleman, Esq
Henry Coleman, Esq
Joseph Cradock, Esq
Asheton Curzon, Esq
Pen Asheton Curzon, Esq
Nathaniel Curzon, Esq
Mr Isaac Carter, Attorney, Leicester
Mr Cradock, Attorney, Loughborough
Mr Cropper, Attorney, Ditto
Mr Ward Cocks, Quarndon
Rev. Mr J. Cant, rector of Knaptoft
Rev. Mr Char. Cave, rector of South Kilworth
Rev. Mr Chambers, rector of Higham
Rev. Mr Clement, rector of Appleby
Rev. Mr Collins, Tamworth
Rev. Mr Rowland Evelyn Cotton, Eastwell
Rev. Mr Cowper, vicar of Ashby-de-la-Zouch
John Darker, Esq
Charles Vere Dashwood, Esq
Edward Dawson, Esq
Thomas Dicey, Esq
Willoughby Dixie, Esq
Mr Edward Davie, Leicester
Mr Dickenson, Leicester
Mr Douglas, surgeon, Loughborough
Mr Dalby, surgeon, Kegworth
Rev. Mr Dickenson, rector of Carlton Curlieu
Rev. Mr Dethic
Mr Eborall, Attorney, Atherston
Rev. Mr Ellis, rector of Leke, Nottinghamshire,
    2 copies
Colonel Fowke
Josiah Fuller Farrer, Esq
Martin Farnel, Esq

Thomas Fisher, Esq
Leonard Fosbrooke, Esq
Mr Fisher of Cossington
Mr Fox, surgeon, Leicester
Rev. Dr Farmer, master of Emanuel College, Cambridge
Rev. Dr Ford, rector of Melton
Rev. Mr Farnham, Quarndon
Rev. Mr Farrer
Rev. Mr Fenwicke, rector of Hallaughton
Rev. Mr Fowler, Hugglescote
Philip Gervase, Esq
Richard Gildard, Esq., London
Richard Gough, Esq., Endfield
George Deligne Gregory, Esq., Harlleston, Lincolnshire
Jonathan Grundy, Esq
Nicholas Grundy, Esq
Richard Green, Esq
Rev. Dr Gresley, rector of Seal
Rev. Mr Greenaway, rector of Nether-Broughton
Rev. Mr Gregory, rector of Langor, Nottinghamshire
Colonel Hastings
John Hallam, Esq., London
Robert Hames, Esq
Edward Hartopp, Esq
Edmund Cradock Hartopp, Esq
George Heming, Esq
Colonel Hemington
William Heyrick, Esq., Beaumanor
Mrs Heyrick, deceased
William Heyrick, Esq., West-Cotes
Arthur Heselrige, Esq
T. Cooper Hincks, Esq., St John's College, Cambridge
William Hood, Esq
Ch. Greve Hudson, Esq
Lebbeus Humphrey, Esq
John Peach Hungerford, Esq
Joseph Hurlock, Esq., London
William Hurst, Esq
Rev. Mr Hanbury, late rector of Church Langton
Rev. Mr Healey, vicar of Loddington
Rev. Mr Heathcote, East Bridgeford, Nottinghamshire
Rev. Mr Hemington, vicar of Thorpe-Arch, Yorkshire
Rev. Mr Higgs, Fellow of Trinity College, Cambridge
Rev. Mr Hitchcock, rector of Bitteswell
Rev. Mr Hunt
Thomas Jee, Esq
N. P. Johnson, Esq
Mrs Johnson
Mr Joyce, surgeon, Billesdon
Rev. Mr Iliff, vicar of Cosby and Wistow
Mr Illiff, Narborough
Anthony James Kecke, Esq
Thomas King, Esq
B. Kidney, Esq
Dr Kirkland, Ashby-de-la-Zouch
Mr Kilby, Queniborough
Samual Leach, Esq
Rev. Mr Lort, Fellow of Trinity College, Cambridge
Rev. Mr William Ludlam, Leicester
Dr Mounsey, physician to Chels. Col.
Edward Manners, Esq
Hugo Meynell, Esq
Ralph Milbank, Esq
Charles Morris, Esq
Miss Mead, Narborough
Samuel Miles, gent., Leicester

Mr Mason, Leicester
Mr Muxloe, Pickwell
Mr Mynors, surgeon, Birmingham
Rev. Mr Middleton, rector of Hathern
Rev. Mr Moore, Appleby
Cosmos Neville, Esq
John Neal, Esq
Mr Newbold, Rothley
Mr Newcomb, Staunton-Harold
Rev. and Hon. Dr Noel
Rev. Mr North, rector of Glen
R.F. Okeover, Esq., Oldbury, Warwickshire
Samuel Oliver, Esq
Welles Orton, Esq
Mr Oldham, Leicester
Charles John Packe, Esq
Peter Pegg, Esq., Beauchief-Abbey, Derbyshire
William Pochin, Esq
Mrs Pochin
Colonel Pochin, 2 copies
Samuel Steele Perkyns, Esq
Mrs Piddocke, Ashby-de-la-Zouch
Mr Pestell, Attorney, Ditto
Mr Pestell, Attorney, Hinckley
Mr Pagett, Ibstock
Mr Pratt, Ravenstone
Rev. Mr Pixell, Durham
Rev. Dr Prior, headmaster of Repton School, Derbyshire
Mrs Tate
Edward Taylor, Esq., official of the Archdeaconry of
    Leicester
Arch. Wilson Taylor, Esq
Thomas Thoroton, Esq
Thomas Tunstall, Esq
F. Fortescue Turville, Esq
Mr Thornley, Ashby-de-la-Zouch
Rev. Mr Topp, rector of Burton Overy
Honourable Henry Vernon
Dr Vaughan, Leicester
William Vann, Esq
James Vere, Esq. junior
Clement Winstanley, Esq
William Woollaston, Esq
S. Pipe, Wolferstan, Esq
Mr Watkinson, deceased, Loughbro'
Mr Joseph Wilkes, Overseal
Mr Thomas Wilkes, ditto
Mr Whittingham, Lynn, Norfolk
Mr S. Wyatt, surveyor, Burton-upon-Trent
Mr T. Wylde, Leke, Nottinghamshire
Rev. Mr Walker, rector of Kibworth
Rev. Mr Willey, rector of Kegworth
Rev. Mr Wyley, rector of Witherley
Rev. Mr Wynne, rector of Gumley
Edward Rooe Yeo, Esq
Rev. Dr Parry, Harborough
Rev. Dr Pegg, vicar of Packington
William Reeve, Esq. junior
Major Revell
Thomas Richards, Esq
Launcelot Rolleston, Esq., Watnall
Colonel Skevington
John Simpson, Esq
Charles Boothby Skrymsher, Esq
Charles Lorrain Smith, Esq
John Christopher Smith, Esq., Bath

Mr Salt, London
Mr Sills, Ditto
Mr S. Statham, junior, Nottingham
Mr Storey, Attorney, Nottingham
Mr Stockdale, Leicester
Mr Stone, Quarndon
Mr Smith, Surveyor, Packington
Rev. Mr Stevens, vicar of Bumpsted-Helion, Essex
Rev. Mr Shaw, rector of Hartshorn, Derbyshire
Rev. Mr Storey, rector of Walton
Governor Tryon
William Tate, Esq., Surry
Benjamin Tate, Esq., Burleigh
Mrs Tate
George Tate, Esq., London

Source: Bodleian Library: Richard Gough's MS
collection for his British Topography, 3rd edition.
Shelfmark Gough. GEN Top 363-6.

INDEX OF PLACE NAMES ON THE MAP

(In Prior's form and spelling)

Ab Kettleby	26		Bens Cliff	22
Abbey Gate	38		Bensford Bridge	44
Abbot Oak	22		Bescoby	28
Agar Nook	22		Billesdon	40
Alder Hall	36		Bilston	34
Alderman Hall	22		Birchwood Hill	22
Allexton	42		Birds Hill	18
Allexton Wood	42		Birstal	24
Alton Grange	20		Bitchby	44
Anbin Wood	34		Bitteswell	44
Ansty	22		Blaby	38
Appleby Magna	18		Blackberry Hill	16
Appleby Parva	18		Blackbrook	22
Arnsby	38		Blackfordby	18
Asfordby	26		Blaston	42
Ashby de la Zouch	20		Boothorpe	18
Ashby Folville	26		Bosworth Mill	46
Ashby Magna	38		Bosworth Toll Gate	46
Ashby Parva	44		Botcheston	36
Ashby Pasture	26		Bottesford	16
Ashwell	30		Bowden Magna	48
Aston Flamville	36		Bowden Parva	48
Atherston	32		Bradgate Park	22
Atterton	32		Bradley	42
Austrey	32		Brand	20
Ayleston	38		Brand Hill	22
			Branston	38
			Branston Hall	38
Bagworth	34		Brascote	34
Bagworth Heath	34		Braunston	16
Bagworth Moats	20		Breedon	20
Baldwin Castle	22		Breedon Lodge	20
Bardon Hall	22		Brentingby	28
Bardon Hill	22		Brickman Hill	36
Barkby	24		Bringhurst	42
Barkby Holt	26		Broad Hill	20
Barkby Thorpe	24		Broadhurst Hill	22
Barkston	16		Brooksby	26
Barlston	34		Broombriggs Hill	22
Barn Park	36		Broughton Astley	36
Barnston	14		Bruntingthorpe	38
Barrat Pool	18		Buckminster	30
Barrow Hill	20		Bull in the Oak	34
Barrow upon Soar	24		Burbage	34
Barsby	26		Burbage Common	36
Barton in the Beans	34		Burbage Lodge	34
Barwell	34		Burbage Wood	36
Battleflat	20		Burleigh	22
Beacon Hill	22		Burleigh Field	22
Bean Hills	32		Burrow	28
Beau Manor	22		Burrow Hill	28
Beaumont Leys	38		Burton Bandals	24
Becks	34		Burton Lazars	28
Beddon Wood	24		Burton on the Woulds	24
Beeby	26		Burton Overy	40
Beggary Nooks	20		Bushby	38
Belgrave	38		Butt House	18
Belton	20			
Belton	42			
Belton Low-wood	22		Cadeby	34
Belvoir Castle	16		Cademan	20

Caldwell	28	Dunton Basset	36
Carlton	34	Dyke Tree	22
Carlton Curlieu	40		
Carthagena	24	Earl Shilton	36
Castle Donington	12	East Langton	40
Catthorpe	44	East Norton	42
Caulk	20	Easthorpe	16
Cavendish Bridge	12	Easton Magna	42
Caves Inn	44	Easton Park	42
Change Wood	36	Eastwell	16
Charley	22	Eaton	16
Charley Hall	22	Edmondthorpe	28 & 30
Charley Knot	22	Elmesthorpe	36
Charter House	36	Elton	16
Chilcott	18	Enderby	36
Church Gresley	18	Evington	38
Church Langton	40	Evington Lodge	38
Clawson Thorns	26	Eye Kettleby	26
Cliff Hill	22		
Cloud-hill Wood	20	Far Coton	34
Coalhill	18	Fenny Drayton	32
Cold Overton	28	Fieldon Bridge	32
Cole Orton	20	Finchley Bridge	42
Cole Orton Common	20	Finney Hill	22
Congeston	34	Fleckney	38
Cop-low	40	Foston	38
Copt Oak	22	Foxton	48
Corbit Hall	20	Freeby	28
Cosby	36	Freeby Gorse	28
Cossington	24	Frisby	40
Coston	28	Frisby on the Wreak	26
Cotes	24	Frith Hall	36
Cotes Deval	46	Frogmores	32
Coton Park	18	Frolesworth	36
Cottesbatch	44	Furze Hill	42
Cottingham	42		
Countisthorp	38	Gaddesby	26
Cranoe	42	Galby	40
Cream Lodge	26	Garendon	22
Croft	36	Garthorpe	28
Croft-Hill	36	Garthorpe Gorse	28
Cropston	22	Gelders Hall	22
Cross Lane	20	Gilmorton	46
Crossing Hand	44	Glen Magna	38 & 40
Crow Hill	22	Glen Parva	38
Crow Mills	38	Glenfield	36
Crown Point	30	Glooston	40
Croxton Banks	16	Glooston Lodge	40
Croxton Kerrial	16	Goadby	40
Croxton Park	16	Goadby Marwood	28
Culloden House	32	Goathouse Hills	22
		Goldsmith Grange	28
Dadlington	34	Gopsall	34
Dalby on the Woulds	26	Gopsall Rough	32
Dalby Wood	26	Gracedieu	20
Dannet Hall	38	Granby	16
Desford	36	Grange	18
Diseworth	22	Great Dalby	26
Dishley Grange	22	Green Hill	22
Doe Bridge	44	Griffy Dam	20
Dog and Gun	38	Grimston	26
Donington on the Heath	20	Grindon	32
Donington Park	12	Grooby	36
Donisthorpe	18	Grooby Pool	36
Drayton	42	Guadalupe	26
Dry Stoke	42	Gumley	40

Hadley	22	
Halfway House	40	
Hall gates	22	
Hallaton	42	
Halsted	42	
Hambleton	38	
Hamer Cliff	22	
Harborough	48	
Harby	14	
Hareston	16	
Harris Bridge	32	
Harrow	34	
Hathern	22	
Hathern Turn	22	
Haughton Hill	20	
Heath End	20	
Hemington	12	
Hether	20	
Hickling	14	
High Cross	44	
Higham	34	
Hinckley	34	
Hoby	26	
Hoethorpe Lodge	42	
Hog Hall	36	
Holt	42	
Holwell	26	
Holwell Hall	22	
Holwell Mouth	26	
Hoo Ash	20	
Hool Hill	34	
Horminghold	42	
Horspool Grange	22	
Hose	14	
Hose Grange	14	
Hoton	24	
Hoton Hill	20	
Houghton Hill	20	
Houghton on the Hill	40	
Howthorpe	48	
Hugglescote	20	
Hugglescote Grange	20	
Humberston	38	
Humberston Bridge	38	
Huncote	36	
Hungarton	40	
Hunters Hill	22	
Husbands Bosworth	46	
Ibstock	20	
Ibstock Grange	20	
Illston Lodge	40	
Illston on the Hill	40	
Ingarsby	40	
Isley Walton	20	
Iveshead	22	
Jericho	28	
Keam	40	
Kegworth	12	
Kegworth Bridge	12	
Kelham Bridge	20	
Keythorpe	42	
Keythorpe Wood	42	
Kibworth Beauchamp	40	

Kibworth Harcourt	40	
Kilby	38	
Kimcote	46	
King Richard's Well	34	
Kings Mills	12	
Kings Stand	36	
Kingston	12	
Kirby Bellars	26	
Kirby Lodge	26	
Kirby Muxloe	36	
Kirkby Mallory	36	
Knaptoft	46	
Knaptoft Lodge	46	
Knight Thorp	22	
Knighton	38	
Knipton	16	
Knossington	42	
Lady Wood	42	
Langar	14	
Langham	28	
Langley	20	
Laughton	48	
Laund Abbey	42	
Lea Wood	22	
Leesthorp	28	
Leicester	38 & 50	
Leicesterford Bridge	28	
Leir	36	
Lewin Bridge	24	
Ley Grange	32	
Lilbourn	46	
Lindley Hall	34	
Little Dalby	28	
Little Thorpe	36	
Lockington	12	
Loddington	42	
Long Clawson	14	
Long Hill	22	
Long Lane	20	
Long Whatton	22	
Loseby	40	
Loughborough	22	
Lount	20	
Lubenham	48	
Lubscloud	22	
Lubsthorpe	36	
Lutterworth	44	
Mancester	32	
Mapplewell	22	
Marefield	40	
Market Bosworth	34	
Market Overton	30	
Markfield	22	
Marston Trussel	48	
Martinshaw Wood	36	
Measham	18	
Measham Field	20	
Medbourn	42	
Melton Mowbray	26 & 28	
Melton Spinney	28	
Merril Grange	20	
Merry Lees	36	
Middleton Mill	42	

Misterton	46	Pampilion Hall	48
Moor Barns	32	Park House	18
Morely Hill	22	Park House	36
Mountsorrel	24	Paske Hall	26
Mowsley	46	Peatling Magna	38
Mucklin Wood	22	Peatling Parva	46
Muston	16	Peckleton	36
Muston Gap	16	Peckleton Mill	36
Muston Gorse	16	Pickering Grange	20
		Pickwell	28
Nailston	34	Pinwall	32
Nailston Wiggs	20	Pinwall Grange	32
Naneby	34	Piper Hole	14
Narborough	36	Pistern Mill	20
Near Coton	34	Plungar	16
Nether Broughton	26	Potters Marston	36
Nether Claybrook	44	Poultney	46
Nether Seal	18	Preston Pans	34
Nethercote	20	Prestop Park	18
New Bridge	26	Prestwould	24
New Inn	40		
Newal Park	36	Quebec House	24
Newberry Wood	20	Quenby	40
Newbold	20	Queniborough	24
Newbold	28	Quorndon	24
Newbold Verdon	34		
Newhouse Grange	32	Ragdale	26
Newton	40	Ratby	36
Newton Burgaland	20	Ratcliff Culey	32
Newton Harcourt	38	Ratcliff on the Wreake	24
Newton Regis	32	Ratcliff upon Soar	12
Newtown Linford	22	Ravenstone	20
Newtown Unthank	36	Rearsby	24
No Mans Heath	18	Red Cow	36
Normanton	16	Red Hall	34
Normanton on the Heath	20	Red Hill	12
Normanton Turville	36	Red Lodge	16
Normanton upon Soar	22	Redmile	16
North Kilworth	46	Redway House	20
Norton	32	Rempston	24
Norton by Galby	40	Robin a Tiptoes	42
Nosley	40	Rockingham	42
		Rockingham Castle	42
Oadby	38	Roe House	32
Oakley Wood	22	Roes Rest	36
Oaks, The	22	Rolleston	40
Oakthorpe	18	Rotherby	26
Odston	34	Rothley	24
Odston Hill	20	Rothley House	24
Old Heys	36	Rothley Plain	24
Old John	22	Rowden	34
Old Park	20		
Orton Gorse	32	Saddington	38
Orton on the Hill	32	Saltby	28
Orton Parva	32	Saltersford Bridge	38
Osbaston	34	Sapcote	36
Osgathorpe	20	Sawley	12
Outwoods	22	Saxby	28
Over Broughton	26	Saxelby	26
Over Claybrook	44	Scalford	28
Over Seal	18	Scraptoft	38
Overton Wood	42	Seagrave	24
Owston	42	Segs Hill	24
Owston Wood	42	Sewstern	30
Oxley Grange	22	Sex Hill	24
		Shackerston	34
Packington	20	Shankton	40

Shardlow Hall	12	Stretton Parva	40
Sharmans Lodge	38	Sulby Abbey	48
Sharnford	36	Sutton	16
Sharp Hill	20	Sutton	36
Shaw Lane	22	Sutton Bonington	22
Shawell	44	Sutton Cheney	34
Shearsby	38	Sutton Heath	34
Sheepshead	22	Sutton Mill	42
Sheepshed Nook	22	Swannington	20
Sheepy Magna	32	Swepston	20
Sheepy Parva	32	Swinford	46
Shenton	34	Swithland	22
Shilton Heath	36	Sysonby	26
Shire Bush	16	Syston	24
Shoby	26	Syston Mill	24
Shrubs	36		
Sibson	34	Teigh	30
Sileby	24	Temple Hall	34
Skeffington	40	Theddingworth	48
Skeffington Lodge	40	Thistleton Gap	30
Skellington	30	Thornton	36
Sketchley	34	Thorp Acre	22
Slawston	42	Thorpe	36
Smeeton Westerby	40	Thorpe Arnold	28
Smisby	18	Thorpe Langton	40
Smockington	44	Thorpe Satchville	26
Snareston	18	Three Queens	30
Snibston	20	Thrinkston	20
Soar Mill	36	Thrussington	24
Soar Stone	34	Thrussington Woulds	24
Somerby	28	Thurcaston	24
South Croxton	26	Thurlaston	36
South Ford	18	Thurmaston	24
South Kilworth	46	Thurnby	38
South Wood	20	Tilton on the Hill	40
Spinney House	28	Timberwood Hill	22
Sproxton	30	Tin Meadow	22
Stainby Lings	30	Tonge	20
Stanford	46	Tooley Park	36
Stanford (Notts)	22	Tugby	42
Stanford Hall	46	Turlangton	40
Stanford Hill	24	Twycross	32
Stanton under Bardon	22	Twyford	26
Stanton Wyvell	40		
Stapleford	28	Ullesthorpe	44
Stapleton	34	Ulverscroft Abby	22
Stathern	16	Upper Grange	20
Stathern Hill	16	Upton	34
Staunton	16		
Staunton Harold	20	Wadland	18
Stephens Gorse	16	Walcote	46
Stewards Hay	22	Waltham on the Wolds	28
Stockerston	42	Walton	46
Stocking Wood	24	Walton Holt	46
Stoke Golding	34	Walton on the Woulds	24
Stonesby	28	Walton Thorns	24
Stoney Stanton	36	Wanlip	24
Stonygate House	38	Wardley	42
Stordon Grange	20	Warren Hills	22
Stoughton	38	Wartnaby	26
Stoughton Grange	38	Weddington Wood	32
Street Hill	26	Welby	26
Street Lane	28	Welford	46
Stretton Hall	38	Welham	42
Stretton in the Fields	18	Wellsborough	34
Stretton Magna	38	West Cotes	38

West Langton	40
Weston by Welland	42
Whatton Mill	22
White Leys	20
White Lodge	28
Whitehouse	18
Whitwick	20
Wigston Magna	38
Wigston Parva	44
Wikeham	28
Wikin	34
Willesley	18
Willoughby Waterless	38
Willowby	24
Wilson	20
Wimeswould	24
Wissendine	28
Wistow	38
Withcote	42
Withcote Lodge	42
Witherly	32
Wiverby	28
Wolsthorpe	16
Wood Gate	38
Wood Thorpe	22
Woodbarrow	42
Woodhouse	22
Woodhouse Eaves	22
Woodwell Head	30
Worthington	20
Wymondham	28
Zouch Bridge	22

Bibliography

a) History of cartography

Harley, J. B. The re-mapping of England, 1750-1800. *Imago Mundi.* 1965: 19, 56-67.

Harley, J. B. The Society of Arts and the survey of English counties, 1759-1809.
(11) The response to the awards 1759-1766.
(111) The changes of policy 1767-1801.
Journal of the Royal Society of Arts. 1964: 112, 119-124, 269-275.

Laxton, P. The geodetic and topographical evaluation of English county maps 1740-1840. *Cartographic Journal.* 1976: 13, 37-54.

b) Reprints of contemporary maps

Several of the eighteenth century county maps have been reprinted with introductions. Particular reference was made to:

Donn, B. *A map of the County of Devon, 1765*, reprinted in facsimile with an introduction by W. L. D. Ravenhill. Devon and Cornwall Record Society, 1965.

Burdett, P. P. *A survey of the County Palatine of Chester, 1777*, reprinted in facsimile with an introduction by J. B. Harley and P. Laxton. Historic Society of Lancashire and Cheshire, 1974.

Burdett, P. P. *Burdett's map of Derbyshire, 1791*, with an introduction by J. B. Harley, D. V. Fowkes and J. C. Harvey. Derbyshire Archaeological Society, 1975. (Reprint of the second edition)

c) Leicestershire sources (in chronological order)

Bray, W. *Sketch of a tour into Derbyshire and Yorkshire, including part of Buckingham, Warwick, Leicester, . . .* B. White, 1778.

Nichols, J. *The history and antiquities of the County of Leicester.* J. Nichols, 1795-1815. Repr. S. R. Publishers, 1971. 4 vols in 8.

Watts, S. *A walk through Leicester.* T. Combe, 1804.

Potter, T. R. *The history and antiquities of Charnwood Forest.* Hamilton Adams, 1842.

Thompson, J. *The history of Leicester in the eighteenth century.* Crossley & Clarke, 1871.

Scott, W. *The story of Ashby-de-la-Zouch.* G. Brown, 1907.

Victoria history of the County of Leicester. Constable/Oxford University Press, 1907-1964. 5 vols.

Firth, J. B. *Highways and byways in Leicestershire.* MacMillan, 1926.

Francis, H. J. *A history of Hinckley.* Pickering, 1930.

Russell, P. *A Leicestershire road (Harborough-Loughborough).* Backus, 1934.

Gimson, B. L. & Russell, P. *Leicestershire maps, a brief survey.* Backus, 1947.

Hoskins, W. G. *Leicestershire: an illustrated essay on the history of the landscape.* Hodder & Stoughton, 1957.

Pevsner, N. *Leicestershire and Rutland (The buildings of England).* Penguin, 1960.

Fox, L. *A county grammar school: a history of Ashby-de-la-Zouch Grammar School through four centuries, 1567 to 1967.* Oxford University Press, 1967.

Davies, J. C. *Georgian Harborough.* Wellandside (Photographics), 1969.

Brown, A. E. *ed. The growth of Leicester.* Leicester University Press, 1970.

Hoskins, W. G. *Leicestershire (a Shell guide).* Faber, 1970.

Pochin, T. *Loughborough in 1770*, edited with introduction and notes by J. D. Bennett. The Book House, 1970.

Simmons, J. *Leicester; past and present. Vol 1, ancient borough to 1860.* Eyre Methuen, 1974.

Daniell, J. *Leicestershire clockmakers: directory of watch and clock makers working in Leicestershire before 1900.* Leicestershire Museums, Art Galleries and Records Service, 1975.

Ashton, N. *Leicestershire watermills.* Sycamore Press, 1977.

Moon, N. *The windmills of Leicestershire and Rutland.* Sycamore Press, 1981.

Foss, P. *The history of Market Bosworth.* Sycamore Press, 1983.